The Natural History of
SPIDERS

THE NATURAL HISTORY OF
SPIDERS

KEN AND ROD PRESTON-MAFHAM

The Crowood Press

First published in 1996 by
The Crowood Press Ltd
Ramsbury, Marlborough
Wiltshire SN8 2HR

British Library Cataloguing-in-Publication Data
A catalogue record for this book is available from the
British Library.

ISBN 1 85223 966 2

Title page: A jumping spider (Salticidae) in a Brazilian
Atlantic coast rainforest.

All photographs by the authors, Premaphotos Wildlife.
Line illustrations by Michael J Roberts.

Typeset and designed by:
D & N Publishing
DTP and Editorial Services
Ramsbury, Marlborough
Wiltshire SN8 2HR

Typefaces used: main text, New Baskerville; captions, News
Gothic; headings, News Gothic.

Printed in Great Britain by BPC Books Limited, Aylesbury,
a member of The British Printing Company Limited

(W) 595ﾗ44ﾆ
638.544ﾟ

CONTENTS

01 Introduction to Spiders

Although in this book we are mainly concerned with the natural history of spiders, we need to understand something of both where they relate to other members of the animal kingdom and something of their external and internal structure in order to have a full appreciation of their lifestyles.

In the first place, therefore, whereabouts in the animal kingdom do those familiar and often maligned creatures, the spiders, fit? There is an assemblage of groups, collectively known as the invertebrate animals, which lack an internal bone or cartilage skeleton and to which belong the worms, the molluscs (slugs, snails, etc.) and the arthropods. The basic diagnostic characteristics of the major groups of arthropods are as shown in the

box (below). It is within one of these groups, the Arachnida, that the spiders belong. It is clear from this that spiders are not insects.

The arthropod groups have in common a tough exoskeleton within which the body musculature and organs are contained. The exoskeleton basically consists of a series of rigid tubes and sets of plates with the muscles running within the tubes and between the plates. In order for there to be some flexibility, to allow movement of the limbs and bending of the body, the exoskeleton is much thinner where joints occur between the plates and tubes. Internally there are many inward protrusions of the exoskeleton to allow for the attachment of the muscles.

The subdivisions within the arthropods have changed somewhat in recent years and the classification of the group shown in the box opposite is now generally accepted by most taxonomists and, those who specifically study the spiders and their relations, the arachnologists.

It can be seen that classification of any living organisms involves a hierarchy, with the superphylum. Arthropoda are divided into several phyla, each phylum then subdivided into superclasses, further subdivided into classes, and so on. Just to make it clear how the system works and before going on to discuss the arachnids and spiders in greater detail, a full classification of a single organism, the widely distributed daddy-long-legs spider, *Pholcus phalangioides,* is shown in the table. You will see that this spider has a common name but unfortunately only a tiny proportion of spiders have been given common names and these differ from country to country or even between regions of a

MAJOR ARTHROPOD GROUPS

Crustacea (crabs, lobsters, prawns, shrimps and woodlice) have five pairs of walking appendages, the first pair may be armed with pincers to assist in manipulating food.

Arachnida (spiders, scorpions, solifuges, harvestmen, whip-scorpions and pseudoscorpions) have four pairs of walking legs. (Pincers in scorpions, pseudoscorpions and whip-scorpions are on modified head appendages.)

Myriapoda have many pairs of walking legs, the centipedes with one pair per body segment and the millipedes with two pairs per body segment.

Insecta have three pairs of walking legs and two pairs (one pair in flies) of wings.

THE CLASSIFICATION OF THE SUPERPHYLUM ARTHROPODA

Phylum Chelicerata

CLASS ARACHNIDA
spiders, scorpions, ticks, mites, etc.

CLASS MEROSTOMATA
king-crabs or horseshoe-crabs

CLASS PYCNOGONIDA
sea-spiders

Phylum Crustacea
crabs, lobsters, shrimps, prawns, wood lice, etc.

Phylum Onychophora
velvet worms

Phylum Uniramia

SUPERCLASS MYRIAPODA
CLASS CHILOPODA
millipedes

CLASS DIPLOPODA
centipedes

SUPERCLASS HEXAPODA
CLASS PROTURA

CLASS DIPLURA

CLASS COLLEMBOLA
springtails

CLASS INSECTA
bugs, beetles, flies, etc.

single country. You will, for example, see the spiders of the genus *Dolomedes* variously referred to as nursery-web, raft, swamp, fishing or water spiders. Confusingly, the 'water spider' proper, this name being used by almost all English speakers, is *Argyroneta aquatica*, a member of a completely different family from *Dolomedes*. It is best, therefore, always to think of individual spider species in terms of their scientific names, since these never change whatever the country or language. You will, in fact, find both common names and scientific names used throughout this volume, the former where they are used widely throughout the English-

CLASSIFICATION OF THE DADDY-LONG-LEGS SPIDER

GROUPING	GROUP	NAME INCLUDES
Kingdom	Animalia	All animals
Superphylum	Arthropoda	All animals with an exoskeleton
Phylum	Chelicerata	Arthropods with unbranched appendages and lacking antennae
Class	Arachnida	The terrestrial chelicerates with four pairs of legs
Order	Araneae	The spiders
Infraorder	Araneomorphae	The 'true' spiders
Family	Pholcidae	The daddy-long-legs spiders
Genus	*Pholcus*	
Species	*phalangioides*	
Common name	daddy-long-legs or rafter spider	

Closely related to the spiders are the tailed whip-scorpions or vinegaroons (Uropygi). Unlike spiders, their pedipalps are adapted for grasping prey and the first pair of legs is much longer and thinner than the remaining pairs. The abdomen is segmented and bears a terminal whip-like flagellum. They are nocturnal hunters but are not poisonous, just grabbing their insect prey in their formidable palps and then crushing them with the heavy chelicerae. The name vinegaroon comes from their ability to squirt a mixture of fatty acids, including acetic, when molested. This is **Mastigoproctus giganteus** from the south of the USA.

The tailless whip-scorpions (Amblypygi) are much flatter versions of the vinegaroons, without the abdominal flagellum, but with much more highly developed pedipalps. They lack poison glands and use the pedipalps to grasp and impale prey before attacking it with their jaws. Their flattened shape suits them for life beneath bark, stones or in cracks in rocks, from which they emerge at night to hunt. This Costa Rican species is feeding on a cockroach it has caught in the rainforest.

The Acari, mites and ticks, are the only arachnid group exceeding the spiders in terms of the number of species described. Many, such as this Arizona desert-dwelling trombidiid velvet mite, are free-living while others are parasitic on both vertebrates and invertebrates or form galls on plants. Like the spiders, they have four pairs of legs, but Acari lack the division of the body into two distinct sections.

speaking world, the latter where common names are local only or where no common name exists.

Within the class Arachnida, the closest relations of the Araneae, the spiders, are the Pedipalpi, which includes the tailless whip-scorpions, the Amblypygi, the tailed whip-scorpions, the Uropygi, and the Schizomida, which resemble the uropygids.

The spiders are an extremely successful group of living organisms, ranking number seven in the world in terms of numbers of species described or likely to be so. They are exceeded in numbers by one other arachnid group, the Acari (mites and ticks) and as might be expected, since they make up the majority of spiders' prey, the five largest insect orders, i.e. the Coleoptera (beetles), Hymenoptera (sawflies, bees, wasps and ants), Lepidoptera (moths and butterflies), Diptera (flies) and Hemiptera (bugs). By the year 1988, approximately 34,000 species had been described from 105 families. Today, with the exception of a few species in the primitive family Liphistiidae, all extant spiders can be referred to one of two infraorders. These are the more primitive Mygalomorphae, often referred to in the text as mygalomorphs or mygalomorph tarantulas and the modern or 'true' spiders the Araneomorphae, referred to as araneomorphs.

Spiders are very old in terms of geological time, the earliest fossil coming from the Middle Devonian period between 374 and 380 million years ago, so they were probably first evolved some 400–420 million years ago. Major speciation of the araneomorph spiders is believed to have taken place around 220 million years ago and from limestone laid down early in the Cretaceous period, which started 144 million years ago, have come fossils of two orb-weavers assignable to modern spider groups. In common with the insects, which like the spiders did not readily fossilize in mineral deposits on account of their relative frailty, the best spider remains come from amber (fossilized tree resin). Many of the spiders in these ambers, which date from as long as 55 million years ago, belong to genera which are still in existence today.

02 Structure and Physiology of Spiders

EXTERNAL STRUCTURE

The body of the spider is subdivided into two distinct sections: (1) a combined head and thorax, the cephalothorax or prosoma; and (2) the abdomen or opisthosoma. Between the two is a narrow, connecting waist, the pedicel. Both of the main body segments may be variously marked, either by showing up the outlines of various internal structures and muscle attachments or by bearing various patterns of pigments. In addition a number of spiders, in particular

The spiders which Western housewives hate most of all are the house spiders of the genus **Tegenaria** (Agelenidae), such as this female scuttling across a carpet. This is the spider which is supposed to come up the plughole into the bath, which of course it doesn't do; it just falls in and then cannot get back out up the smooth sides. It clearly shows the main spider characteristics: the body in two sections, the lack of segmentation, the pair of palps at the front and the four pairs of walking legs.

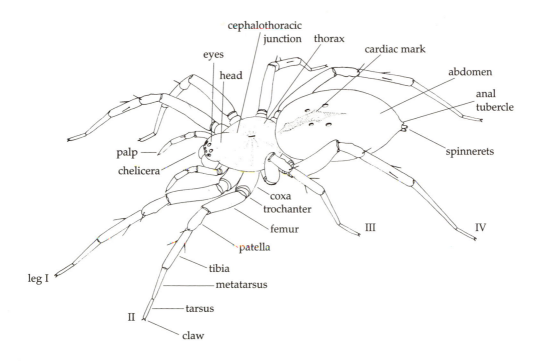

The external structure of a generalized araneomorph spider from above.

the jumping spiders of the family Salticidae, are covered in iridescent hairs which turn them into veritable jewels when illuminated by the sun's rays.

Like other arthropods, the spiders possess an outer exoskeleton, the cuticle, which is similar in structure to that of insects but has an extra layer in it. The major structural component is chitin and as well as supporting the body and serving as an attachment for muscles, the exoskeleton protects the spider and reduces water loss from its body. There are also intuckings of the outer cuticle, particularly in the cephalothorax, which form an endoskeleton for the attachment of muscles working the sucking stomach and the legs.

THE CEPHALOTHORAX

The upper surface of the cephalothorax is covered by a tough shield or plate called the carapace and it is usually fairly easy to make out the line on this which is the demarcation between the head and the thorax. In some families, but notably the Linyphiidae, the carapace has evolved into all sorts of weird shapes, especially in the males, which seem to be associated with courtship and mating in these spiders. On the front and on top of the head region are the eyes, primitively four pairs but in some families three, two or one pair only. The size and arrangement of these varies from family to family and is an important diagnostic feature in spider classification.

Viewed from the underside of the cephalothorax on the head region are visible a pair of jaws (chelicerae), a pair of pedipalps (often just called 'palps') and between these a small plate (the labium), marking the floor of the mouth, which is attached to the basal plate of the thoracic region, the sternum. On either side of the of the labium are the maxillae, which are used in crushing and

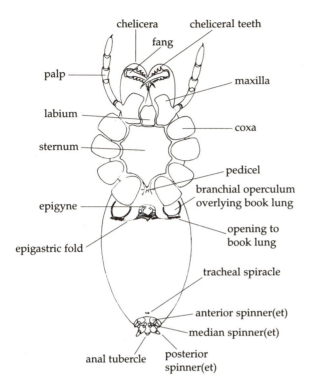

chelicera   cheliceral teeth

fang

palp

maxilla

labium

coxa

sternum

pedicel

branchial operculum overlying book lung

epigyne

opening to book lung

epigastric fold

tracheal spiracle

anterior spinner(et)

median spinner(et)

anal tubercle   posterior spinner(et)

The external structure of a generalized araneomorph spider from below.

filtering the food. On the thoracic region as well as the sternum there are the four pairs of walking legs. The pedipalps lie on either side of the head behind the jaws and they resemble legs but do not have a metatarsal segment. The palps of female spiders are always simple but in males the tarsal segment is modified as a mating aid. In the more advanced spider families the palpal tarsus can become extremely complicated in structure, assuming quite bizarre shapes when fully inflated.

The paired legs resemble those of the insects and the names applied to each of the sections are the same in both groups. One major difference is the presence of an extra segment, the patella, which lies between the femur and tibia in the spiders. Although the legs of spiders differ greatly in length and thickness between families or even within members of the same family, they lack the modifications associated with digging, swimming, etc. found in

BITING IN SPIDERS

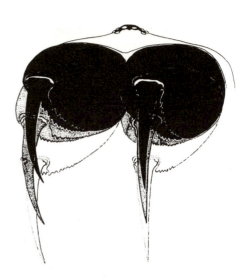

the downward strike of the paraxial chelicerae of a mygalomorph spider

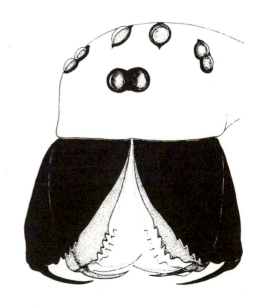

the sideways pincer action of the diaxial chelicerae of an araneomorph spider

BITING IN SPIDERS

The jaws are attached at the front of the head and each consists of a basal segment, which is often sharply toothed along the inner edge, and hinged onto this a sharply pointed fang. The latter, which is used to pierce the body of the spider's prey and inject poison into it, often lies in a groove along the basal segment. Towards the end of each fang is a tiny hole through which the poison passes. Primitively spider jaws lie paraxially, i.e. along the horizontal axis of the body and thus the spider has to raise its front end to strike forward and down onto its prey. From this has evolved the more advanced diaxial system, where the jaws lie at right angles to the line of the body and close towards one another in the manner of a pair of pincers. The paraxial system requires the prey to be on a firm surface and is fine for ground-dwelling spiders but the diaxial system suffers no such constraints, the jaws striking against each other, and is of equal use whether the spider lives on the ground, on water, on flowers or leaves or in a web and the majority of present-day spiders possess this more adaptable system.

A male **Aname** species mygalomorph spider of the family Dipluridae rears up and bares his fangs at the threatening form of the photographer in Western Australia. The paraxially striking chelicerae with their massive base and sharply pointed fangs show up clearly as do the modified tarsi on the end of the palps, which he will use during mating. Also visible on the tibia of the front legs are the pointed spurs which he uses to hold onto the female and the many hairs, including the very fine trichobothria, which are an integral part of the spider's sensory system.

insect legs. There are minor differences between groups, for example hunting spiders usually have just a pair of claws at the leg apex whereas web dwellers have an extra claw. These extra claws hook over the silk web-lines and, by forcing them against a series of barbed hairs on the underside of each foot allows the spider to wander around its web. A number of hunting spiders have dense rows of short hairs called scopulae along the underside of the terminal leg segments. The ends of these hairs are split thousands of times, giving them a high capillary attraction and allowing the owner to walk around on very smooth surfaces. In the cribellate spiders, there is a single or double row of spines, the calamistrum, along the upper side of the metatarsus of the fourth pair of legs, which is used to comb out the hackled band so characteristic of these spiders.

THE ABDOMEN

Unlike the cephalothorax and the abdomen of insects, the spider abdomen has a relatively thin covering (integument), which, although not so good from a protective point-of-view does allow considerable stretching, as when a female spider is filling with developing eggs. With the exception of the primitive family Liphistiidae, there is no real external sign of the segmentation so obvious in most other arthropod groups. In shape, it can vary from very long and narrow through broad and flat to totally globular, with all the permutations in between.

There is little to be seen on the upper surface of the abdomen, save in those species which possess bizarre, horn-like extensions. On the underside, however, from front to back, the following may be seen, though individual families do not necessarily possess all of them. First, there is a pair of semicircular marks which represent the outlines of the paired book lungs and their external openings. Behind and between these, in females only, may be found the epigyne, a special structure associated with the spider's unique mating technique. There then follows the epigastric furrow, running across the abdomen and into which open the male and female reproductive systems. Towards the rear of

the abdomen is the single, centrally spaced tracheal spiracle opening into one of the two alternate spider gas-exchange systems and at the tip of the abdomen is the anus through which waste products are expelled. Surrounding and/or in front of the anus are the paired spinnerets from which silk is extruded. These vary in number present and structure and are important in spider classification.

INTERNAL STRUCTURE

Spiders possess all of the systems we associate with members of the animal kingdom though, unlike insects, they have two different kinds of gas-exchange system.

THE ALIMENTARY CANAL

At the front end of the alimentary canal is the mouth. From this runs the oesophagus, its posterior end developed into the 'sucking stomach', which plays a very important role in feeding. As in insects, the oesophagus has an impermeable cuticular lining. Following the oesophagus is the midgut, which is not lined with cuticle but instead is lined with selectively permeable cells associated with the production of digestive enzymes and absorption of the digested food. A number of sacs may extend out from the wall of the midgut, thus increasing its surface area considerably. In certain families, they are so extensive as to extend forwards from the abdomen into the cephalothorax. Branching off from the posterior section of the alimentary canal, the hindgut, is a sac, the cloaca, which stores the waste products until they can be passed out through the anus.

THE PHYSIOLOGY OF FEEDING AND DIGESTION
Spiders are relatively unusual in that the initial digestion of their prey takes place outside the body. Once the latter has been subdued, either by being injected with poison or by being wrapped, or

Not all spiders have a straightforward rounded outline, indeed quite a number of species in the family Araneidae, the orb-weavers, have flattened bodies with bizarre extensions on the abdomen. This is a female thorn spider **Gasteracantha versicolor** on her web in rainforest in Madagascar. A number of theories have been put forward to explain this unusual body form, including that it prevents birds from getting a good grip.

both, then digestive enzymes from the front end of the alimentary canal are brought into play. In those spider families that lack teeth on the basal cheliceral segment, holes are cut into the prey with the fangs and the enzymes are injected through these. As the internal organs of the prey are liquified so they are sucked out and more enzymes are pumped in. Thus at the end of feeding, the prey remains recognizable but as just an empty husk. Spiders with cheliceral teeth, however, mash up their prey, pouring enzymes onto it as they do so,

again sucking up the resulting liquid food for further processing. By the end of such treatment, the prey is usually unrecognizable.

The partially digested prey, mainly fluid but containing some particulate solids, is now sucked into the oesophagus and on into the midgut by the action of the sucking stomach. Any remaining solids are filtered out through bristles around the mouth and in a filter system in the throat. The final stages of digestion of the food and absorption of the resulting products takes place in the midgut.

Spiders basically fall into two categories: they either break their prey up with their jaws as they feed and leave an unrecognizable mess when they have finished or they inject digestive juices and suck up the resulting liquid, leaving an empty husk as the remains. The flower spider **Misumena vatia** (Thomisidae) is widespread in Europe and temperate North America. Here she is feeding on insect prey and, because her jaws are very small, this is essentially what the prey will look like when she has finished her meal.

THE ROLE OF THE POISON GLANDS

Compared with their insect prey spiders are rather delicate creatures with the virtually unprotected abdomen particularly vulnerable to damage. Consequently it is a great advantage if the prey can be quickly neutralized and this is the role of the spider's poison. The poison itself is manufactured in the poison glands and then passes along a narrow duct and out through the small opening on each fang. There is a pair of these glands, one for each fang. In the mygalomorph spiders they are fairly small and lie inside the cheliceral base but in the higher spiders they are larger, extending well back into the cephalothorax in some cases. Each gland is surrounded by bands of muscle which can contract to provide a rapid delivery of the poison into the prey.

The poison itself is mainly made up of neurotoxic compounds but it also contains some protein-digesting enzymes. It is very fast acting and a small spider like the theridiid *Enoplognatha ovata* can, for example, subdue a bumble-bee 20 times its size in a matter of seconds.

THE CIRCULATORY SYSTEM

As with most invertebrate animals, spiders have an open circulatory system, i.e. most of the 'blood' (haemolymph) flow is through the body cavity around the main organs, rather than in discrete vessels as it is in vertebrates. A tubular 'heart' lies along the dorsal side of the abdomen with a main artery passing forwards through the pedicel into the cephalothorax and a second passing backwards into the abdominal cavity. Two or three pairs of openings called ostia are found on either side of the heart and it is through these that blood enters. The blood is pumped forwards and backwards from the heart, backflow being prevented by valves at the beginning of the anterior and posterior aortas and by the ostia. From the front end of the heart blood flows to the head, along the appendages and then finally makes its way back into the abdomen and back to the heart. The abdomen itself receives blood from the posterior aorta and from arteries branching from the side of the heart. In those spiders with book lungs, blood returning from the cephalothorax passes over these, picking up oxygen, since the blood does contain an oxygen-carrying pigment, **haemo-cyanin**. Most of this oxygen-carrying blood is supplied to the cephalothorax, since in the majority of spiders the abdominal organs receive direct supplies of oxygen from the tracheal system via the local blood supply. Although spider blood lacks any equivalent of the mammalian red blood cell, it does contain cells concerned with defence against infection and healing of wounds.

MECHANISMS OF GAS EXCHANGE

In the earliest spiders, the only means of breathing was by means of two pairs book lungs, a situation which still remains true for the mygalomorphs and the small, primitive araneomorph family, the Hypochilidae. In some araneomorph families, e.g.

the Pholcidae or daddy-long-legs spiders, just one pair of book lungs is retained. In the remaining araneomorph spiders, the posterior book lungs have been replaced by a tracheal system similar to though not as extensive as that found in the insects.

A book lung consists basically of a series of air spaces interleaved with a series of blood spaces like the leaves of a book. Oxygen diffuses from the air space within the book lung across the cuticle and into the blood space. The leaves of the 'book' are kept separated by rows of pillars spanning the air spaces. Some researchers have reported rhythmical movements in the book lungs which may represent breathing movements. In the tracheal system tubes are kept open by rings of chitin but unlike those of insects, those derived from the posterior book lungs do not branch but run in parallel trunks from the tracheal spiracle to the various organs. In those spider families where, however, the anterior book lungs have also evolved into a tracheal system, the tubes are branched.

The advantage of the tracheal system over book lungs is that it gives more efficient gas exchange, thus allowing a higher degree of activity, and there is a reduced water loss, very important for the higher spiders, most of which, unlike many mygalomorphs, do not live in the higher humidity of a subsoil tube. Those families which have only tracheal systems are in fact amongst the tiniest of spiders and as a result they have a very high surface area to volume ratio and a consequent high water loss from the body surface. They do, however, compensate for this by living amongst leaf litter and under stones where the air humidity remains fairly high.

THE EXCRETORY SYSTEM

The excretory system in spiders closely resembles that of the insects in structure and function, the structures which perform the main process having the same name, the Malpighian tubules, although the origin of these is different in the two groups. These secrete nitrogenous waste, mainly in the form of guanates, which are passed into the cloaca to be stored before being passed out of the anus. Also concerned with excretion are the prosomal coxal glands, which open to the exterior on the coxa of the legs. Although two pairs of these still exist in the giant trapdoor spiders and the mygalomorph tarantulas, they gradually become reduced in higher spider families and, although they may still be present, they are no longer excretory in function.

REPRODUCTION

Internally the reproductive organs of spiders resemble those of other arthropods. In males, a pair of coiled testes in the abdomen join to form a common duct which opens to the exterior at the centre of the epigastric furrow. The elongate, paired ovaries of the female also lie in the abdomen and join to form a common oviduct terminating in a uterus, which opens to the outside in the epigastric furrow. Also present is a pair of spermathecae or seminal receptacles, in which sperm taken in during copulation is stored until egg-laying.

Spiders have an unusual copulatory mechanism. In other arachnids and in some insect groups, the males produce a sperm packet, the spermatophore, which is picked up directly by the female into her genital opening. Alternatively, the males may possess a penis for introducing sperm into the female. In spiders there is no penis but instead insemination is carried out by the modified terminal palpal segment of the male. This modification can be simple or very complex but at its centre lies the palpal organ, which forms the sperm reservoir and from which a narrow tube, the embolus runs to the exterior. This functions as a simple bulb pipette which can be used to both suck up and squeeze out the seminal fluid. The way in which the process of sperm induction into the palp takes place is described in detail in Chapter 05.

In the giant trapdoor spiders, the mygalomorph tarantulas and certain more primitive araneomorph spiders, the male palp just has this basic

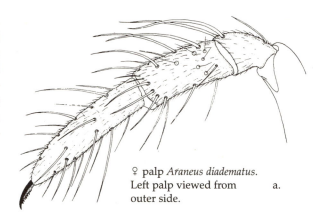

♀ palp *Araneus diadematus*.
Left palp viewed from outer side.   a.

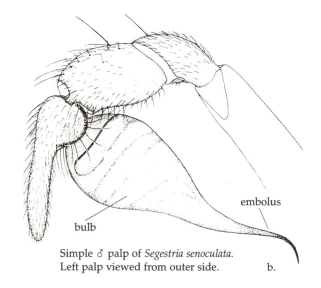

bulb   embolus

Simple ♂ palp of *Segestria senoculata*.
Left palp viewed from outer side.   b.

Spider palps.

a. the unmodified palp of a female spider.
b. the palp of a male spider modified for introducing sperm into the female. This is the simple type of palp found in mygalomorph males and some male araneomorph spiders. Semen is pumped from the reservoir (bulb) and into the female through the embolus.

simplicity (*see* figure above). The embolus is introduced into the female's uterus during copulation, the seminal fluid is squeezed out and then passes into the spermathecae. In the more advanced spiders, the male copulatory apparatus is rather complex and works in conjunction with an extra set of apparatus in the female, the epigyne. This lies centrally just in front of the epigastric fold and internally it contains the spermathecae, one on either side with tubes which carry sperm into them and a second set which carries the stored semen into the uterus when it is required. Externally, the epigyne is sclerotized, its structure varying from species to species.

The complex male palp (*see* figure below) bears sclerotized projections such as hooks and spines, which fit into grooves on the surface of the epigyne and these are elevated into position prior to copulation by increasing blood pressure within the palp. The copulatory apparatus is, however, normally kept collapsed in order to protect the delicate pumping apparatus. Only the correct palp will fit into the appropriate epigyne, and as a result, the mechanism is very good at ensuring that successful mating can occur only between individuals of the same species. In these higher spiders, the long, slim embolus is actually introduced directly into the sperm duct leading to each individual spermatheca.

LIFE-CYCLE

Like all animals, spiders start off as fertilized eggs which then undergo embryonic development before they hatch out. Development takes place within the eggs which in many spiders are inside a silken cocoon produced by the female spider to protect them. Most spiders emerge from the egg as a prelarva, which, although recognizable as a spider, is unable to move and has the limbs and jaws incompletely developed. The prelarva continues to develop inside the egg-sac at the expense of its stored yolk and may then moult to form another prelarval stage or directly to the more advanced larval stage, which still has little mobility but has the legs and jaws fully differentiated and fairly well-formed spinnerets. The larva continues to develop at the expense of its yolk and after a further one or two moults becomes the free-living first-stage nymphal spider which, apart from its size and non-functional sex organs, resembles the adult. It now catches its own prey and grows and moults up to ten times before eventually becoming a fully grown

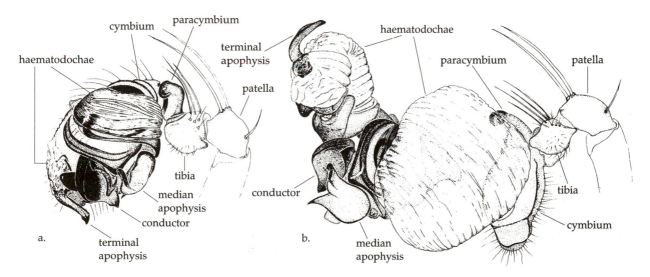

The left palp of a male garden spider (**Araneus diadematus**) viewed from the outer side showing the complexities associated with its fitting into the correct epigyne.

a. the palp in its deflated form.
b. the palp in its expanded form, with the haematodochae filled with blood under pressure, ready to be inserted into the female's epigyne.

Female spiders from at least two families carry their young around on the top of their abdomen for several days after they emerge from the egg-sac. This is a **Trechalea** species (Trechaleidae) from Argentina and her babies are still not able to feed themselves. They will eventually moult to become free-living nymphs and will then leave her protection.

mature adult. The number of nymphal stages relates to the eventual size of the adult, larger species undergoing more moults than smaller ones.

GROWTH

The only part of the spider's body which can stretch to any extent is the abdomen. In order for it to grow, therefore, the immature spider has to go through a series of moults or ecdyses, which involve the growing of a new exoskeleton and the shedding of the old one. In common with other arthropods and following a period of feeding, the spider's outermost cell layer, the epidermis begins to produce a new cuticle beneath the old one. At the same time, it secretes enzymes which begin to digest useful chemicals out of the old cuticle for recycling. The new cuticle is soft and folded so that it can be expanded after the old one is cast.

Prior to actually moulting, the spider stops feeding and becomes inactive. When it is ready to moult, it either hangs from a thread or, in the case of the mygalomorph tarantulas, it lies on its back. The spider will emerge head first from its old cuticle and in order to facilitate this, the heartbeat increases and blood is pumped into the cephalothorax, increasing its volume considerably and decreasing that of the abdomen. The result of this increased volume and

A European female nursery-web spider, **Pisaura mirabilis**, who has just completed her moult. She is hanging head-down from her old skin (exuviae) and has flexed her body and appendages to expand the new cuticle to its full size. Since it has already hardened and attained its normal coloration she will soon be lowering herself down on a length of dragline and resuming her normal life.

pressure is to rupture the already weakened old cuticle. Helped by movements of the jaws, this splits across the head and down the sides of the cephalothorax above the legs, the whole carapace then swinging up and back. Further movements and contractions of the abdominal muscles now cause the split to extend along the side of the abdomen, which eventually becomes free of the old cuticle. As the abdomen is coming free, so the legs, jaws and palps are withdrawn from the old cuticle, the most difficult part of the whole process. The spider now flexes its legs and stretches the new cuticle before it eventually hardens off and develops its normal colour on exposure to the air. At this stage, although the cephalothorax has increased considerably in size, the abdomen is smaller than before moulting as a result of the blood which was pumped out of it. As, however, it can stretch to some extent, it will increase in size as the spider feeds and grows prior to its next moult.

Once they are adult, the araneomorph spiders undergo no further growth or moults, except for swelling of the female abdomen with eggs. The longer-lived mygalomorph females, however, which can live in excess of 20 years, continue to moult throughout their lives. This enables them to replace lost or damaged surface sensory and urticating hairs, all of which are grown anew before each moult.

THE NERVOUS SYSTEM

The nervous system of spiders is much more condensed than that of other arthropods, the main nervous centres being situated in the cephalothorax. Above the oesophagus lies the supraoesophagial ganglion, effectively the spider's brain, with nerves connecting to the eyes, and the nerve centres controlling the jaws. Nerve fibres run from this either side of the oesophagus down to the much larger suboesophageal ganglion which has sections supplying the palps and legs. From the hind end of this ganglion, nerves run through the pedicel to supply the various abdominal structures.

THE TACTILE SENSES

Since the majority of spiders are nocturnally active, when sight is of lesser importance, it is their tactile senses which show a high degree of sophistication. Like other arthropods, spiders possess sensory structures, which tell them the position of their jaws, palps and legs. More important from the natural history viewpoint, however, are those structures which inform them about what is happening in their immediate surroundings. The spider has to be able to respond to stimuli coming in from two main sources, potential prey and possible enemies, and accordingly has to distinguish between them. The stimuli to which it has to be sensitive are mainly vibrations, either through the ground or substrate, such as a leaf, on which they are perched, or through the web. Alternatively, they also have to be able to respond to air movements created by flying prey.

Most spiders are very hairy creatures, one of their less-appealing characteristics to humans. Most of these tactile hairs have a connection to the nervous system and clearly they must therefore play an important role in the spider's sensibility. That this is so can be proved quite simply, for touching but a single hair will elicit an immediate reaction of some kind from a quiescent spider. In the wild, the spider will have such hairs in contact with the substrate on which it is standing or with the web in which it is lodged; vibrations brought about by prey will be detected and the spider can respond accordingly.

Movements of the air, as from an insect's wings, or low frequency sounds are picked up by a different kind of hair, the trichobothria. These are much less numerous than the tactile hairs, being found along the legs, and they are referred to as 'touch at a distance' receptors since the spider is able to orientate to sound produced by a spider of the opposite sex or to a buzzing insect without being able to see it. Experimental removal of the trichobothria seriously impairs this ability.

Vibrations through both the substrate and the air, in the form of sounds, not only stimulate hairs but also a type of receptor called the slit sense organ. These are situated in the cuticle, mostly on the legs and they respond when the cuticle undergoes some mechanical stress. One particular form of these sense organs, the lyriform organs, are used in web-building spiders to detect movements of the web induced by trapped prey.

CHEMICAL SENSES

These are what we refer to as taste and smell and there is ample evidence that spiders can do both. When approaching prey in the web, spiders will touch them with the tarsi of the front legs and with the palps. Microscopic investigation has revealed the presence of taste hairs on both of these structures and further evidence from rejection behaviour after biting distasteful prey indicates that spiders may also have some sense of taste located in the mouth region. 'Taste' seems also to be involved in courtship, for male spiders find wandering females by following their silken drag-lines. These are probably coated with pheromones which are detected by the male's tarsal chemoreceptors.

Situated on the tarsus of each leg are the tarsal organs which appear to respond to airborne chemical stimuli, in particular pheromones produced by members of the opposite sex.

VISION

With the exception of a number of cave-dwelling species, all spiders possess at least one and up to four pairs of eyes. The degree of development of the eyes and their ability to form images varies very much from family to family. In those spiders which are completely nocturnal or which catch their prey in webs, the eyes are usually small and probably have a limited ability to form images. They can, however, detect changes in light intensity as night follows day and vice versa and they can also respond to large shadows, allowing them to show the correct escape response if threatened by a potential predator.

Eye development and visual acuity is at its highest in those spiders which catch prey without the use of a web and notably in families whose members are active, daylight hunters. These include the wolf spiders (Lycosidae) and lynx spiders (Oxyopidae), which spend much of their time sitting around waiting for prey to pass. Once seen, it is followed and jumped on. Paramount amongst the active hunters, however, are the jumping spiders (Salticidae); they do not sit and wait for prey to come to them, but

The contrasting faces of two jumping spiders (Salticidae) showing how in one family there is some difference in eye arrangement. The **Thyena** species from Madagascar (*left*), with its homopteran bug prey, has the commonest arrangement whilst that of the leaf jumper **Lyssomanes viridis** (North and Central America) is less common (*below*). The huge jaws on the males are a feature of this genus. The largest eyes, the anterior medians, are used to fix on and line up prey before leaping on it.

EYE ARRANGEMENTS IN VARIOUS SPIDER FAMILIES

a. *Dysdera* (Dysderiidae), a six-eyed
   nocturnal hunter.
b. *Xysticus* (Thomisidae), a sit-and-wait
   daylight hunter.
c. *Evarcha* (Salticidae), a jumping spider,
   an active daylight hunter.

d. *Pardosa* (Lycosidae), a wait-then-rush-and-
   grab daylight hunting wolf spider.
e. *Pholcus* (Pholcidae), a daddy-long-legs
   spider, a small-eyed web builder which often
   takes other spiders as prey.
f. *Araneus* (Araneidae), a small-eyed orb web
   builder.

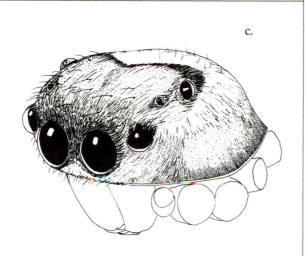

c.

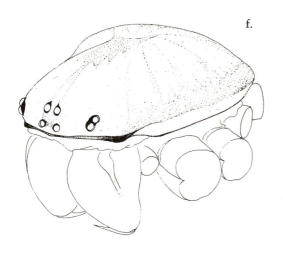

f.

These diagrams are also an indication of how eye-arrangement and general shape of the cephalothorax are of use in spider taxonomy.

actively search for it to the extent that during daylight hours they are seldom still. It is research on this large-eyed family which has yielded much of our knowledge on how spiders see.

The Salticidae are eight-eyed spiders, the most typical arrangement being to have them in three rows of four, two and two eyes. In a number of genera, there are somewhat different arrangements relating to alternative hunting strategies. The front row of eyes is composed of two forward-facing pairs. The largest of these and the ones with which jumping spiders 'look at' you when you are observing them are the anterior median (AM) eyes. On either side of these is one of the pair of smaller anterior lateral (AL) eyes. Just behind these is a pair of small, posterior median (PM) eyes, about which little is known and then further back on the side of the carapace is the pair of moderately sized posterior lateral (PL) eyes.

Structurally, the eyes show many basic similarities, any differences relating to their special roles. Each has a transparent outer cornea and lens, which is part of the cuticle, and below this is the vitreous body made up of transparent cells. The innermost layer is the retina with its connections to the central nervous system. In the anterior median eyes, the light-sensitive portion of the retina points towards the light and unusually there are four distinct layers of these cells instead of the more usual single layer. The spider is able to focus its anterior median eyes, not as we do by altering the shape of the lens but instead by altering the position of the retina in relation to the lens. In the remaining eyes, the light-sensitive portions of the cells points away from the light as it does in the human eye.

The field of view of the salticid eyes is shown in the figure on the following page. The widest field of view is obtained by the posterior lateral and anterior lateral eyes and when hunting it is one or other of these which is most likely to pick up the movement of prospective prey. The spider now swivels its highly mobile cephalothorax towards the source of the stimulation until the anterior median eyes fix upon it. Once they have done so, the spider is able to stalk and eventually spring upon its prey. There is some evidence, from at least

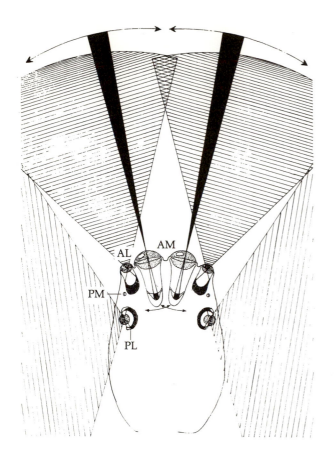

AM – anterior median eye. Visual field of about 10° but movement of retina gives total field of about 50°. There is no overlap.

AL – anterior lateral eye. Visual field of about 50–60° with some overlap frontally of about 25° and binocular vision.

PM – posterior median eye.

PL – posterior lateral eye. Visual field 120–130°

The field of view of a typical jumping spider. These large-eyed daylight hunters have a wide all-round field of view to help them locate prey and accurately focusing anterior median eyes which help them, once prey has been located, to line up on it for the final leap. The posterior median eyes are reduced in both size and function.

one jumping spider studied, that the anterior lateral eyes continue to play a role after detection, allowing it to jump at or follow more active prey.

SPIDER SILK

It has always been assumed, but for no good reason, since spiders and insects have very separate evolutionary lines, that spider silk is structurally similar to that of the other great silk producers, the lepidopteran larvae. Thus, the silk used by silk moth larvae in the production of their cocoons has attracted the greatest research on structure and has ultimately become a benchmark for all silk threads.

However, spider and lepidopteran silks may have very different structures, though the protein keratin, a component of hair and feathers in vertebrates, is common to both. Considering that the roles of spider and moth silks are very different, then these structural differences become very plausible.

Silk threads from the silk moth larva are known to consist of bundles of strands of totally disordered chains of amino acids (the building blocks of proteins), winding untidily in all directions within the fibre. When the thread is stretched these chains are straightened, setting up tensions within them as when a spring is stretched. When the pull on the thread is released, the chains then resort to their prestretched state, just as the stretched spring would. Although this silk is strong, spider silk is much stronger and this may in the main be due to the much more organized structure of the fibres. At present, the possible structure of just the drag-line of various species of the araneid genus *Nephila* has been elucidated. It appears that this silk consists of a flexible tube surrounding a central core. The tube consists of bundles of microfibrils winding in parallel spirals along the length of the thread, with fewer fibrils spiralling in the opposite direction to give a lattice-like structure. The inner core does not appear to be fibrous in structure. There also appears to be an outer membrane covering the fibril sheath, which almost certainly provides a waterproofing layer for the fibre. The similarity between this arrangement and that of the nylon ropes used in bungee-jumping merits some consideration.

SILK PRODUCTION

Since it first evolved as a means of lining the burrows of the earliest species, silk has played a major role in ensuring the success of the spiders as a group. Several different types of spider silk have so far been recognized, each produced by its own particular kind of abdominal gland. Each type of silk is produced in a liquid form which is then extruded through spigots at the apexes of the abdominal spinnerets (*see* figure right). There are three pairs of these spinnerets, which are believed to have evolved from pairs of abdominal appendages (originally used in female spiders to hold her eggs against the abdomen), for each produces a double strand of silk. Alternatively, in the cribellate spiders, multistranded silk is extruded from the cribellum, homologous to the anterior median spinnerets of ecribellate spiders. This multistranded silk is combed out by the calamistrum (*see* page 29), a row of bristles on each hind leg, to form the so-called hackled band of the cribellate spiders. As well as being able to select a particular silk from a particular gland for a specific purpose, the spider is able to control the properties of an individual length of silk by manipulating it in some way as it is extruded. The spigots appear to contain valves which can control the diameter of the threads and by altering the pull on the silk as it is exuded and hardens in the air, so its strength can be altered. Thus, the harder the pull on the silk as it is extruded, the stronger it is. Silk is in fact very strong, some types exceeding the strength of a steel thread of the same diameter.

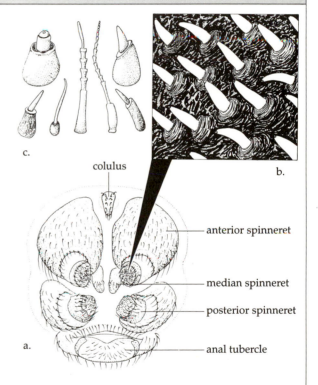

c.

colulus

anterior spinneret

median spinneret

posterior spinneret

b.

a.

anal tubercle

a. the arrangement of the spinnerets in the araneid spider **Zygiella x-notata**.
b. an enlargement of the tip of an anterior spinneret to show the spigots through which the silk is extruded.
c. a selection of spigots from a number of different spiders to show their shape and arrangement, which relates to the different types of silk they produce.

A view from behind of a female **Amaurobius** lace-weaver combing out hackled band silk. The silk is being extruded from her cribellum, with the calamistrum on her right-hand hind tarsus. Her rather untidy web with its strands of hackled-band silk is clearly visible.

SILK FUNCTION

Although it probably evolved as a means of lining, and thus waterproofing, the burrows of the earliest spiders, silk now plays many roles in the life of the average spider, though its involvement in egg-sac production means that greater use of it is made by females. Individual kinds of silk are manufactured by different types of gland for diverse purposes. The aciniform glands, for example, produce the silk used for wrapping prey. In female spiders, this soft silk is also used as the immediate covering for the eggs within the egg-sac. The tough outer silk layer on the egg-sacs is, however, manufactured by the cylindrical glands, which are not found in male spiders. The silk for the dragline, which all spiders lay down as they go about their daily rounds, is extruded from the minor ampullate glands, which, along with the major ampullate glands, also produces structural silk in many spiders. Other glands individually manufacture the core fibres of the capture spiral in orb-web spiders, the sticky globules which coat these, the hackled band of the cribellate spiders and the cement used to attach other silks to the substrate.

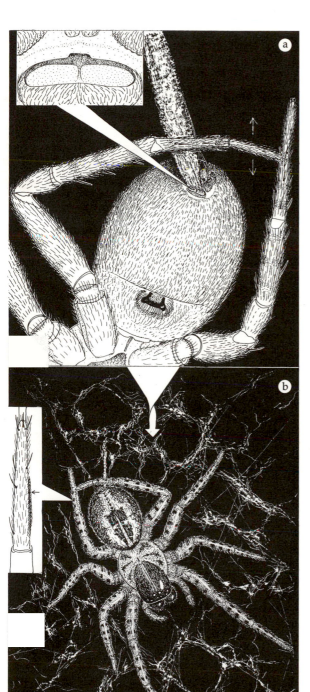

Laying down of hackled band silk by a cribellate spider.

a. The underside of a female **Amaurobius** spider as she combs out the strands of silk from the cribellum using the calamistrum on the metatarsus of her left hind leg. In order to comb she has placed the tip of her left leg against the tarsus of the right leg and both move in a rapid back and forth action to tease out the strands of silk as they are extruded. INSET. The cribellum.

b. The same spider from above showing her untidy web of hackled band silk as she combs out more to add to it. INSET. A hind leg metatarsus with the calamistrum arrowed.

(*Below*) A diagram to show how an araneid spider holds onto its web. The silk is held between the median claw and the flexible serrated bristles or auxillary foot claws. To let go of the silk the spider lifts the median claw and the thread springs clear, the outward curve of the serrated bristles keeping it clear of the larger paired claws.

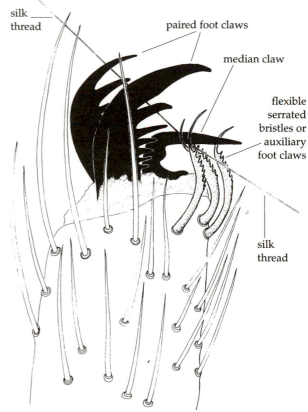

silk thread

paired foot claws

median claw

flexible serrated bristles or auxiliary foot claws

silk thread

STICKY CAPTURE THREADS VERSUS THE HACKLED BAND

There can be no doubting the fact that the aerial orb-web, with its ability to exploit such a great diversity of flying insects, is the ultimate prey-capturing device of spiders. The orb-web has evolved in two distinct, though fairly closely-related families, the Uloboridae and the Araneidae. The Uloboridae are a cribellate family which, with their sister family the net-casting deinopids, encompass just 300 species. In comparison, the orb-web constructing araneid spider family has more than 2,500 species and also vastly outnumbers the uloborids (in terms of the absolute numbers of individuals) in existence at any one time. Unlike the araneids, the uloborids lack poison glands and just wrap their prey; they build a horizontal rather than a vertical orb-web. These differences may be a major determining factor in the relative success of the two groups but it is also possible to relate their success to the differences in the prey-capture components of the uloborid and araneid orb-webs.

What parameters must be met by an aerial web if it is to be 'economically' successful as far as the spider is concerned? Firstly, it must be able to constrain the prey until the spider arrives to bite or wrap it. Secondly, it must be able to absorb the energy imparted by the prey, when it collides with the web, with the minimum amount of damage to the web itself. Thirdly, and perhaps less obviously, its manufacture needs to expend the least amount of energy but with the maximum amount of return in terms of prey captured. In order for it to meet the first requirement of restrainment, silk must be relatively lax, so that the prey finds it difficult to obtain a purchase on it, by which means it could pull itself off the sticky surface and escape. In order to meet the second requirement, however, the silk needs to be both strong when stretched and with a degree of elasticity, properties which will also assist in resisting the effects of being blown around in strong winds. Its elastic recoil, though necessary must not, however, be too violent otherwise it would throw the prey back out of the web. In order to fulfil the third requirement, the silk needs to be as thin as possible, thus using the minimal raw materials, and it must require as small amount of

energy in production as is possible. If we compare the silk of an araneid, the garden spider *Araneus diadematus*, with that of a cribellate orb-web builder, the former has, to some extent, achieved these ends more successfully than the latter.

The success of the garden spider's capture spiral is a result of the interaction between the structure of its silk and the way the silk is exploited in the web. As the core silk of the capture spiral is extruded, it is coated with a layer of very viscous fluid from a different set of glands. This fluid takes up water from the atmosphere, and as it does so, it separates into numerous discrete sticky droplets along the core silk. Now, silk is normally dry and relatively stiff, this dryness being maintained by a waterproof outer coating. When wet, the silk will certainly stretch but will not recoil, so if the silk were not waterproofed, a shower of rain would cause the whole web to collapse. The difference between the capture fibres, which are not proofed, and the scaffolding fibres, which are, is in fact most noticeable after rain, when the latter remain tight and the capture fibres hang in a series of loose loops between them.

Why then is capture silk wet? The answer lies in those droplets and their high surface tension. The figure opposite shows how the system works. It can be seen that inside each droplet, long lengths of the core silk are coiled up and held their by the surface tension. If a capture thread without these coils was hit by an insect it would stretch to its full length and, although it would actually become stronger, once fully stretched and with little recoil, the insect's struggles would soon break it. The coils inside the droplet, however, maintain tension within the capture thread as a whole. As the struggling insect pushes against the thread trying to break it, so it gets longer, not just by stretching but by unreeling from the droplets. As the insect relaxes, or pushes or pulls in other directions so the droplets reel in any slack, keeping the whole system taut and intact. This increases both the chance that the prey will get stuck on the sticky droplets and the chance the spider will arrive to subdue it.

a.

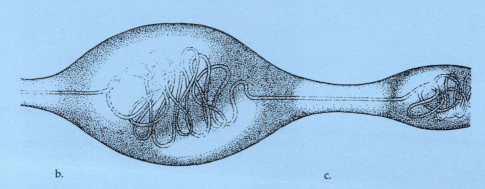

b.   c.

A comparison between sticky araneid and fluffy hackled band silk.

a. viscous globules strung along a line of araneid capture spiral silk.

b. an enlargement of the globules to show how the strands of core silk are effectively 'wound up' inside them, allowing line to be paid out and then 'reeled in' as prey struggles on the web.

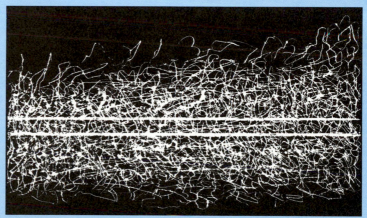

c. a highly magnified view of multi-strands of cribellum silk laid down over scaffolding lines to produce hackled band silk.

The capture threads of the cribellate uloborid spiders are very different from those of the garden spider (*Araneus*). True, they have core fibres but instead of being coated with sticky fluid they are covered in a combed-out mass of very fine fibres of dry silk, which have been extruded from the hundreds of tiny spigots on the cribellum. Each of these fibres is in fact only ¹⁄₂₀th the diameter of the *Araneus* silk. The effect of the combing is to cause the threads to puff up along the core fibres so that the hackled band bears some resemblance to a spring. Although not covered with a sticky agent, it is, in mechanical terms, 'sticky', possibly due to electrostatic forces induced while combing and/or

because the mass of fine threads entrap the hairs and bristles of insect prey. The struggles of the insect are absorbed by stretching of the core fibres and accompanying breakage of some of the finer fibres. It tends to be longer lasting than the garden spider's capture spiral and in the long run, is probably just as effective at catching prey.

The true success of the garden spider's capture spiral therefore seems to lie in its economy of production. It requires considerably less in the way of raw material in its manufacture than does the hackled band and the energy expended in its production is much less than that required to comb out the latter, which is a long and painstaking process.

03 Classification of Spiders

As a result of new approaches to the study of taxonomy, spider classification has changed a great deal over the past two decades with the result that families once thought to be distantly related are now considered very close, and vice versa. One of the problems was that, in the past, relationships were often based simply on the sharing of primitive characters with the result that some families contained species which had not evolved from a common ancestor. The classification system that it used here is, therefore, the best compromise for the group as a whole based on present-day knowledge.

Previously, the spiders were separated into three main suborders, the first comprising the primitive giant trapdoor spiders, with their still segmented abdomens, the second the mygalomorph 'tarantulas' and the third the araneomorphs, the so-called 'true spiders'. (It should be made clear that the term 'tarantula' should strictly speaking apply only to one European species of wolf spider, or at least to members of its genus *Lycosa*. Nowadays, however, it is equally applied to the hairy mygalomorph spiders such as the bird-eating spider and its relatives.) The giant trapdoor spiders of the Liphistiidae, the only remaining family within the suborder Mesothelae, are now, however, considered to be a sister group to all of the other spider families in the suborder Opisthothelae. Within the Opisthothelae there are, then, the two major infraorders, the Mygalomorphae, the bird-eating spiders and their kin with 15 families and the Araneomorphae, all of the other spiders, with more than 70 families. Reference to the cladogram opposite will enable understanding of the relationship between these groupings and between the various spider families as a whole.

What now follows is an overview of those spider families which, as a result of their accessibility or their outstanding behaviours, are most likely to be encountered. Those in **bold** lettering are the families most likely to be encountered on a day-to-day basis. The common names for the groups, where they exist, are those that appear most often in the literature.

LIPHISTIIDAE (GIANT TRAPDOOR SPIDERS)

The liphistiids are the only spiders surviving today that retain dorsal tergites (sclerotized plates) on the abdomen, which show us that the group as a whole evolved from an ancestor with a clearly segmented abdomen. Other primitive and observable features are the downward striking jaws and the four pairs of spinnerets placed well forward of the anus on the underside of the abdomen. Internally, they have two pairs of book lungs. They live in tubular holes dug in the ground and as their common name indicates they build trapdoors to cover the entrance. In some species, a ring of trip-lines extends from the mouth of the burrow. They are sit-and-wait predators, rushing out of their holes to catch passing prey detected by vibrations or as they contact the trip-lines. The distribution of the liphistiids is limited to Japan, China, Sumatra and South East Asia.

MYGALOMORPH SPIDERS

The spiders in the mygalomorph families retain, some but not all, of the more primitive characteristics of the preceding group in that they have

CLADOGRAM OF SPIDER FAMILIES

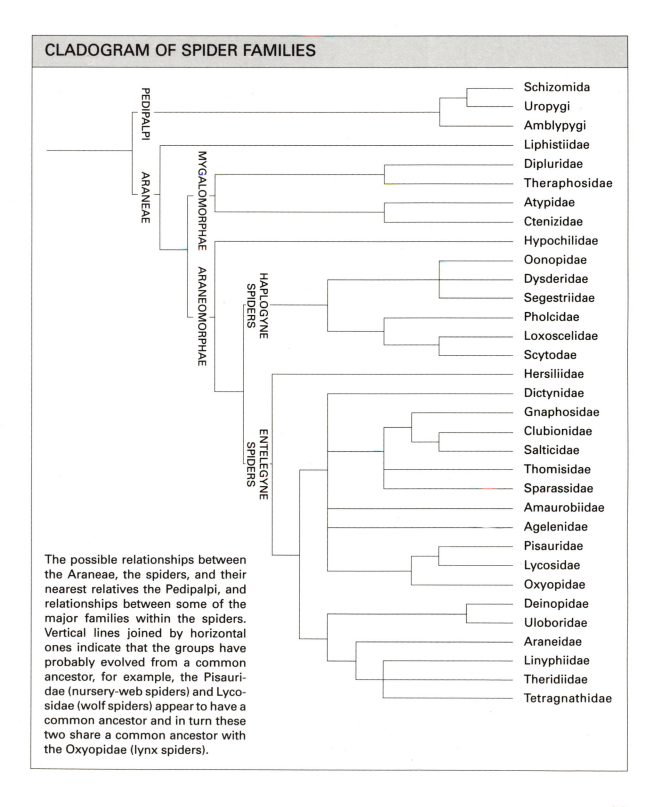

The possible relationships between the Araneae, the spiders, and their nearest relatives the Pedipalpi, and relationships between some of the major families within the spiders. Vertical lines joined by horizontal ones indicate that the groups have probably evolved from a common ancestor, for example, the Pisauridae (nursery-web spiders) and Lycosidae (wolf spiders) appear to have a common ancestor and in turn these two share a common ancestor with the Oxyopidae (lynx spiders).

downwards striking jaws and two pairs of book lungs. On the other hand, the abdomen never shows any segmentation and the anterior median pair of spinnerets have disappeared completely and the anterior laterals are reduced or also missing. One consequence of this is that they produce fewer kinds of silk than the araneomorph spiders and make less use of it in their everyday lives. They vary in body size from midgets less than 1mm long to giants 9cm long, awesome spiders which seem even larger due to their long legs. Most species spend the greater part of their lives in burrows and it is males that are wandering around in search of females that are most likely to be encountered.

CTENIZIDAE (TRAPDOOR SPIDERS)

Like the giant trapdoor spiders, the mygalomorph trapdoor spiders dig tubular burrows in firm ground and in all but a few species cap this with a specially manufactured hinged cover. In order to help them to dig, the ctenizids possess on the end of the basal cheliceral segment a series of teeth forming a rake or rastellum. A number of related, smaller, lesser-known mygalomorph families share this characteristic. Like most tube-dwelling spiders, they are sit-and-wait predators, rushing from their burrows to pounce on passing insects.

DIPLURIDAE (SHEET- OR FUNNEL-WEB SPIDERS)

This is a family which has gained notoriety in recent years due to the inclusion in it of members of the genus *Atrax*, including the Sydney funnel-web spider, whose bite is highly toxic to humans. They have well-developed spinnerets with which some diplurids construct a tubular retreat and, radiating from its entrance, a sheet-web which can approach 1m in diameter. These are fast-moving spiders, with the best eyesight of all mygalomorphs, rushing out of their lair to catch prey which lands, struggling on the sheet web. Other members of the family live in burrows but in soft soil, since they lack the digging rastellum of the ctenizids. The majority of this family are tropical or subtropical in their distribution.

THERAPHOSIDAE ('TARANTULAS' OR BIRD-EATING SPIDERS)

The majority of this family are hairy spiders with a pair of 'brushes' or clustered hairs on the ends of the legs which allow them to climb on smooth surfaces. The terminal segments of the spinnerets are long and slim and extend beyond the end of the abdomen. Many of them live in burrows, without caps, from which they emerge short distances to catch prey. Some of the South and Central American species have become tree-dwellers, occasionally feeding on birds from the nest. They reach their greatest distribution in the Americas but are also found in Africa (notably the baboon spiders), Asia and Australia. Though large and fearsome in appearance, they are relatively gentle souls and a number of species are popularly collected as pets.

ATYPIDAE (PURSE-WEB SPIDERS)

A common feature of the mygalomorphs is that they line their burrows with silk but the Atypidae have extended this use as a unique method of prey capture. These spiders extend the silk tube either across the ground or up the trunk of a tree in the form of a closed purse. They then lie in wait in the tube and plunge their long, sharp chelicerae from within into any prey item which walks over it. In order to open the tube so that prey can be dragged in, they have a row of sharp teeth along the edge of the basal cheliceral segment against which the fangs close. Purse-web spiders retain one primitive characteristic not found in other mygalomorphs, i.e. a single dorsal

(*Above right*) A male western desert tarantula **Aphonopelma chalcodes** wandering around the Arizona desert at night in search of a female. He is a member of the Theraphosidae, which are typically very hairy mygalomorphs.

The purse-web spiders of the mygalomorph family Atypidae are much less hairy than other mygalomorphs. **Atypus affinis** is a European species with a purse which lies along the ground. The female normally spends all of her life within her silken tube but in this instance she has been temporarily removed from it.

plate (tergite) at the base of the abdomen. Living permanently in tubes they tend to be less hairy than other mygalomorphs. They are North American, Eurasian and African in their distribution.

ARANEOMORPH SPIDERS

The araneomorphs, with their diaxial chelicerae, tracheal systems, abilities to make many types of silk and their complex sexual apparatus are more advanced than the mygalomorphs. Their greater number of families, species and extant individuals is a pointer to their greater biological success. One characteristic where they appear more primitive than the mygalomorphs, however, is in their retention of the anterior median spinnerets, either as the cribellum in cribellate spiders or as the apparently non-functional colulus of ecribellate spiders. The subdivision of the araneomorphs into the Haplogynae and the Entelegynae is based upon the structure of the female reproductive system. The haplogynes lack specialized fertilization ducts while they are present in the entelegynes, usually in the company of an epigyne, the males then having complex palps.

HYPOCHILIDAE (LAMPSHADE WEAVERS)
This araneomorph family retains primitive characteristics which in some ways make it a link between the present group and the mygalomorph spiders. Their mygalomorph characters are the possession of two pairs of book lungs, the venom glands restricted to the basal cheliceral segment and a similar arrangement of ostia in the heart. Their araneomorph character is the presence of a cribellum. The arrangement of the jaws, however, is intermediate between the two groups, though interestingly they are closer to those of the mygalomorphs than those of the araneomorphs. They are long-legged spiders building lampshade-shaped webs in the form of a net of hackled-band silk below which they hang to await the arrival of prey items. One species, *Hypochilus thorelli* is quite common in the mountains of the south-eastern USA.

HAPLOGYNE FAMILIES

In these families, the male palps are simple and the females lack an epigyne.

OONOPIDAE (SIX-EYED SPIDERS)
These are tiny spiders, no more than 1–2 mm long. They usually live amongst leaf litter or under stones where they are hunters rather than web-builders. A number of them are brightly coloured and some have plates variously placed on the dorsal surface of the abdomen. They are perhaps best known for one or two tiny species, both in Europe and America, which live in domestic situations and may be seen after dark running around on the huge expanses of walls and ceilings, hoping to encounter suitable prey.

DYSDERIDAE (SIX-EYED SPIDERS)
This family is included on account of one species alone, the cosmopolitan woodlouse spider, *Dysdera crocata*. This spider has enormous jaws, needed to pierce the tough integument of its favoured prey. It has been spread around the world by man and may be found by turning over stones which catch the sun and under which it is damp enough to attract woodlice. Strangely, if there are ants present then the spider will be absent. It is said to have a painful bite.

SEGESTRIIDAE (TUBE-WEB SPIDERS)
Another family of six-eyed spiders with very tubular bodies and the front three pairs of legs directed forwards for grasping prey. They live in tubes in crevices in walls or rocks or in holes in trees from which radiate a series of trip-lines like the spokes of a wheel. If a wandering insect touches a trip-line, the spider rushes out and grabs it.

PHOLCIDAE
(DADDY-LONG-LEGS SPIDERS)
This family earns its common name from the fact that its members have extremely long legs in relation to their bodies. It is best known for those species which are man's camp followers and are now cosmopolitan in distribution. They are usual-

The daddy-long-legs spiders of the family Pholcidae have a nearly circular carapace and very long legs in relation to their body length. This female of the very widespread species **Pholcus phalangioides**, which is common in houses and under stones in warmer temperate regions, is feeding on eggs which she has stolen from the jaws of another female of the same species.

LOXOSCELIDAE
(BROWN OR RECLUSE SPIDERS)
These are small-to-medium sized, six-eyed spiders, rather drab brown in colour and known for their notoriety as being poisonous to man. There are many species in the Americas and they are also found in Africa and Europe, *Loxosceles rufescens* being virtually cosmopolitan. They spin untidy webs in dark spaces under rocks, in holes in the ground and unfortunately in buildings, where, in their encounters with man, they may cause serious bites.

SCYTODIDAE
(SPITTING SPIDERS)
This is another family of six-eyed spiders with a characteristic domed carapace, the dome accommodating the enlarged venom glands. The latter pro-

ly eight-eyed though a pair has been lost in a few species and the bodies are usually either globular or somewhat elongate. They build untidy webs under stones, in caves or cellars or in the corners of rooms. The cosmopolitan *Pholcus phalangioides* is a common house species, and among its prey it numbers the much larger and fiercer house spiders of the genus *Tegeneria*.

duce, as well as poison, a glue, which is shot out in a stream from the tip of each fang, immobilizing insect prey. Most likely to be encountered is *Scytodes thoracica*, which has been introduced into most countries by man. It is small, the females attaining just 6mm in length and is a nocturnal hunter, walking around over walls and ceilings in search of its prey.

ENTELEGYNE FAMILIES

In these families, the males usually have complex palps and the females paired copulatory pores and usually an epigyne, though there is some reversion to a more haplogyne condition in a few genera in some families.

HERSILIIDAE (TWO-TAILED SPIDERS)

This is a family of mainly tropical spiders which live on the trunks of trees, their coloration tending to merge in with that of their surroundings. Their most obvious characteristic is their very long posterior spinnerets, the 'tails' in their common name, which can be as long as the whole abdomen. They hunt actively on the tree bark, running rapidly away when threatened with their 'tails' held vertically above the abdomen.

GNAPHOSIDAE (GROUND SPIDERS)

The ground spiders live, as their name implies, mainly on the ground where they live under stones and other debris, emerging mainly at night to hunt for prey. They are flattened-tubular spiders,

The two-tailed spiders of the family Hersiliidae are unmistakable with their very long posterior spinnerets. This is a **Hersilia** species with the family's typical flattened body form and cryptic coloration. Careful inspection reveals the strands of silk that the spider lays down on the tree to act as triplines for prey.

The Gnaphosidae are short-sighted hunters who spend the hours of daylight under stones and bark, emerging at night to forage. Turning over a piece of rock has revealed this European gnaphosid, **Drassodes lapidosus**, often called the stone spider.

The members of the family Dictynidae are in the main small spiders which build their webs on plants. Many of them are rather drably marked in browns, greys and blacks though a number, such as this female **Nigma puella** from Europe, are quite pretty. They are cribellate spiders using hackled band silk to trap their prey. One of the other characteristics of the family is that the males and females often cohabit.

usually drably coloured in blacks and browns, though some species are much brighter. A species which is becoming more widespread around the world, since it lives with man, is *Herpyllus blackwalli*, a mouse-grey spider which scuttles around on walls after dark and which does indeed resemble a small mouse, thus its common name of mouse spider. The Gnaphosidae are a large family with some 2,200 species worldwide.

CLUBIONIDAE (RUNNING SPIDERS)

Spiders of this family closely resemble the gnaphosids in appearance, though they tend to be less flattened. The posterior median eyes are circular, rather than oval as in the gnaphosids, and the arrangement of the spinnerets is somewhat different. Again, many species are brown or black though clubionids are more likely to be found living and hunting on plants or by day. The family includes a number of excellent and interesting ant-mimics, with some tropical species being almost indistinguishable from real ants.

SALTICIDAE (JUMPING SPIDERS)

This is the largest of the spider families, with in excess of 4,000 species already described, and they are found throughout the world though are at their

An **Acragas** species jumping spider, mimicking a mutillid wasp, from the Brazilian rainforest.

A jumping spider in rainforest in India. Typical of the Salticidae, it has a high-fronted carapace with large eyes and the front two pairs of legs sturdier than the hind legs.

greatest abundance in tropical regions. They are a family whose members, though mainly small spiders, are likely to be seen since most of them are day-active hunters, wandering around in all situations in search of their prey. Many of them are patterned and brightly coloured, or both, as a result of their patches of iridescent hairs, and their inherent curiosity of anything that moves means that they will often stop to examine it further. They tend to be short and compact, though a few are long and slim and some are ant-mimics. Their most noticeable characteristics are their eight eyes (the large anterior medians are clearly visible), their highly mobile cephalothorax and their stout front two pairs of legs. They are the real hunters of the spider empire and their common name of jumping spiders is well chosen for they not only run around, but jump quite happily from perch to perch in search of prey.

THOMISIDAE (CRAB SPIDERS)

The Thomisidae are lie-in-wait ambushers with broad squat bodies reminiscent of crabs and, like the jumping spiders, they do not build webs. They possess eight eyes, some of which may be on the end of lateral protuberances, and the front two pairs of legs are sturdier than the others and adapted for grasping prey. Many are highly camouflaged, no doubt to hide them from predators, since they often sit conspicuously on flowers or leaves waiting for prey. Some species have long slim bodies and lie along plant stems where they are both well camouflaged and can expect prey to approach within grabbing distance. One subfamily, the Philodrominae (family Philodromidae according to some authorities), are more active and wander around on leaves and even in buildings in search of prey. The family has a worldwide distribution.

SPARASSIDAE (HUNTSMAN OR GIANT CRAB SPIDERS)

Referred to by some authorities as the family Heteropodidae, they are more common in the tropics, although at least one species, rare at that, is found in the British Isles. On average, they are larger and more flattened than the previous family and many of them have the legs rotated so that they stick out to the side, and all pairs point forwards. Some tropical species live alongside man and are tolerated because of their use in catching pest insects such as cockroaches.

The huntsman spiders of the family Sparassidae are very flattened spiders with laterigrade legs. This **Holconia (Isopoda) immanis** giant huntsman is lying in wait for prey at night in rainforest in Queensland, Australia.

AMAUROBIIDAE (LACE WEAVERS)

The lace weavers are cribellate spiders which usually build untidy tangles of web in dark holes, often expanding them outwards to cover neighbouring surfaces. Most obvious about these webs are the thick, fluffy, bluish-white strands of hackled-band silk associated with cribellate spiders. In Europe one species, the window spider, *Amaurobius fenestralis*, builds its web on and sometimes in houses. The amaurobiids are in the main robust spiders and the cribellum on the underside of the female abdomen is easily distinguishable with a good magnifying glass. Until fairly recently the Amaurobiidae were thought to be closely related to the Dictynidae (*see* page 39), even to the extent of being considered to be members of a single family. They are now reckoned to be much more distantly related, deserving their separate family status.

AGELENIDAE (FUNNEL-WEB OR SHEET-WEB SPIDERS)

Not to be confused with the mygalomorph funnel-webs, which build similar structures, this family includes the well-known house spiders of the genus *Tegenaria*, whose males so often frighten people in the world's temperate regions as they run about the floor in search of females, sometimes falling into the bath as they do so. The family is made up of around 1,000 species worldwide and the majority build a tubular retreat which opens out onto an expansive sheet-web. The famous water spider, *Argyroneta aquatica*, which builds a bell-shaped web under water in which it lives in a bubble of trapped air, is sometimes included in this family though of late it has been placed in its own family, the Argyronetidae.

PISAURIDAE (NURSERY-WEB SPIDERS)

Spiders of this family resemble somewhat those of the Lycosidae (below) and in some texts they have been called wolf spiders. Other common names of pisaurids are water, raft or fishing spiders because members of one genus, *Dolomedes*, which get quite large, are able to run on the surface of water where they catch their prey. The females carry their egg-sacs around with them in their jaws and place them in a silken tent when they are ready to hatch, remaining on guard over them for a time.

LYCOSIDAE (WOLF SPIDERS)

Although there is an overall similarity between the lycosids and the closely related pisaurids, close examination will reveal that the eyes are on average larger, the posterior lateral pair set back quite far on the carapace in some genera. Wolf spiders have always been thought of as active hunters but recent research has shown them to be more in the way of sit-and-wait predators, prepared to move their pitch every so often. Most of them live on the ground, some digging burrows from which they emerge to

Some of the larger wolf spiders of the family Lycosidae are very attractively marked though seldom seen because of their nocturnal habits. This female **Lycosa** from Spain digs a burrow in which she passes the daylight hours.

hunt and there is little doubt that their fairly large eyes help them to spot prey, which they then pounce on. Other stimuli must also be involved, however, since many of them are nocturnal. Female wolf spiders also carry their egg-sacs around with them but attached to the spinnerets, leaving their jaws free for action at all times. The wolf spiders in the genus *Lycosa* are amongst the largest of the araneomorph spiders and some of them are quite handsome in appearance. The wolf spiders have a worldwide distribution.

OXYOPIDAE (LYNX SPIDERS)

Whereas the wolf spiders hunt on the ground, so the lynx spiders have adopted the life of a hunter on plants. Typically, they have a noticeably pointed abdomen, spiny legs and fairly large eyes, though not as large as those of the jumping spiders. They combine periods of active hunting, when they will happily jump from leaf to leaf, with periods of sit and wait. Female lynx spiders do not carry their egg-sacs but affix them to the plant on which they live and stand guard over them.

The lynx spiders hunt actively on plants in search of their prey. The anterior lateral eyes, the large pair on the front of the head of this South African **Peucetia** species, are the most important for forward vision, compared with the anterior medians in the jumping spiders with their similar life-style.

DEINOPIDAE (OGRE-FACED OR NET-CASTING SPIDERS)
This is a small family of cribellate spiders found in the world's tropical regions, only likely to be seen on a nocturnal foray but with a very interesting life-style. They have long, slim bodies and are alternatively called stick spiders, but their most noticeable feature is the large pair of posterior median eyes giving them their 'ogre face'. Uniquely among spiders the deinopids construct an elastic net and then, holding it in the front two pairs of legs and hanging from a scaffolding web they throw the net over passing insects.

ULOBORIDAE (CRIBELLATE ORB-WEAVERS)
The common name of these spiders comes from the tufts of feathery hairs found on the front legs. Once thought to be a more primitive family on the basis of their being cribellate, it is now realized that the uloborids are closely related to the araneid spiders (below), the major world orb-web family, but they have retained the use of the cribellum. The relative merits of the hackled band *versus* the sticky trap-line have already been discussed in Chapter 02. The uloborids are unique in that they lack venom glands. Many of the family, which numbers around 200 species, are tropical though the triangle spiders of the genus *Hyptiotes* are found in temperate regions.

ARANEIDAE (ORB-WEAVERS)
Members of this family are perhaps the most noticed of all spiders since they are the major builders of that supreme flying insect trap, the orb-web. The archetypal araneid is a stout spider with a globose abdomen which sits either at the centre of, or in a lair close to, its orb-web. There are, however, many exceptions to this, for in the tropics a number of araneids have bizarre spines sticking out of the abdomen and in other genera the abdomen may be elongated, flattened or even triangular. A number of araneids have even given up using the orb-web and notable among these are the bolas spiders, which spin a large globule of sticky silk on the end of a short line and trap moths on it as they fly past. Araneids of one kind or another are found throughout the world with about 2,600 species reckoned to be included within the family.

This is one of two varieties of the marbled orb-weaver **Araneus marmoreus** sitting feeding on her silk-wrapped prey. It has the typical build of the family Araneidae and the small eyes of a spider which does not rely on sight for prey capture.

LINYPHIIDAE (SHEET-WEB SPIDERS)
This is a family of small-eyed spiders which are very abundant in the temperate regions of the world. They are more elongate than either the web-builders discussed above or below, and the majority of them live a secretive life amongst grass and detritus, in leaf litter, under stones, etc. Quite commonly they have stridulating ridges on the

A female sheet spider **Linyphia triangularis** (Linyphiidae) with a shield bug which she has caught in her sheet web.

chelicerae. They are divided into two main sub-families, the Linyphiinae and the Erigoninae. The former contain the largest members of the family, a number of whom build their webs in more obvious places on bushes and trees and where the spiders themselves may be found hanging beneath the main sheet. The erigonines, commonly called 'money spiders' in the British Isles, are much smaller, often black and the males of a number of species have bizarre extensions on the ocular region of the head. The linyphiids are great 'balloonists' and in late summer and autumn, countless millions of them may be floating around in the breeze at the end of a short length of gossamer. Around 3,700 species have been identified to date, making them the second largest of the spider families.

THERIDIIDAE (COB-WEB OR COMB-FOOTED SPIDERS)
Whereas the araneids have had great success with the orb-web so the theridiids have had similar success with the scaffold-web, since, with around 2,200 species, this family approaches the latter in

The members of the spider family Tetragnathidae are often long and slim like the European grass spider **Tetragnatha extensa** illustrated here. This genus constructs a horizontal orb-web though it may also be found sitting stretched along a plant stem in a cryptic pose (*left*).

abundance. The name 'comb-footed' derives from the presence of a row of enlarged hairs on the tarsi of the hind legs which help them to fling silk over their prey to subdue it.

TETRAGNATHIDAE (BIG-JAWED SPIDERS)

The common name of these spiders comes from the fact that many members of the family have noticeably elongated mouthparts. Both sexes from the genus *Tetragnatha* have on their jaws projections which interlock during their face-to-face mating. Many of the family are long, slim, long-legged spiders which build a typical orb-web. Recently added to the family are the world's largest orb-weavers of the genus *Nephila* and the rather less elongate spiders of the genus *Meta*. Not all of them are web-users, however, for spiders of the genus *Pachygnatha* hunt for their prey amongst grass and other thick vegetation. Members of the Tetragnathidae may be found in most parts of the world.

04 Feeding in Spiders

The connection between spiders and webs is so powerful in the minds of the general public that any spider seen scurrying along the ground is immediately assumed to be lost. In reality, a large percentage of the total known number of spiders manages to make a good living perfectly well without the aid of any kind of web. Even some former web-builders have given up the use of silk and gone back to a life of sneak-and-pounce or patient ambush. Examples include adult *Pachygnatha* (Tetragnathidae), which are active prowlers among vegetation, although the juveniles still spin small webs, and *Drapetisca socialis* (Linyphiidae) in which the highly cryptic adults live on tree trunks. Conversely, in some spider families which are overwhelmingly committed to prey capture without a web, such as jumping spiders, there is the occasional exception which employs silk to snare its prey.

The quality of a spider's eyesight tends to dictate the techniques available for obtaining a meal. The short-sighted hunters set some kind of trap, as in trapdoor spiders, or wait in ambush in some locality which acts as a catchment area for insects, such as a flower, as practised by crab-spiders. Other short-sighted hunters, such as gnaphosids and clubionids probably acquire most of their prey by accidentally bumping into it. This is likely to happen sooner rather than later in spiders which often live among an abundance of prey under stones, among

The European spider **Drapetisca socialis** (Linyphiidae) has dispensed with the complex scaffold web typical of its family and spends the day sitting cryptically on tree-trunks in woodland.

grass tufts, etc. Among the sharp-sighted hunters, the wolf spiders may also sit around a great deal and wait for something to chance by, but are then able to home in on a target from some distance and make a kill with extreme accuracy. This is especially true of the jumping spiders, the most mobile of hunters, which spend most of their lives on the prowl in active pursuit of their prey.

AMBUSH STRATEGIES

The ambush seems to have been the original strategy adopted by spiders before the more sophisticated silk-based methods were developed. For mygalomorph spiders, being large, fat, heavy and somewhat lumbering and clumsy in their movements dictates that the ambush should be set under some kind of cover, such as a burrow. However, some large tropical tarantulas rely on a cloak of darkness to provide security and hunt at night in the open on tree trunks and rocks.

TRAPDOOR AND PURSE-WEB SPIDERS

Trapdoor spiders are among the least-often noticed of all spiders. Their beautifully camouflaged front doors are unlikely to be spotted by chance, and can be infuriatingly difficult to find even when a careful search is being made in a likely spot, such as a gently sloping bank sprinkled with dead leaves, moss and lichens. The females are the real stay-at-homes, the true agaraphobes of the spider world, never voluntarily venturing forth more than a short distance from the cosy protection of their silk-lined burrows. Here they spend the whole of what can be a considerable lifespan lasting many years – as many as 20 years in some species. However, in the most primitive ctenizids such as *Nemesia*, the spider habitually leaves its burrow in close pursuit of prey.

During burrow-digging operations, the spider harnesses its long and powerful fangs as a pair of

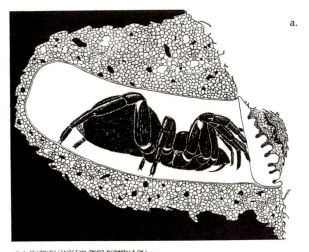

a.

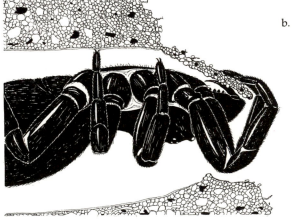

b.

a. An idiopine female trapdoor spider from Kenya holding her trapdoor shut with her front legs. (Black = bark, particulate = soil, white = silk.)

b. Moulding the door with chelicerae and front legs.

picks to prize loose the soil. This is then gripped in the chelicerae and each pellet of excavated soil is then taken laboriously up to the surface for disposal. Two basic types of door are employed: the more primitive 'plug type' or 'cork type.' which is moulded from pellets of spoil resulting from burrow-digging operations. This is reinforced with silk and swings open on a silken hinge which constitutes an extension of the burrow-lining. The more advanced 'wafer-type' is excised from the top of the sealed silken retreat.

Plug-door construction is basically similar in all species so far observed. Starting from the silk hinge and working downwards, pellets of soil are squeezed into place on the developing door by the chelicerae, palps and legs. The material is then cemented in place with silk from the spinnerets. As the door grows in size, the spider pauses now and then to tug it powerfully inwards to test the fit. The whole process can take 6–12 hours, and even then, this may not be the end of the story, as doors are often reinforced and thickened over time. The door forms an effective barrier to enemies, although only as long as it can be held firmly shut. Some spiders do this with their fangs, others use their back legs, while at least one uses its front two pairs of legs, leaving its fangs free for a retaliatory strike at the intruder should it gain entrance.

Sitting quietly inside a closed burrow waiting for a meal to wander within grabbing range on a regular basis would, at first sight, seem to offer a fair guarantee of slowly starving to death in a ready-made grave. Surprisingly enough, this does not happen for three main reasons. Firstly, ground-dwelling insects and other arthropods are usually extremely common in most environments, particularly after dark. Secondly, unlike many spiders, which tend to be fussy eaters, trapdoor spiders will tackle just about anything, especially woodlice whose distasteful defensive secretions cause them to be rejected in a hurry by most spiders. Thirdly, minute vibrations created by the prey's feet as it walks along overhead penetrate the soil clearly enough to be picked up by the spider, poised ready behind its door. In the ctenizid *Cyrtocarenum cunicularium* from Greece, feeble low-frequency vibrations of between 1 and 100Hz in the earth can elicit a capture-pounce from a spider behind a door which is only very slightly ajar, and with none of the occupant's limbs protruding. Unlike many open-air sit-and-wait ambushers (such as thomisids), *C. cunicularium* will prepare for further action only a short time after making a kill, rather than confining itself to one meal at a time.

In some trapdoor spiders, there will be no capture-strike unless the prey actually blunders against the door, behind which the spider lies ready to fling the door open, grab the prey and

dart back inside, all accomplished in a single slick operation almost too rapid for the eye to follow. The spider will always try to keep its rear legs firmly in contact with the burrow, but in extreme situations, where a valuable target would otherwise be missed, the spider will rush full tilt out of its burrow before careering back inside, bearing its prize. Some species leave the door slightly ajar with the front legs sticking out. This expedites rapid reaction, while the ample provision of hairs on the legs enables the early detection of vibrations caused by approaching prey.

The odds against something stumbling across or even making a close approach to a door only some 15mm across are obviously not good. These unattractive odds are considerably shortened by those species which extend the range of their prey-detecting systems. This usually means surrounding the door with a fan of silken alarm lines, constituting an early-warning system. By maintaining its legs in contact with these trip-wires, the spider can capitalize on prey which would otherwise have ambled undetected past the relatively narrow door. *Arganippe raphiduca* is one of a number of Australian species which economize on valuable resources by substituting twigs for the silk, arranged like fingers around the burrow entrance and with just short silk connections. The merest touch on the tip of one of these twigs by a passing insect alerts the spider to come rushing forth and pounce.

The purse-web spiders (Atypidae) dispense with an actual door, but instead continue the silken lining of their burrows outwards to form a finger-like above-ground extension. In the European *Atypus affinis*, this lies inconspicuously among grass on the ground or concealed under a stone, but in the American species it is usually extended upwards along a tree trunk. Much as in trapdoor spiders, the waiting purse-web spider depends on pure chance to send a meal strolling across her silken tube. She then reacts with incredible speed and accuracy to spear the invisible insect through the silk with her very long curved fangs. Having impaled her victim, she cuts a hole in the silk with her serrated jaws, pulls the prey inside and then tidily repairs the damage before commencing to feed.

EATING MEAT – BUT ONLY AS LONG AS IT IS TASTY

Some of the giants among spiders leaven their mainly invertebrate diets with a sprinkling of vertebrates such as frogs, lizards, mice or small birds. A number of the large tropical theraphosids such as *Avicularia* are even known as bird-eating spiders, although poultry probably figures on the menu only on an occasional and purely opportunistic basis. However, some South American tarantulas such as *Lasiodora* and *Grammostola* seem positively to prefer vertebrate prey such as frogs, lizards and small snakes and apparently shun mere insects. Similar tastes are also evident in the ctenid *Cupiennius coccineus*, a large rusty-brown wandering spider which is

common in certain tropical rainforests in Costa Rica. At night the heavyweight and quite formidable females either wait in ambush on vegetation, or else creep stealthily across the broad rainforest leaves, stalking frogs whose loud resonating type of calling would send vibrations through the leaves which the hunter can home in on using the sensitive lyriform slit-organs on its feet. In this species, these can also detect airborne sounds, of which those made by small tree frogs such as the harlequin frog (*Hyla ebraccata*), a common prey during its highly vocal mating season, would be of a frequency which the slit organs are particularly suited to detect. In fact, many spiders have similar organs on their feet, which are in effect their 'ears'. A captured frog is soon reduced to a shapeless pulp as it is turned over and over and mashed thoroughly in the spider's jaws.

Not all frogs are equally vulnerable. In the spider's rainforest home one of the commonest bite-sized frogs, the strawberry arrow-poison frog (*Dendrobates pumilio*), is seemingly immune to attack. The frog's brilliant red and blue skin secretes extremely potent nerve toxins, whose existence is advertized to visually hunting predators (such as birds) by the bright 'do not touch' warning colours. These cannot be perceived by the wandering spiders, either by day or at night, yet even so, the spiders reject the frog unharmed after the briefest touch with the palps and legs. It seems that the mere 'taste' of the frog's skin is enough to invoke disgust and rejection by the spider, using the contact chemoreceptors situated on the tips of its front legs and palps.

This sense of taste by touch is common to many (perhaps all) spiders and plays a vital role in rejection of prey which could potentially harm the spider. Sometimes, however, the chemoreceptors fail to sound the alarm bells in time, and the spider unwisely bites a chemically-protected prey item. The result usually follows quite rapidly, as the spider promptly spits out its meal and staggers off in apparent

*A large **Cupiennius coccineus** wandering spider (Ctenidae) feeding on a harlequin-patterned tree frog in a Costa Rican rainforest.*

Like many spiders, this **Phidippus** *sp. jumping spider (Salticidae) in Mexico is not averse to feeding on chemically protected insects, in this case a warningly coloured arctiid moth.*

distress to some spot where it can 'vomit' and wipe liquid off its chelicerae against a nearby leaf. However, in general, spiders are noteworthy for their willingness to make do with chemically-protected prey which would be quickly rejected by other predators. For example, burnet moths (Zygaenidae) are extremely distasteful and contain a massive dose of highly poisonous hydrogen cyanide, yet are apparently accepted as prey by at least some spiders.

The other group of spiders which often catch vertebrate prey is the so-called fishing spiders in the family Pisauridae. These large handsome spiders can run with ease on the water surface, although they prefer to adopt a waiting stance at the water's edge. Their prey often consists of insects which have fallen into the water. Their helpless struggles to escape generate surface ripples which the waiting spider detects through its sensitive feet in contact with the surface film. However, some species such as *Dolomedes triton* certainly also capture larger prey which are quite at home in the aquatic environment, such as small fish, frogs and tadpoles. These betray their presence by producing ripples whenever they break the surface. *D. triton* has proved capable of identifying the epicentre of this concentrically spreading wave at a distance of up to 18cm. Unfortunately, capture attempts resulting from such long-range detection are only about half as successful as those made accidentally by a prey being helpful enough to surface close to the waiting spider. The main handicap seems to be the spider's difficulty in distinguishing between prey-generated ripples and those, so confusingly numerous, caused by leaves or twigs falling into the water. When it does make contact, the spider is a capable fisher, using its substantial chelicerae to gaff slippery fish up to four-and-a-half times its own weight. One American *Dolomedes* is thought to dispense with pure chance, and actually encourages fish to come and be caught by 'angling' for prey, dabbling the front legs in the water as 'bait'.

Trechalea magnifica, which inhabits small streams in the Central American rainforests, is another wolf spider with unusual tastes. Unlike *Dolomedes*, it is active at night, and includes in its diet small freshwater shrimps, a gastronomic item so far unreported from any other spiders with fishing habits.

In many of the more advanced non-mygalomorph spiders, such as the segestriids, the silken tube of the retreat is constructed inside a pre-existing cavity, such as a hole in a wall or rock. It is then extended outwards to form a funnel whose mouth is often surrounded by silken trip-wires. Old walls are often a mass of such webs, although only at night do the spiders come and sit at the mouth of their lairs.

STAKE-OUTS ON FLOWERS

What better place to lie in wait for an insect than on a flower? After all, flowers exist for the sole purpose of attracting insects as pollinators. Yet despite this, relatively few spiders actually cash in on the advantages offered by flowers as productive real estate, probably because of the dangers inherent in spending large amounts of time in full view on such an exposed site. Dedicated flower-squatters therefore tend to be restricted to those species which can adequately blend into their background, namely a relatively small number of crab-spiders. The most familiar and abundant of these is the so-called flower spider (*Misumena vatia*) which is common on both sides of the Atlantic. In the British Isles, its favourite flowers tend to be either white or yellow, a choice dictated by the spider's ability to change its colour back and forth (over a period of a few days) to match both these colours. In springtime, when there is a shortage of flowers, the overwintered (usually white) juvenile spiders often perch on

Unlike most web-building spiders, crab spiders (Thomisidae) do not store prey, but deal with only one prey item at a time. The hive bee **Apis mellifera** walking past this female flower spider **Misumena vatia** occupied with feeding on a fly in England is therefore perfectly safe from attack.

leaves, where their resemblance to a bird-dropping is not insignificant, and they certainly manage to capture a regular supply of insects. However, with the appearance of a suitable flower, the spider will gravitate towards it, even from a considerable distance, despite its poor eyesight, which dictates the need to wait for prey to come within very close range. In two instances (observed by one of the authors), two plump white juvenile females suddenly disappeared from leaves on which they had been faithfully sitting for over two weeks. A day or two later, two similar-looking females appeared on the newly-opened white flowers of a rowan tree (*Sorbus aucuparia*) right above the spiders' former position. If these were indeed the same females, they must have detected the flowers 3m above them and then reached them by a long and tortuous route up the trunk and out along the branches. How a mere spider (and short-sighted at that) could make the mental connection between the presence of a distant trunk and a possible path up to the flowers directly overhead is a mystery.

When waiting for the arrival of prey, *Misumena* sits with its front legs outstretched at the sides, ready to snap shut on the victim in a pincer movement. The spider's venom is particularly powerful, usually acting in seconds, especially when the bite is delivered in the favoured position in the neck, through which the main nerve ganglions run. However, if the bite strikes home elsewhere, delaying its effectiveness, the spider will cling on to the flower tenaciously with its back pairs of legs until its struggling victim finally succumbs. This potent venom is a characteristic of all spiders which lack a web to help restrain the prey until the venom takes effect (i.e. crab-spiders, wolf spiders, lynx spiders, jumping spiders, etc), eliminating the need for wrapping of the prey with silk. *M. vatia* does not fight shy of tackling even large stinging insects such as bumble-bees, but once it is occupied with feeding on its prey, any further visitors to the flower are in no danger. Unlike in most web-building spiders, the crab spiders, along with wolf spiders and their ilk do not store prey, dealing with only one meal at a time. It is therefore not unusual to see a hoverfly walking back and forth quite

safely across the plump body of a *M. vatia* female preoccupied with feeding.

The most bizarre flower spiders are the superb South American species of *Epicadus* whose abdomens are deeply corrugated with a series of humps which aid the spider to blend into the flower. Despite this, flower spiders are basically easy prey for those of their enemies with the most finely-tuned sensory apparatus. This is amply demonstrated by the fact that spider-hunting wasps in the USA often provision their nursery-cells almost exclusively with dozens of paralysed *M. vatia*, plucked repeatedly off flowers despite their wonderful camouflage. Numerous species of *Thomisus*, *Misumenops* and *Misumenoides* also specialize on flowers. In the British Isles, the plump pink *T. onustus* usually settles on pink heathland flowers such as heather (*Calluna vulgaris*), cross-leaved heath (*Erica tetralix*) and bell-heather (*Erica cinerea*). Not all crab-spiders, however, practise the art of ambush on flowers. The many small brown species of *Xysticus* in Europe lie in wait on leaves, rocks, soil or sand, although they will also perch on flowers. Here, despite being more conspicuous than *M. vatia* and its like, they still make a reasonable living. The green densely hairy *Heriaeus hirtus* from Europe specializes on perching invisibly among hairy-leaved plants.

WOLF AND LYNX SPIDERS

These names are applied to three groups of agile spiders belonging to the families Lycosidae and Pisauridae (wolf spiders) and Oxyopidae (lynx spiders). As applied here the term 'wolf spider' is something of a misnomer, for the concept of a pisaurid or lycosid joining, wolf-like, with its fellows to run down their prey in a long and exhausting hunt is somewhat wide of the mark. In reality, most wolf spiders are sit-and-wait predators, not really so different from crab-spiders. The commonest European species, *Pardosa amentata,* is frequently seen in suburban gardens scurrying busily around, but such apparently purposeful activity is a little misleading, as it is probably the arrival of the observer which is responsible for the action. In fact, studies of this species have established that it really spends most of its time sitting around for something to come within range. When it gets fed up with one particular spot, it moves, but surprisingly enough this is not related in any way to how good the pickings have been, although moves do tend to increase with rising temperatures. Even so, the spider is engaged in actual walking for less than four minutes out of each 24-hour period – some wolf!

The commonest of the European pisaurid wolf spiders *Pisaura mirabilis* (also called the nursery-web spider – *see* Chapter 05) is similarly sedentary. It prefers to devote long periods to basking comfortably on leaves low down near the ground, relaxed but watchful until a meal shows up. When this happens, the spider emphatically demonstrates that it is wide awake by exhibiting considerable agility and amazing precision targeting – one of the authors has watched apparently somnambulent individuals of this species spring into action by flinging themselves almost vertically upwards to pluck a passing fly out of the air. The acuity of vision needed to accomplish such a feat is obvious, facilitated by the battery of relatively large forward-facing eyes. It is also essential to obtain a good grip with the front legs so that they can press the prey against the fangs, giving the venom time to take effect. In web-building spiders, the web itself performs such a restraining service, but in wolf spiders 'sticky feet', substantial claw-tufts comprised of adhesive hairs, serve the purpose.

Many pisaurids build prey-catching webs in the juvenile stages, but abandon this habit when adult. Web-building in adults is restricted to relatively few species, such as *Euprosthenops*, *Vuattouxia* and *Tetragonophthalma* from Africa and *Inola* from Australia. In *Architis nitidopilosa* from the American tropics, the adult catching-web is three-dimensional and amazingly variable in shape, although it always has a funnel at one side leading to two broad vertical sheets. However, this spider's adoption of the web-based lifestyle seems to be almost grudging, for it will still leap *Pisaura*-like into the air to catch passing insects, and likewise does not wrap its prey in silk, unlike 'proper' web-building spiders such as araneids and uloborids. However, some spiders with wolf-like habits do enswathe their prey, such as the two-tailed spiders *Hersilia* and *Tama* (Hersiliidae) which use their long paired spinnerets (the 'tails') to enwrap a victim as the spider runs round and round it, trailing silk. Two-tailed spiders generally lurk as sit-and-wait predators on tree trunks, escaping observation due to their very flattened outline and cryptic colours. Such sedentary spiders can become very attached to a 'favourite' site. Thus, the huntsman spider *Holconia* (*Isopoda*) *immanis* from Australia tends to have one or two preferred ambush spots where it sits night after night for month after month. It will jump on just about anything which comes along, from centipedes, spiders and stick insects to beetles, moths and lizards. These range in size from less than 1cm to around 10cm, reflecting the ability of such a large and sturdy spider to overpower even relatively large prey.

Lynx spiders have similar habits, loafing about for hours on end upon leaves, but quick to intercept prey from these relatively stable attack platforms. The green lynx spider (*Peucetia viridans*) is a familiar sight in the southern USA and throughout Mexico and Central America, with several very similar-looking species also common in Africa and Madagascar. *P. viridans* is probably typical by having a very catholic diet which frequently includes other spiders and members of its own species. Cannibalism is also common in wolf and jumping spiders, which are bound to make regular encounters with smaller members of their species. As they make easy targets, it is not surprising that they are taken, confirming what has long been thought, that spiders probably kill more spiders than any other source. Some of these are specialists on spiders (*see* later in this chapter), but few spiders will resist the temptation to make an easy meal of a relative, particularly a junior. In the American wolf spider (*Lycosa lugubris*), around one-sixth of all prey is thus composed.

As recently as 1983, the long-held view that lynx spiders had long ago dispensed with the use of webs in the adult stage was contradicted when a web-building species, *Tapinillus longipes,* was discovered in a tropical rainforest in Costa Rica. It builds a non-sticky sheet-web with a knock-down scaffold, similar to those built by agelenids and linyphiids, but does not wrap its prey at any stage.

This Kenyan **Peucetia** sp. lynx spider (Oxyopidae) has caught a dragonfly by leaping on it.

GOING FOR THE HIGH JUMP

The most artful, athletic, sharp-eyed, colourful, entertaining and personable of the visual hunters are the jumping spiders in the family Salticidae. Their most endearing trait is their common habit of turning their tiny heads upwards to peer intently and with apparent comprehension at the enormous face looking down on them. Jumping spiders are constantly on the prowl, progressing in a characteristic jerky fashion, peering in all directions for signs of a possible meal, always ready to crouch cat-like for the pounce. Although able to launch an attack from as much as 14 times their body length away, they also share a cat's habit of trying to sneak up on their target as closely as possible, body-hugging the substrate, before taking the final plunge. Launched powerfully upwards with their back legs, their front legs held out forwards, they hold their fangs outstretched, ready to grasp and pierce the target upon landing. They can also track flying targets and are ready to pounce accurately as soon as they land.

A jumping spider's amazing hunting prowess is all thanks to its visual system, which is by far the sharpest and best organized of all spiders. The pair of large forward-facing headlamp-style principal eyes are responsible for acute vision, while three pairs of smaller eyes detect motion. In a typical attack sequence, the salticid detects a prey's movements with its secondary eyes and then turns to fixate the target with its primaries. These are focusable miniature telephoto lenses and enable the salticid to distinguish and recognize potential prey from as much as 30cm away. The narrow field of view intrinsic to the 'telephoto' design of the primary eyes is compensated for by their mobile eye-tubes (having both rotational and side-to-side movement) and the extreme mobility of the head.

The visual dexterity of jumping spiders is ably backed up by a surprising degree of intelligence. In fact, jumping spiders are the 'intelligentsia' of the spider world, capable of problem-solving feats which would defeat any other spider. For example, *Phidippus pulcherrimus* is capable of working out an alternative and lengthy detour to get within range of a fly sitting on the far side of a gap too far to be bridged with even the mightiest of leaps. The spider's 'intellect' seems evident by its ability to work out in advance the route to be taken to reach its goal, and then actually to follow this itinerary without actually being able to see its final destination, perhaps for some considerable time, until it is almost on top of it. *Phidippus* is probably typical of salticids in its facility for recognizing the type of prey to be dealt with, and therefore the best way of mounting the attack. When coping with looper caterpillars whose defensive reaction consists in regurgitating gobs of unpleasant liquid, the spider avoids becoming contaminated by rapidly dragging its victim backwards, leaving a trail of vomit harmlessly staining the leaf. With large and possibly dangerous prey, the spider first circles around so that it can pounce from the rear, while ants are treated with considerable respect and held away from the body, keeping it clear of the bite or sting. Jumping spiders also tend to reduce the speed of their advance as they near a 'touchy' target such as a fly, thereby reducing the chances that it will spot the hunter and fly away.

As jumping spiders do not deploy silk to facilitate immobilization of prey while the venom takes effect, the latter has to be particularly powerful, although it would still be logical to assume that large prey several times the spider's own size would be too much of a handful. In fact, salticids frequently attack and overcome amazingly large insects, including those which are themselves fierce predators, such as dragonflies and katydids. The secret of such giant-killing feats seems to lie in the incredible tensile strength of the spider's dragline. This is securely fastened to the substrate at the rear before any capture jump is hazarded. Strenuously struggling prey which could otherwise push itself free by heaving mightily with its legs against the substrate is rendered helpless by being dropped into mid-air on the drag-line, along with its attacker. By constantly maintaining a firm grip with its jaws, the spider has now bought time for the prey to become enfeebled through exhaustion combined with the effects of the venom.

This trapeze act also comes in handy when attacking *Pogonomyrmex* and other ants which can instantly release an alarm pheromone. Within seconds this can bring dozens of the victim's fellows running to the rescue. By doing a quick bungee jump with its prey, the spider can confidently get on with its meal, while the ant's would-be saviours mill around helplessly up above, unable to descend the spider's slender drag-line. Another use for the vertical drag-line is to provide an isolated and inaccessible mid-air position where the spider can slumber the night away in relative safety.

A rather stockily-built and heavily muscled *Euryattus* species from Australia routinely practises aerial interceptions from a running leap, and also routinely tackles large prey by dropping on a drag-line. It uses pure muscle to subdue its victim, something which its rather weak venom fails to do.

Prey capture by a few of the more primitive jumping spiders is still accomplished with the aid of silk. In other salticids quantity use of silk is reserved for the construction of nests in which they sleep, moult, lay eggs and sometimes mate. *Spartaeus spinimanus* and *S. thailandicus* from South East Asia adorn the surfaces of tree trunks with large sheet-webs, beneath which the spiders lurk, lunging through the silk to capture any prey – mostly moths – which strikes the web. Unlike in the purse-web spider, the salticid then has to make its way laboriously out onto the web surface to haul its prey back inside, rather than cutting a slit for direct admission.

THE WEB-BUILDERS

Webs come in all shapes and sizes, using silk which is sticky or dry, multi-stranded 'hackle-banded' or simple. Sometimes its use is hardly more advanced than in the trapdoor spiders. *Plectreurys tristis* (Plectreuridae) from the deserts of the southwestern USA builds a small but very strong non-sticky sheet-web beneath stones. Whereas most spiders rapidly convert their prey into a glutinous messy blob by chewing it in their chelicerae, while copiously coating its surface with large quantities of digestive fluids, *P. tristis* merely seems to make a series of tiny feeding chinks in the hard exoskeleton of its prey (particularly beetles) through which it squirts digestive juices. The spider then sucks back the liquified contents, leaving the skeleton largely intact. The stinking defensive chemicals released by ground beetles (Carabidae) when attacked seem to be ignored by the spider, another example of how relatively impervious spiders seem to be when faced with chemical defences which would instantly deter other predators.

FUNNELS, TUBES, SHEETS AND SCAFFOLDS

The notorious Sydney funnel-web spider (*Atrax robustus*) is but one of a menagerie of spiders which skulk inside a funnel which opens out onto a sheet-like web whose design fits it mainly for tripping-up hopping and walking insects. True funnel-web spiders are members of the Mygalomorphae, but some of the most familiar kinds of true spiders construct similar kinds of webs, especially the *Tegeneria* house spiders (Agelenidae), whose webs are so much a feature of dark unswept corners in garages and outhouses around the world.

A sheet-web leading into a funnel draped across a small bush or among grass and low vegetation is likely to be *Agelena* or (in America only) *Agelenopsis*. The broad sheet web of the labyrinth spider (*Agelena labyrinthica*) is not armed with gum, so relies on causing the incoming insect to flounder helplessly on the obstacle-course maze of trip-lines above the main sheet. Even thus hampered, it may still be fortunate to stagger towards the edge of the sheet, demanding quick detection and attack by the spider.

A scaffold of threads above the sheet causes flying insects to come crashing downwards. As in all spiders, the web's owner can come hurtling across its treacherous surface with consummate ease to dispatch a struggling insect, never seeming to put a foot wrong among the confusion of silk, despite having eight of them to cope with. The geometry of the tarsal claws with their long hairs probably helps, but it is the accompanying lyriform organs which probably make a major contribution to the spider's sure-footed speed, constantly feeding back information about the precise angle of each foot and the tensions in the legs. In this way the spider always 'knows' exactly how each of its feet is interacting with the complex surface of the web. As in most of these sheet-web spiders, the prey is picked up in the chelicerae and hauled back to the cover of the funnel, to be consumed in safety.

The most abundant webs in temperate countries are made by the money spiders in the family Linyphiidae. Although the web is much smaller, its basic design is broadly in line with that of the araneid *Cyrtophora hirta* described above, having a broad sheet (which can be convex or concave) surmounted by scaffold-lines and secured below by guy-lines. The spider has to react promptly to the arrival of prey, there being no sticky silk to ensnare it.

The familiar hammock web of the sheet spider **Linyphia triangularis** in England. Note the upper and lower scaffold lines above and below the sheet.

A MEDLEY OF WEBS

Acusilas gentingensis from Malaysia is an araneid in the group Cycloseae. The web is remarkably loosely constructed, with a gap of 45° at the top. Incorporated into the centre of the web is a leaf which the spider uses as a retreat. Remarkably enough, the web of *A. malaccensis* is nothing more than a platform extended from a leafy retreat, representing a mere 45° sector of a complete orb web, just about the size of the sector missing from the web of *A. gentingensis*. By contrast, the web of *A. coccineus* is a more or less complete orb. This illustrates the great variety of web geometry found within just three species of a single genus.

The horizontal orb-web of the Australian *Cyrtophora hirta* (Araneidae) is constructed upon a scaffold of interlacing threads projecting above and below the orb. Unusually for an araneid, *Cyrtophora* webs do not contain any viscid silk, even on the spirals. The total diameter of the structure may reach 1m, with the orb platform itself measuring some 15–20cm across. The periphery of the orb is pulled upwards into a more or less concave shape by the tension in the upper scaffolding. This 'knockdown' zone also acts to bring flying or leaping

Acusilas gentingensis. *Web and retreat formed by rolled leaf.*

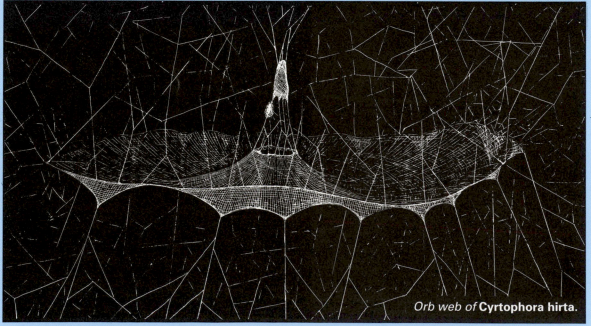

Orb web of **Cyrtophora hirta.**

insects tumbling down onto the orb below, where the spider rapidly pounces on them. When rushing to bite and wrap its prey, the spider does not trail a drag-line behind it from the hub, unlike in all other araneid types. If an insect becomes lodged in the overhead tangle-web and fails to fall, several species of *Cyrtophora* have been seen to help it on its way by vigorously shaking the web beneath the stranded insect. This does not seem to happen in other araneids, but has been observed in *Psechrus argentatus* (Psechridae) which has a similar type of web to *Cyrtophora*.

In an idiosyncratic habit highly uncharacteristic of other orb-web builders *C. hirta* ignores the arrival of a second insect once a meal has already been secured and stored in the web. Storage always takes place in the hub, never at the capture site as happens in some araneids. The webs of adult females tend to be surrounded by groups of satellite webs, probably occupied by the main web's own offspring. This could represent a step on the road to the kind of communal living seen in other members of the genus.

The webs of the cosmopolitan genus *Episinus* (Theridiidae) are generally of a greatly reduced minimalist design aimed at trapping prey moving over the ground. *E. maculipes* from Europe has one of the most reduced of all webs, but sites it above ground in bushes and low trees, where sticky blobs liberally applied to the lower threads seem to be amazingly effective at trapping an adequate supply of prey. This mainly comprises plant bugs and lacewing larvae which are fairly mobile on the leaves at night. The webs are also quite large and can span gaps of up to 20cm between branches.

The Central American *Drymusa dinora* (Scytodidae) spends its life beneath logs where its rather simple permanent web, consisting of a few simple tangled threads, is built across crevices and horizontal tunnels in the rotting wood. Its purpose is apparently limited to warning the spider that something has entered and to slow down its movements. This then gives the spider time to rush and build an extra trapping-web at its own end of the tunnel, after which it races past the prey to block up the entry point with yet more silk. The prey is now effectively trapped, and the spider can move in to administer the first bites. Groggy from the venom beginning its work, the prey usually staggers around within the trap for while, but

Episinus maculipes *female on web.*

the spider does not take much notice until its movements slow to the point where it can be safely wrapped in silk. If something really large or fierce comes through the front door, the spider stays out of the way until the intruder has safely passed right through. With bulky heavyweight beetles quite often blundering unstoppably through (only to be expected in the spider's type of habitat), but in so doing only destroying the minimal permanent web, the spider economizes on the silk that would be regularly destroyed should the permanent web be larger. In its present thrifty arrangement, the spider only deploys extra silk when it is going to yield material benefits.

Such a prey-capture method is very different from that practised by the celebrated *Scytodes* spitting spiders. By spitting a meshwork of gooey threads from their chelicerae, the target is immediately stopped in its tracks, firmly cemented to the substrate.

The 5mm long nocturnal *Scoloderus cordatus* (Araneidae) from Florida builds a huge perfectly vertical web in the shape of an upside-down ladder up to 1.2m long, taking as much as three hours of continuous labour. The extended upper part of the web, surmounting the spider-containing orb, consists of a dense mesh of sticky threads designed to catch moths. Moths usually escape from normal araneid webs because their scales quickly rub off when they touch the sticky spirals, rendering them clogged and ineffective. By fluttering vigorously, the moth can usually struggle free, in effect by harmlessly 'shrugging off' a small part of its coat. However, when a moth strikes the perfectly vertical and very dense sticky mesh of the ladder web, its struggles initially rub off some scales, but the mesh prevents it from breaking free. By thrashing about, it merely trickles ever downwards, rubbing off more and more scales until eventually bare patches begin to appear, when the web can finally take a conclusively firm grip. An hour before dawn, the spider dismantles its web and eats it. Although the expansive web represents a major investment, it does permit the spider to exploit with maximum efficiency a prey item usually wasted by most spiders, namely moths. By recycling the web at dawn, the owner minimizes any losses in the system.

In contrast to the considerable investment in time and material made by *Scoloderus cordatus* in web construction, *Wixia ectypa* (Araneidae) takes less than two minutes, just around dusk, to rig up its simple device. The web consists of non-sticky silk and is usually placed more or less horizontally in the crook of two branches. The radii are tethered to the branch

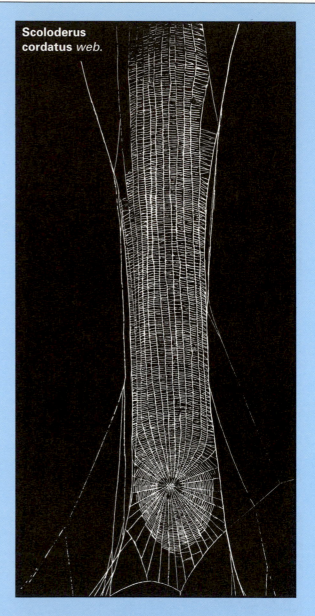

Scoloderus cordatus *web.*

with multiple attachment strands, which perform the prey-detecting function, alerting the spider when an insect walking along the branch touches one of the strands. The spider then carries out the unusual task (for an orb-web spider) of actually having to subdue a prey item which has a firm hold on a solid substrate. It does this by running around and around the branch and over the prey, enswathing the whole lot in silk before biting. Dangerous prey, such as predatory stinkbugs with their long lance-like stabbing

Wixia ectypa *web.*

horizontal triangular section of an orb-web with a mid-line thread dividing the triangle in half. From these frame-threads hangs down a series of sticky loops, which are securely fastened to the mid-line thread, but fastened to the outer frame threads with an easily broken joint. An insect colliding with the sticky spanning threads breaks the fragile joint and is left hanging downwards on the thread. This is so securely suspended from the mid-line thread that the insect can whirr around in circles on the end of its tether without breaking it loose from its attachment. The spider merely has to dash up, heave its booty upwards on its fishing line and give it a bite. This slick yet economical design has much in common with the reduced web of another araneid, *Poecilopachys australasiae* from Australia.

Arcys nitidiceps (Araneidae) from Australia (illustrated overleaf) has taken the reduction of the orb-web to its logical limit by restricting it to just a single non-sticky horizontal suspension thread. After dark the spider hangs from this line (from 10–90cm long) with its front legs stretched out to its sides, much like an expectant crab-spider. Indeed, during the day this is exactly how *Arcys* species behave, for they abandon their nocturnal webs and position themselves in thomisid-like ambush on leaves. Several other araneids have completely abandoned their webs and always ambush prey in this way, including *Archemorus* and *Celaenia*.

mouthparts, are left strictly alone, presumably because the spider's capture technique provides inadequate safeguards during wrapping. This strange process enables the spider to take advantage of one type of prey – namely crawling insects – which are not adequately covered by normal orb-web spiders.

A *Pasilobus* sp. (Araneidae) from New Guinea builds a web which in the elegance of its design and operation can be said to have evolved one step ahead of the normal orb-web. *Pasilobus* builds a

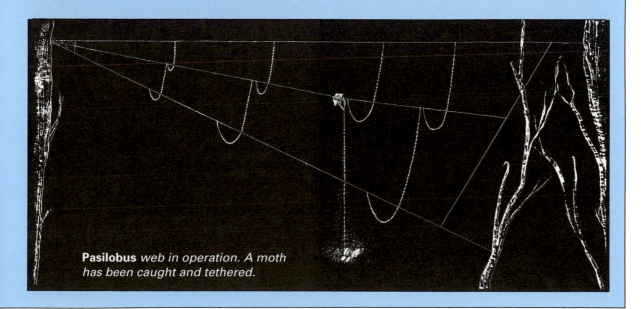

Pasilobus *web in operation. A moth has been caught and tethered.*

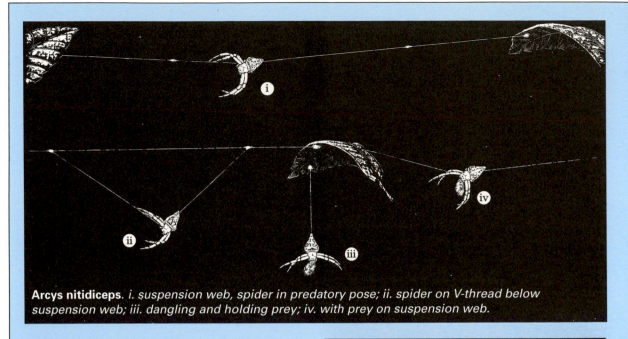

Arcys nitidiceps. *i. suspension web, spider in predatory pose; ii. spider on V-thread below suspension web; iii. dangling and holding prey; iv. with prey on suspension web.*

At least six species of *Miagrammopes* (Uloboridae) from the American tropics have also greatly reduced their webs; in *M. simus*, there is just a single catching line hanging down vertically from a horizontal thread on which the spider waits. Unlike in *Arcys*, *Miagrammopes* webs use sticky cribellar silk. The spider pulls the silk taut with its legs, and then gives it a quick tug when an insect strikes home, abruptly following up by allowing the silk to droop suddenly, enmeshing the insect in loops of sticky thread. As there is no evidence that these webs actively attract prey, in contrast to *Phoroncidia studo* (*see* below), it might be thought that the reduction of a web to just one or two threads would result in a very poor rate of captures. In fact, tests with artificial single-thread sticky lines in New Guinea captured an amazing average of four insects per day. This surprising rate of success may be due to the difficulty experienced by insects in spotting a single thread, compared with the relatively conspicuous full or partial orb, which may be noticed in time to take avoiding action. The habit of hanging by the legs from non-sticky lines on spiders' webs is also widespread in tropical flies (Diptera), and may also contribute towards the success of single threads armed with a generous measure of a glue.

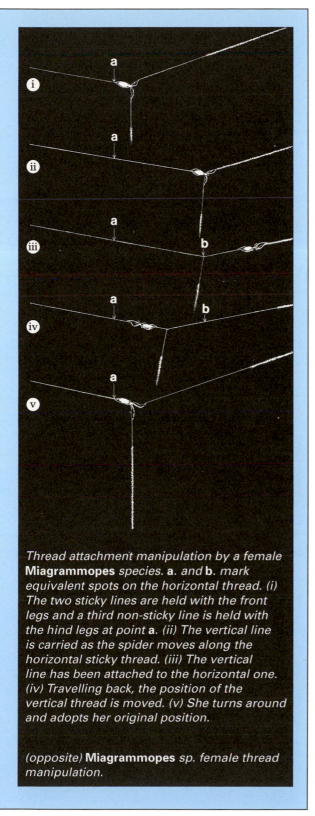

Thread attachment manipulation by a female **Miagrammopes** species. **a**. and **b**. mark equivalent spots on the horizontal thread. (i) The two sticky lines are held with the front legs and a third non-sticky line is held with the hind legs at point **a**. (ii) The vertical line is carried as the spider moves along the horizontal sticky thread. (iii) The vertical line has been attached to the horizontal one. (iv) Travelling back, the position of the vertical thread is moved. (v) She turns around and adopts her original position.

(opposite) **Miagrammopes** sp. female thread manipulation.

Linyphiids are interesting for their inability to digest their own silk, so consequently they cannot recycle their webs when they become battered and worn, but have to abandon them and start afresh.

At first sight, the scaffold-webs (or space webs) built by theridiids look disorderly. In reality, such webs are more organized than these first impressions would convey. The fact that they lack the sheet of other webs while retaining the scaffold probably accounts for their chaotic appearance. The web's core is more densely provided with criss-crossing trip-lines than the outer areas, while many of the threads are coated for part of their length with sticky globules, which make it difficult for an insect to escape. Some species build their webs close to the ground and include a series of drop-lines with sticky ends, the so-called 'gummed feet' designed to catch insects passing on the ground below.

Theridiids are famous for fearlessly going in for the kill against insects much larger and more

Despite their small size, theridiids have a reputation for pluck. This **Enoplognatha ovata** female has caught a fierce European **Vespula** sp. social wasp many times larger than herself. This is the plain form of the spider; other forms have prominent strawberry markings.

heavily armed than themselves, such as bumble-bees and wasps. Such giant-killing acts probably stem from the theridiid habit of slowing the prey down by flinging a mesh of sticky threads at it from a safe distance. This helps to calm things down before the spider darts in to inflict a series of light-ning bites containing a particularly potent venom. Just how potent this can be is of course obvious when, pitted against not a tiny insect but a huge human being, the minute amounts of poison injected by *Latrodectus* spp. (widow spiders) can have such a devastating and even fatal effect.

Some theridiids have greatly narrowed down their field of prey capture. *Chrosiothes tonala* from Mexico specializes on wingless soldier and worker termites, but catches them using a most peculiar and possibly unique method. The spider 'sniffs out' the nearby presence of termites by detecting their scent. It then tracks towards them by using a most curious method of wafting out horizontal lines one after the other a short distance above the ground, forming a bespoke aerial ropeway to reach its quarry. When a good supply of termites is encountered, the spider picks them off one at a time and attaches the corpses to vertical hoists sus-pended from the overhead ropeway. This, being under tension, springs upwards and hauls the ter-mites off their feet one at a time. Eventually the spi-der makes off with the whole catch in a bundle holding 20 or more corpses weighing some 20 times as much as their captor.

As detailed below, evolution towards simplifica-tion and reduction of the web has proceeded in a number of orb-web spiders (Araneidae and Ulo-boridae) but has also taken place in some theridi-ids such as *Episinus* and *Phoroncidia*. In *P. rotunda* and *P. quadratum,* the process of reduction has almost reached its logical limit and the 'web' con-sists of a mere single partially sticky strand. How such a minimal web manages to catch anything has always been a mystery, but evidence on *Phoroncidia studo* from South America indicates that the single-line thread employed may actually attract prey directly. A mature adult female uses her body as a bridge at one end of a more or less horizontal thread some 50-cm long, most of which is sticky.

Males of tiny sciarid flies seem to arrive at the web with greater regularity than would be expect-ed by mere chance. What is more, they seem to show a close interest in the web and touch it with their front legs, whereupon they instantly become trapped by the gluey silk. The waiting spider does not make a move until several flies have managed to gum themselves up, and then she moves towards them by rolling up the sticky line in front of her, while paying out a fresh dry thread behind, thus acting as a moving bridge.

ENGINEERING EXCELLENCE – THE ORB-WEB

For most people, the seemingly symmetrical per-fection of the orb-web of a common garden spider (*Araneus diadematus)* glistening with dew on an autumn morning is the epitome of the spider's art with silk. The orb-web is an intricate yet very eco-nomical method of capturing mostly airborne prey while reducing the amount of material required to an absolute minimum. As silk is expensive to pro-duce in terms of consumption of bodily resources, the orb-web is an elegant answer to the problem of capturing prey, although the ability of most spiders to recycle the nutrients invested in the web by tak-ing it down and eating it when it is no longer ser-viceable does reduce any losses quite drastically. In view of the essential 'rightness' of the design, it should not perhaps be surprising that the basic plan of the orb-web has been evolved indepen-dently by two families of spiders, independently reaching the same solution to the problem of max-imum efficiency in catching insects using silk: the Araneidae (using sticky silk from the spinnerets to build the spirals and dry silk for the radii); and the Uloboridae (using fluffy sticky cribellar silk laid across a warp of spinneret silk). However, in both these families the basic plan is modified in a multi-formity of ways, so that various reduced portions of the orb-web may be constructed by various species, leading in some to an almost complete reduction in the use of silk, while a few have even given up the use of silk altogether and reverted to an ambush style of life as seen in crab-spiders (Thomisidae).

This angular orb-weaver **Araneus angulatus** female in England is neatly rolling up her whole web into a compact ball, a process which took just a few seconds. She then ate the silk. In this way, almost the entire material needed for construction of the next web can be derived from material recycled from the old one. There may also be a bonus in terms of pollen and micro-organisms trapped on the silk.

The perfect orb-web, in this case made by the grand argiope **Argiope aemula** (Araneidae) in an Indian forest.

FROM THE ORB-WEB TO THE SINGLE THREAD

As the basis for discussion of other web-types we can take the web of *Araneus diadematus*. This is a basically vertical prey-catching array consisting of a series of sticky spirals laid down upon a spoke-like series of non-sticky radial threads. Like many araneid spiders, *A. diadematus* spends much of its time resting at the web's hub, monitoring the tensions and vibrations in the silk with its sensitive legs. These will instantly convey information about the precise position of an arriving insect for as in any web-building spider, the web of *A. diadematus* is

an extension of its senses, which are thereby extended outwards to the further limits of the web's reach. As the webs of some spiders (e.g. *Nephila, Caerostris*) can be several metres across, this means an enormous increase in effective prey detection and trapping range compared with the total spread of the spider's unaided legs.

When not at the hub, the female *A. diadematus* sits in her retreat to one side of the web, but monitors events therein by holding on to a signal thread. In many araneids, the web is not entirely symmetrical, the hub sometimes being placed slightly higher than centre. This is because the spider can run

While sitting at the upper corner of her web, this European garden spider female **Araneus diadematus** keeps in touch with events by holding on to a radial line with her left front leg.

faster downhill than up, so putting the hub nearer the top allows equal access times to all parts of the web. Spiders which build horizontal orb-webs place the hub in the centre of a symmetrical circular web, for obvious reasons.

In *A. diadematus* the hub is central, but the spider treats the upper and lower parts of the web differently during construction. As it can reach the lower part fastest, with less chance of an insect escaping, it invests more in this area, making the spirals closer and coating them more densely with sticky globules. The area nearer the hub also receives a closer spacing of spirals than the periphery, which always takes more time to reach allowing insects a better chance of escape.

A highly modified orb-web is made by several species of *Wendilgarda* which belong to the small mostly tropical family Theridiosomatidae. The looped webs are draped across streams, whose turbulent surface is stroked by numerous vertical lines. These are connected to the surface tension of the water surface, a design which is unique both in construction and operation, for it serves to trap insects which are floating downriver on the water.

A further bizarre variation on the normal araneid web is made by *Paraplectanoides crassipes* from Australia (illustrated overleaf). In this amazingly long-lived species, the females may live nine years or more, compared with the normal araneid maximum lifespan of one year. Web-nests occur close to the ground underneath bushes and fallen logs. The spider starts out by rigging up a series of horizontal radial lines with a central hub, and then encloses the whole lot in a 'radiotelescope style' dome-like covering of silk. She never gets around to adding the normal spiral threads to the radials within. The latticework of silk forming the outer envelope is decorated with whatever bits of detritus happen to be lying around, such as leaves and twigs. In its early juvenile stages, the food consists solely of springtails (Collembola), but later instars switch to an exclusive diet of cockroaches. Upon entering the nest, these forget where the entrance was and career wildly about on the wall until the spider picks them off.

Wendilgarda (Theridiidae) web above a stream in Central America. There is a fairly fast flow from left to right. The sticky threads are held in tension in the water.

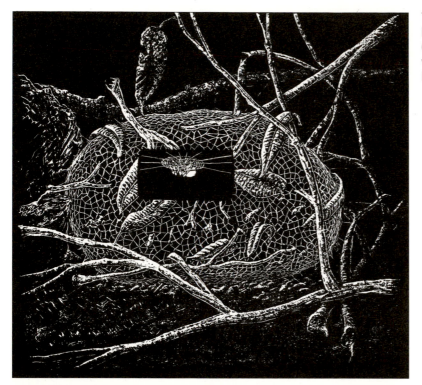

The strange web of
Paraplectanoides crassipes
(Araneidae) from Australia,
with the female depicted within
hanging from the hub.

Micrathena gracilis is
'primitive' within the Araneidae in
biting prey first before wrapping.
This female is feeding on a
butterfly in Mexico. Butterflies
are not common prey in the
normal orb web.

DEALING WITH THE PREY

The sequence of steps taken by an orb-weaving spider to deal with newly arrived prey varies somewhat according to the family of spiders involved, or even the genus, and to the type of prey which has turned up. With uloborids the first act is to wrap the prey in silk, there not being much alternative really given that venom glands are not present in uloborids, so biting only takes place as the spider starts to feed.

Even within the single family Araneidae, a range of techniques is employed, some being regarded as more 'primitive' than others. *Micrathena* and *Nephila* belong to the 'primitive' school, in that they use the so-called 'bite-wrap' attack, giving a good long bite upon first contact and then using silk mainly as a packaging material for transfer back to the hub for consumption. The more 'advanced' method, as employed by *Argiope*, is to stand back at a relatively safe distance and wrap the prey first, throwing silk on it from a distance using the back legs. This greatly reduces the risk of the prey escaping as it is now temporarily bound to the web, after which it is comprehensively trussed in more silk. The spider accomplishes this rapidly and with great dexterity, nimbly rotating the prey rotisserie-style while pulling a stream of silk directly from the spinnerets. As it wraps, the spider moves its abdomen from side to side in an arc, thereby ensuring that the whole of the prey is evenly covered. If the prey is too large and heavy for such deft manipulation (such as with a dragonfly or cumbersome beetle) the spider simply leaves it and then runs round and round it, trailing silk. Only when the prey is thoroughly bandaged and immobilized will the now mummy-like blob of silk be finally approached for the intimate contact needed to administer a 'short bite'. This whole process is designed to keep the spider's vulnerable body clear of retaliatory manouevres by flexible-jointed prey such as wasps, which can push themselves through extreme contortions in order to bring their meat-mangling jaws or lethal sting to bear on a careless spider.

As it happens, many spiders can tell when something unwanted and unpleasant like a wasp drops in, and it is probable that at least some of these hazardous arrivals announce themselves by a particular kind of web vibration induced by their buzzing struggles. Some individuals of *Araneus diadematus* will unhesitatingly rush down to do battle with a wasp despite its intimidating buzzing, while others will approach the striped horror with evident reluctance and, with manifest caution, cut it free from the web by severing the lines one at a time, always maintaining a respectable distance. In fact the same spider may be the performer in both acts, depending on whether it is early or late in the season, and thus how frequently wasps are encountered. It seems that spiders will often refuse to attack dangerous prey items at first, but gradually get the hang of coping with them, so that as their performance improves, so does their success rate.

Some prey is not life-threatening to the spider unless actually used as food. The taste may not be conducive to the spider, so the prey-capture sequence is nipped in the bud as soon as the chemoreceptors in the spider's palps and legs make contact with the prey. Thus a *Cyrtophora* will almost always subdue a harmless blowfly by going straight in and biting, but reverses its tactics and applies silk upon first contact with hazardous prey such as stinkbugs (Pentatomidae), which can discharge a blast of powerful chemical deterrent, and also wasps. Interestingly enough, stratiomyid flies, which are excellent visual mimics of wasps, are also wrapped first. This suggests that they may also mimic the wing-vibration frequency characteristic of wasps. Wasp-mimicking hoverflies are normally attacked without hesitation by all spiders, even visual hunters such as salticids which do not perceive and react to the wasp-like pattern. Stinkbug discharges can momentarily knock a spider senseless, forcing it to interrupt its attack to recover and clean its legs and palps of the offending chemical. Bombardier beetles can fight back with an even more powerful explosive discharge of hot gas. Even this military-style hardware is within the capacity of some spiders to counteract, such as *Argiope* which manages to deal with the problem by adopting a very stand-off cautious type of wrapping from the maximum possible distance. The spider then waits around until the beetle shoots its chemical batteries into exhaustion while struggling to break free of its silken bindings.

Spiders such as *Nephila,* which cannot vary their attack and always dive straight in and bite first, could suffer problems in dealing with chemically defended prey. In practice, accidents can usually be avoided either because there is often enough information transmitted by the behaviour of the prey itself, or after a quick and relatively risk-free 'taste' contact with the legs. When the trapped insect is particularly unwelcome, the spider takes the logical action and cuts it free from the web. If this can be accomplished while wasting the minimum amount of energy and silk, then so much the better. Such economical release procedures are easy with certain South American ithomiine butterflies which enter the webs of *Nephila clavipes.* Instead of thrashing around frantically in a futile attempt to escape, the butterfly exhibits an incredibly laid-back attitude and simply hangs there, motionless, its wings outspread in a strange rigid posture. This very absence of commotion seems to give advance warning to the web-owner of the fact that the new arrival is unpalatable and therefore is not going to be imminently figuring on the menu. Thus alerted, the spider launches into its 'cut-and-dump' routine.

Instead of charging down and biting the butterfly, the spider strolls down rather sedately and briefly touches the insect with outstretched forelegs, pedipalps and chelicerae, using its chemotactic senses to confirm that the butterfly is indeed a distasteful reject. The spider then carefully bites the silken snags around the butterfly, carefully cutting it free and removing most of the silk from its wings. During all this manhandling (which can even involve getting a firm grip with the chelicerae and heaving the butterfly through the web by the thorax) the butterfly sustains its rigid posture. This is in the best interests of both parties. Just one small struggle would trigger an automatic bite from the spider. That means needless loss of expensively produced venom (a protein), a sickeningly distasteful experience and loss of web silk. The spider finally disposes of its unwanted garbage by dropping the butterfly free, upon which it often

takes wing before it has reached the ground, such has been the spider's care and thoroughness in its release. The fact that the butterfly's behaviour and 'flavour' are the critical decision-makers for the spider, rather than colour and pattern is indicated by the numerous *visual* ithomiine-mimics which are unhesitatingly treated as normal prey. Interestingly enough, while rejecting ithomiines, *N. clavipes* seems to accept all heliconiines, which are rejected by most birds, showing yet again that spiders are discriminating in their tastes.

Even when palatable, a lepidopteran usually stimulates a response different from the normal 'wrap-bite' procedure common in spiders such as *Argiope argentata.* As already mentioned, the scales which smother the wings and bodies of butterflies and moths are rapidly shed on to the spider's sticky silk, enabling the insect to escape relatively quickly by casting off part of its dispensable overcoat along with the encumbering web. With quick immobilization being essential with such slippery customers, *Argiope* dashes in for a 'long bite' which quickly curbs any struggle, following which bobbin-fashion wrapping can commence. The normal silk-throwing preliminaries are omitted, apparently because the spider recognizes a lepidopteran through brief contact with its heavily scaled surface texture.

Once prey has been bitten and wrapped, it is cut free from the web and carried back to the hub or to a retreat on one side of the web for consumption. Small prey will merely be carried in the chelicerae, but large bulky items are suspended from the spinnerets aided by one or both of the hind legs. Large bulky items such as dragonflies, with wings and legs sticking out at awkward angles, are thoroughly trussed with their limbs strapped down to their sides, thus making for easier transport without snagging the web. *Argiope argentata* seldom repairs the hole left in its web after prey extraction, although some spiders, such as the garden spider (*Araneus diadematus*) mend the damage as they are cutting the wrapped prey free.

In their methods of dealing with specific types of prey sheet-web spider are also quite flexible. *Agelenopsis aperta* administers a succession of short bites to anything which could fight back, such as ants, wasps and heavily-jawed beetles. The spider shows a remarkable ability to recognize the relevant offensive hardware on these insects, such as the sting of a wasp at the rear end, the jaws of a beetle at the front end, or the heavily spined kicking legs of a grasshopper, and takes appropriate countermeasures by securing such weaponry to the web with silk. By contrast, harmless moths and flies receive the full direct long bite to the thorax, and the spider hangs on tightly regardless of how much the victim bucks and flaps and drags its attacker around the web.

(*Above*) This bank orb-weaver **Araneus (Larinioides) cornutus** female in England is carrying to her lair a damselfly belayed to her spinnerets and hind leg.

The silver argiope **Argiope argentata** is a more 'advanced' araneid in wrapping prey first before biting. This female is feeding on a butterfly in Costa Rica.

THE ENIGMA OF THE STABILIMENTUM

It has been shown that many insects can see and avoid spiders' webs, dodging around or over them at the last moment. Web silk therefore has to be as thin and transparent as possible while still being adequate for the primary task of restraining prey. Web invisibility is also improved by the fact that spiders often site their webs where they will be least conspicuous.

Why then should some spiders go out of their way to make their webs as conspicuous as possible by adding one or more bands of thickened silk to form a prominent white structure known as a stabilimentum? Some stabilimenta are definitely of a camouflaging nature (e.g. *Cyclosa*, see Chapter 07) but in *Argiope* the purpose of the stabilimentum has

long been the subject of much speculation, experimentation and dispute. First, why should juvenile and adult stages of the same species construct differently shaped stabilimenta? While juveniles generally fashion a disc of densely woven white silk, which provides a resting place during the day, the adults construct linear stabiliments. In their perfect form these are in the form of a St Andrew's Cross, made of zig-zag ribbons of glistening white silk. The spider sits in a gap left in the centre, not against the stabilimentum as in juveniles. The perfect cross is less common than a partial form, represented by a vertical line or perhaps a diagonal, or even just a single arm of the cross. At some mid-point in their

*A juvenile **Argiope flavipalpis** on her disc-shaped stabilimentum in a Ugandan rainforest.*

*A grand orb-weaver **Argiope aemula** sits in the gap in her cross-shaped stabilimentum in an Indian forest.*

of attracting insect pollinators. The silk used in the rest of the *Argiope* web reflects very little ultraviolet light compared with most other web silks, making the stabilimentum and spider stand out like a beacon to ultraviolet sensitive insects, such as bees. In a study of the insects caught in *A. argentata* webs over a single year in tropical America, bees represented over 60 per cent of the total, which included a very varied range of insects. These included eagle-eyed dragonflies, crickets, grasshoppers, bugs, flies and small numbers of beetles. As would be predicted, a high percentage of the moths and butterflies which collided with the webs managed to escape after losing just a few scales, confirming just how difficult it is for a normal web to capture these non-stick insects.

The juvenile's dense disc-like stabilimentum can also come in handy as a parasol. When the sun's rays fix upon a web and start to cook its occupant, the spider can hardly just up stakes and move to a cooler spot. Similarly, if it vacates the hub it may risk losing any insects which arrive. By staying put, the spider has to endure a considerable heat overload. Its first reaction is to stilt up as high as possible on its legs and tilt the tip of its abdomen towards the sun. Many kinds of spiders from different families adopt this measure as a built-in response, which reduces to a minimum the bodily cross-section exposed to the heat. If this is still not sufficient, a juvenile *Argiope* merely has to dodge around to the far side of its stabilimentum. This dense white shiny disc acts as a perfect reflector, keeping the spider on the shaded side relatively cool.

Recently, it has been suggested that the huge yellow orb-webs built by *Nephila* might in effect comprise one huge stabilimentum. The web of *N. clavipes*, especially in exposed sites, is often golden, hence the common name golden orb-weaver. The main prey in many habitats consists of stingless bees, which are quite strongly attracted to the flower-like yellow reflections given off by the web. In darker situations, such as in forests where yellow is inadequately reflected, its use would be of little practical advantage as an attractant. So then the spider modifies the composition of its silk and turns out a more or less white product, which is difficult to see in the dim light, increasing its utility for capturing more generalized prey.

development, the juveniles make the switch from one form to the other.

One explanation surmised that the stabilimentum makes the web more conspicuous, thus preventing birds from flying through and wrecking it when the spider is absent from the hub. However, as the author has seldom seen an *Argiope* anywhere but the hub (out of many species and hundreds of individuals seen around the world) this explanation is not convincing. The discovery that both the spider itself and the stabilimentum could possibly attract certain types of insects was therefore most interesting. They do this by strongly reflecting ultraviolet light, as do many flowers with the prime object

THE SPIDER SOPHISTICATES

ANGLING WITH SILK – THE NET-CASTING SPIDERS

It is to Europe's eternal loss that not a single example of the remarkable net-casting or ogre-faced spiders (Deinopidae) is found within its bounds. Indeed, one has to travel to the southeast USA or

A **Dinopis** sp. ogre-faced spider wrapping a beetle which she swept out of the air only a minute or two after completing her net one night in a Costa Rican rainforest.

southern Africa to find any examples from a more or less temperate area, most species being overwhelmingly tropical.

During the day, a *Dinopis* is quite unremarkable, perched motionless, its legs projecting fore and aft, the very epitome of a broken twig. As dusk rouses the winged nightguard from their daytime sleep, so too does the *Dinopis* stir and sets in train the preparations for the night's action. It starts by laying down a simple scaffold of lightweight silk, destined merely as support for the construction of a much more sophisticated miniaturized web – the net. This is made from dense strands of white silk combed from the cribellum to form a rectangular net. While still attached to the scaffold, this is under some degree of tension. The spider now grips each corner with its four front legs and cuts the completed net free, whereupon it sags considerably as the tension is released. It remains in this collapsed state while the spider waits, head down for prey to arrive, but is instantly expanded to its full size when thrown over a passing insect. With its prey secured, the spider commences to feed before constructing a new net and resuming the hunt.

Some species specialize on flying insects, while others target those passing on the ground or on vegetation. *Dinopis longipes* from the tropical rainforests of Panama stations itself above the dense hurrying columns of leaf-cutting ants (*Atta* spp.), which are such a feature of these forests. The Australian *Dinopis subrufus* also captures ground-dwelling insects, but will tackle anything which passes. *Menneus unifasciatus* from the same area positions itself opposite grass stems in order to target insects (mostly small cockroaches) which scurry up them. Most deinopids are renowned for their huge eyes which greedily drink in every glimmer of light (hence the name 'ogre-faced spiders'), so essential for accurately aiming the net at a small moving target at night. The challenge of precisely tracking small dark prey running on the dark earth therefore demands exceptional measures. *D. subrufus* solves the problem by squirting a splash of white faeces on to the proposed killing zone. When a dark insect runs across the white bull's-eye, the spider can hardly miss it.

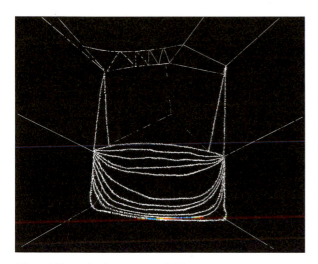

(*Above*) The cribellate snare of **Menneus unifasciatus** is about 2cm across.

(*Right*) The female is poised ready to cast her net upon an insect walking up the nearby grass-stems.

LETTING FLY WITH FLYPAPER – THE BOLAS SPIDERS

There are few more intriguing and bizarre hunters than the bolas spiders, which are distributed around the world in the following way: *Mastophora* (21 species) and *Agatostichus* (two species) in the Americas; *Cladomelea* (three species) and *Acantharanea* (six species) in Africa; *Ordgarius* (nine species) in Asia and the Australasian region. Unfortunately, despite the wide range of some genera, such as *Mastophora*, the spiders themselves are very rarely seen. This may partly be due to genuine scarcity on the ground, and partly because the adults are so difficult to spot during the day, often resembling bird-droppings or a bump on a twig. Bolas spiders are araneids, and therefore descended from orb-weaving spiders, but have reduced their webs to a mere sticky ball attached to the end of a short thread.

Only after nightfall does the spider become active. First she constructs a horizontal line from which she suspends a vertical thread, embellishing its lower end with a sticky ball. The whole process

takes only one or two minutes. This is the bolas. In some species, the operator swings this continuously for some time until she catches an insect; in others swinging only starts when the spider senses an approaching insect – probably by detecting the hum made by its whirring wings. This might seem a risky way of catching a meal, but in reality the spider's prosperity is not dependent on mere chance. *Mastophora* and probably all bolas spiders, ensure a plentiful supply of food by actively luring their prey to come and be captured. In the South American *M. dizzydeani* (American readers will need no explanation of the significance of the chosen name; for other readers, the spider was named in honour of one of the greatest baseball pitchers of all time, Jerome 'Dizzy' Dean) the prey (always male moths of the family Noctuidae) constantly seems to approach from downwind of the immobile spider. Completely hoodwinked by the spider's chemical mimicry, the male moths track upwind, guided by a pheromone deliberately released by the spider which mimics the sexual attractant released by female moths. The spiders pay close attention to the vital wind direction, and will shift through 180° soon after the wind has done likewise.

Even though the moths practically offer themselves as dinner and flutter around suicidally close to the spider, they are still not easy targets, and the wildly swinging spider misses with half her attempts. When she does score a hit, the glue on the ball manages to penetrate through the moth's detachable scales and sticks directly to the body; few victims escape. If her chemical siren-song draws a blank after 20 minutes or so, the spider eats the ball, apparently because it dries up and loses its 'bite' after a while. The capture techniques used by *M. dizzydeani* net an average of just over two captures per night, about the same as nocturnal spiders with conventional orb-webs.

Males and immature females probably capture prey directly without the use of a bolas. This is similar to the spider *Taczanowskia* from South America, which behaves much as in *Mastophora* but uses the legs directly to seize prey attracted by the pheromone which is released.

ANT-EATING SPIDERS

Most predators shun ants, even though they usually represent the most abundant and easily obtainable of all potential prey. However, just as certain mammals and lizards specialize on ants, so does a small band of spiders, in addition to the *Dinopis longipes* mentioned above.

Steatoda fulva (Theridiidae) in Florida specializes on capturing *Pogonomyrmex badius* (harvester ants). For much of the day the flow of these combative short-tempered legions in and out of the crater-like nest entrance is too constant for the *Steatoda* to risk an approach. However, during the heat of mid-afternoon the ants close down

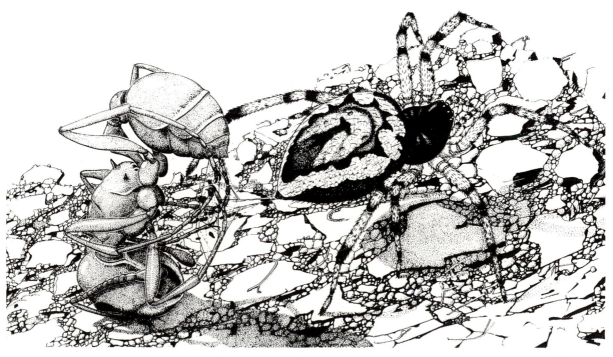

A **Euryopis coki** female towing a **Pogonomyrmex** harvester ant on a thread attached to her spinnerets.

operations for a few hours, giving the spider the chance to hustle in and build a web directly above the nest's doorway. The first few ants to emerge in the cool of the evening walk straight into the trap and become entangled. In their struggles to escape the ants release a mandibular gland alarm secretion which unwittingly brings more of their nest-mates hurrying to their aid, only to end up in the same position. Even the bulldog-jawed soldiers are beaten in their attempts to remove the exceptionally sticky silk, and the ants eventually give up, close the entrance down and construct a fresh one a short distance away.

Another harvester ant, *P. owyheei,* is attacked by the theridiid *Euryopis coki* in the American northwest. Several spiders (up to a dozen) may lie in wait on the stony nest-mounds, tethering emerging workers to the ground with a length of silk flung by the legs. *E. funebris* in Virginia hunts ants (or at least sits around until an ant bumps into it) on trees at night, fixing them to the bark with masses of thrown sticky silk. Members of the Oecobiidae do likewise, especially *Oecobius annulipes* which also specializes on ants. These two theridiids therefore exhibit the greatest reduction of silk use known in the family.

Zodarium frenatum (Zodariidae) restricts its attentions to guard-ants of *Cataglyphis bicolor,* ambushing them near the nest entrance at night. Another zodariid, *Habronestes bradleyi* in Australia, targets the extremely irascible and pugnacious meat-ant (*Iridomyrmex purpureus*). Workers from different nests often engage in duels during which alarm pheromones are released to summon aid. It is just as likely to bring *H. bradleyi* at the run, the spider having 'tuned in' to the ant's alarm pheromones, a most elegant way of being guided to a meal.

Several crab spiders specialize on ants. *Strophius nigricans* from Brazil usually attacks from the rear. If forced to confront its prey, the spider holds its front legs well up out of the way of its adversary's limb-severing jaws. A more cunning ploy is to present the ant with the corpse of one of its fellows, which acts as a distraction and keeps it occupied while the spider launches an assault from the rear and lifts the ant off the ground. A suitable corpse is almost always on hand, as *S. nigricans* does not

An **Aphantochilus** sp. spider (Thomisidae) carrying a cephalotine ant by the neck.

discard its prey, but runs around holding the empty skeleton aloft. This offers some degree of protection against the spider's enemies, for it resembles an ant ferrying a dead nest-mate, a common enough sight. The corpse also doubles as a shield, being proffered to worker ants who come too close for comfort. Similar behaviours are also found in the thomisid *Aphantochilus rogersi*, which brilliantly mimics its exclusive prey, namely armoured spiny cephalotine ants.

Few jumping spiders capture ants even when they are available, but a few specialize on them. Some also mimic their ant prey both visually and behaviourally, such as *Cosmophasis* from Africa and *Tutelina similis* from the USA.

SPIDER-EAT-SPIDER

As mentioned above, more spiders probably fall victim to other spiders (including older members of their own species) than to any other predators. In most cases, such attacks are opportunistic, just one part of a broad spectrum of prey being captured. However a number of spiders from various families are specialists in the skilled assassination of other spiders, and indeed will spurn any insect, even one which is there for the taking. Such a high-risk lifestyle obviously demands special talents as a hunter, and indeed stealthy, manipulative and downright deceitful about sum up the 'personality profile' of the successful spider-killer.

Members of two families, the Mimetidae and Archaeidae, are completely restricted to preying upon other spiders. The mimetids are often called 'pirate spiders'. The hunting technique employed by *Mimetus maculosus* from New Zealand is probably fairly typical. It is able to enter the webs of other spiders and walk upon the unfamiliar silk with relative ease. Such sure-footedness in 'foreign' webs is an essential prerequisite for any web-invading killer. However, *M. maculosus* is not equally at home in every type of web, preferring sticky orb-webs and space-webs and shunning cribellar silk. Whereas most spiders blunder around in confusion when on a strange web, the mimetid makes steady progress with its characteristically slow and methodical pace, seldom adhering to the gluey lines and able to free itself quickly when it does. Rather than proceed directly towards its target, which would be asking for trouble, the invader lies still for a while and then begins quivering and plucking the web, imitating the arrival of an insect. If the web-owner responds in the usual way, then it is rushing to its execution. Mimetid venom is both powerful and apparently spider-specific, and *M. maculosus* uses its extravagantly spined legs to corral its victim until the venom takes effect. However, if a noticeably swift and vigorous response indicates that the proposed prey is going to be more than the invader bargained for, the mimetid makes a rapid exit by dropping to safety on its dragline. Occasionally, the invader is too slow to get the message and pays with its life. The riskiest confrontations tend to be with a long-legged opponent such as *Pholcus*, itself a spider-killer with an impressive ability to cast smothering quantities of

silk from some distance with its long thin legs. An interesting variation on this procedure is exercized by *Ero furcata* from Europe, which can entice female spiders to their death by imitating the courtship web-pluckings of the male.

The process of spreading misinformation – vibrating a stranger's web like an arriving insect in order to lure the occupant to its death – is known as 'aggressive mimicry' and is widespread in spider-eating (araneophagic) spiders. The spindly-legged rafter spider, *Pholcus phalangiodes,* usually places its large untidy non-sticky non-cribellate webs in houses, often in a corner where walls and ceiling meet. In comparison with the gangling lightweight build of a *Pholcus*, a *Tegeneria* house spider would seem a pugilistic heavyweight, with little need to take care to avoid tripping over the outer lines of the rafter spider's web. Yet *Pholcus* is undaunted. Leaning out as far as possible from the edge of its web, it hurls a welter of silken lines across its larger adversary until it is pinned down and can be safely bitten. The rafter spider also pussy-foots its way on tip-toe into the webs of other spiders and captures them using aggressive mimicry. Its small thin feet seldom adhere to sticky webs, and when they do, the spider either pulls them free or bites away the offending silk, often adding some familiar easily-trodden threads of its own to smooth further progress. It is least at home hunting amaurobiids on their sticky cribellar sheet-webs. *Pholcus* sometimes loses a leg in a silk-throwing tit-for-tat with a theridiid, but has a habit of escaping with its life when the chips are down. It will also enter foreign webs to steal wrapped prey and egg-sacs, chewing and slobbering on the latter's dense silken wrapping until it can inject enzymes into the interior. The dissolved contents can then be sucked back up in one go like soup.

One of the most versatile of the araneophagic spiders is *Taieria erebus* (Gnaphosidae) from New Zealand. It is perfectly well able to catch insects on its own account, but also thieves them, along with egg-cases, from the webs of other spiders. It even enters the legitimate prey-catching business by building a small web of its own. It also trespasses in foreign webs to catch the owners by using aggressive mimicry. However, unlike the rafter spider, it is most at home on densely woven webs of cribellar silk. It will even take over segestriid webs for several days after killing the owner, taking advantage of the latter's superior web-building skills to catch a few extra insects without having to work for it. *T. erebus* is also gruesomely effective at chewing its way into silken nests occupied by jumping spiders.

An Indian species of *Chorizopes* is unusual in being an araneophagic araneid. It also has an unusual hunting technique. It enters the web of its intended victim, usually much larger than itself, without bothering with any pretence of stealth. When the web's owner responds by shaking the silk to warn the trespasser off, the *Chorizopes* replies in kind with its own equally combative reply. When the owner then rushes down to sort out the problem, and finds that it is facing a midget of an adversary, it piles straight in without hesitating. This is its undoing, and just what the *Chorizopes* has been angling for, a chance to use its unexpectedly huge chelicerae and long fangs to lethal advantage in close combat. One of its favourite targets, species of *Leucauge*, have adapted to all this and often respond by severing part of the web so that the section holding the *Chorizopes* collapses and leaves it isolated.

THE REMARKABLE ABILITIES OF *PORTIA* – SPIDER EGG-HEAD

Versatile though *T. erebus* might be, the prize for sheer virtuosity must surely go to *Portia*. Several species are known from tropical Africa, Asia and Australasia, and they are probably the most unusual of all jumping spiders, as

well as the most 'intelligent'. The local race of *P. fimbriata* from Queensland seems to be especially gifted, reaching a pinnacle of behavioural diversity. Like all members of the genus, *P. fimbriata* resembles a squashed dead leaf on legs. This makes it difficult to spot, even when moving with its characteristic slow robot-like shuffle. This style of progress, allied to its strange unspider-like appearance, seems to be one of the keys to its success. Other jumping spiders simply fail to recognize *Portia* as a threat when it is stalking them in the open. It is also quite at home on sticky two-dimensional orb-webs, cribellar webs or non-sticky and sticky space-webs. It enters such foreign webs to kill the

This is what its victim sees as a **Portia schultzii** jumping spider creeps up on it in Kenya. No wonder other salticids fail to recognize it as a threat.

builder, poach prey (even taking it from the very mouth of the owner) and steal eggs. Its method of dealing with an egg-sac is to rip it open and scoop the eggs towards its mouthparts with its legs.

P. fimbriata shows its true virtuosity when practising its finely-honed art of aggressive mimicry, in which it has no peers. For example, when entering the web of *Pholcus phalangioides*, itself a highly accomplished slayer of other spiders, a *P. fimbriata* usually manages to lure the spider to its death without setting off its defensive 'whirling' behaviour. It is equally adept at employing aggressive mimicry in a wide range of webs, despite their differing vibratory qualities. In this it owes its success to its use of trial and error. Upon first setting foot in a web, *Portia* transmits a wide-ranging set of vibratory signals on the basis that at least one of them will stimulate a reaction from the owner – such as web-plucking. When this finally happens, the waiting *Portia* uses this feedback to narrow down its broadcasts to the one which evoked the reaction. This constitutes a remarkable mental feat for a spider, as it is necessary to recall which was the last type of vibration used.

A prodigious memory is also necessary for making the circuitous prey-approaching detours which are typical of *Portia*. Sometimes the spider spends nearly 15 minutes with its destination out of sight, yet finally fetches up at the correct point, having calculated and remembered the whole route in advance – and that even includes moving *away* from the destination at some point, using so-called 'reversed detouring'. This kind of mental route planning is useful when the chosen prey is an orb-web spider. For the best chance of success, the *Portia* needs to gain a vantage point above the web, so that it can drop down on its drag-line in front of the spider and grab it. It is in its ability to calculate the possibly complex route to the vantage point – such as a branch – that *Portia* excels. Detouring is actually known from at least seven other salticids, but is probably best developed in *Portia*.

Portia also stealthily stalks spiders in their webs, which is a potentially perilous enterprise. To reduce the risk it often waits for a chance to take advantage of a 'smokescreen', such as a gust of wind, to mask its movements as it advances across the web. This reduces both the chances of a dangerous headlong counter-attack (*Portia* is sometimes killed by its intended victim) and of the target making a bolt for it when it detects the invader's characteristic movements; these apparently signal 'danger' to some spiders.

When tackling female *Euryattus* jumping spiders in their nests, the Queensland *P. fimbriata* entices the occupant to emerge by copying the courtship display of the male *Euryattus*, vibrating its body on the nest. The deception has to be good, for it seems that *Euryattus* is at least one jumping spider which *does* recognize *Portia* as an enemy.

DEWDROP SPIDERS

Most *Argyrodes* dewdrop spiders (Theridiidae) have given up the predatory lifestyle and sponge a living off other spiders in their webs (*see* discussion below on kleptoparasites). However, a few still carry on the tradition of killing for a living, while some of the spongers will not hesitate to prey on their hosts, given a risk-free chance.

Argyrodes (Ariamnes) attenuatus from Costa Rica, a weird creature resembling a long thin twig, builds a very simple non-sticky web consisting of a few intersecting lines. This does not actually function as a trap, but rather provides a convenient alighting place for ballooning spiders and for tiny 'trapeze' flies. These latter have a habit of hanging suspended at night on the non-sticky horizontal lines of spider's webs. The chance that the web will be encountered is increased by the length of the lines, which can reach 2m, and the spider employs extreme caution when approaching the resting flies, so as not to alert them to its presence.

An *Argyrodes (Rhomphaea)* from New Zealand builds a simple web in bushes on which other kinds of spiders frequently wander. It also leaves this web and invades those of other spiders. It lures these close with aggressive mimicry and then scoops them up in a very simple but effective sticky net which it holds in its legs.

Kleptoparasitic dewdrop spiders are generally vastly smaller than their hosts. These are therefore

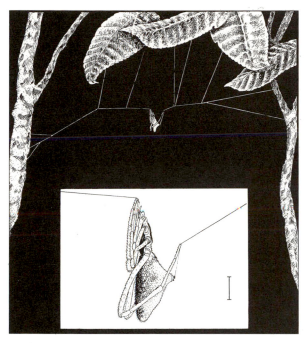

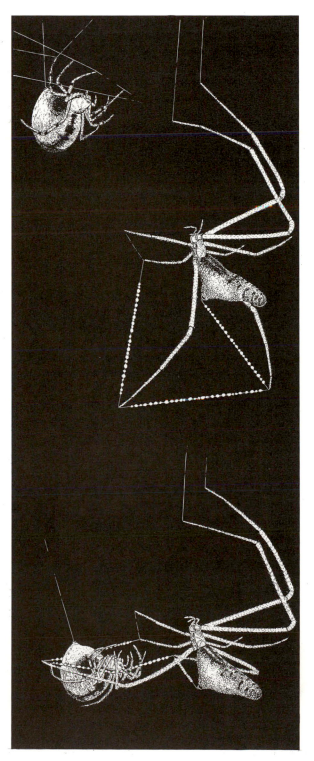

(*Above*) A New Zealand species of **Argyrodes** (**Rhomphaea**) (Theridiidae) in her simple snare. The scale bar is 1mm.

(*Right*) **Argyrodes** (**Rhomphaea**) with her simple triangle net which she casts over a theridiid spider.

safe from attack except when soft and vulnerable during and just after moulting, when they may fall victim to an opportunistic *Argyrodes* on the make. Some species of *Argyrodes*, such as *A. baboquivari* and *A. fictilium* are as large, or larger, than their normal hosts, and often take them as prey. The former regularly captures adults of the communal spiders *Philoponella oweni*, which do not seem able to detect the presence of the killer in their web, even when it is taking a heavy toll of their spiderlings.

THE BODY-SNATCHERS

As briefly mentioned above, most *Argyrodes* are kleptoparasites within the webs of much larger spiders, such as *Argiope*, *Araneus*, *Agelena* and *Nephila*. Being so minute compared with their hosts, it might be thought that their scrounging and thieving depredations would be of small consequence to their host's well-being, but in fact this is often not the case.

Argyrodes elevatus is a particularly common inhabitant of the webs of *Argiope argentata* and *Nephila clavipes* in tropical America. The latter's web is a large fine-meshed orb provided back and front with an extensive barrier web of irregular mesh

and with the hub placed off-centre in the upper third of the orb. Prey items are normally stored at or near the hub. *A. elevatus* generally loiters inconspicuously on the barrier web, connected to the orb's radii by signal threads which warn of events in the centre. The actions of a host spider wrapping an insect in silk transmits a characteristic series of vibrations through the web. These are decoded by the waiting *Argyrodes* as 'food has

The slight tremor caused by the sucking-stomach of the giant golden orb-weaver **Nephila clavipes** spider alerts an **Argyrodes** sp. dewdrop spider to the presence of a meal in Brazil.

arrived'. The same message is involuntarily conveyed by a *Nephila* which has started to feed. The pumping and sucking actions in the stomach of this huge spider are carried through to its legs which then oscillate the web in a recognizable way. The *Argyrodes* will also choose their moment well and make a rapid beeline towards a *Nephila* which is busy wrapping, being able to cast caution to the winds while the host is too preoccupied to notice the tiny vibrations caused by the advancing thieves. They may also move onto the prey while the host is busy administering its prolonged bite to a victim, which may last several minutes. They will have to be prepared to move fast when the host begins to wrap, otherwise they could end up being spliced together with the prey.

By contrast, when a host is busy feeding, the thieves advance with extreme caution, gradually easing towards the giant until they can sup the digestive juices so liberally dribbled on the prey. *Nephila* is such a messy feeder that these juices usually soak the mangled prey to the extent that it shines wetly. Being so tiny, and therefore with minimal digestive fluids on tap, *Argyrodes* cannot in fact feed on large insects unless they have already been predigested by the host.

The host rushing off to deal with an incoming insect is often the signal for an *Argyrodes* to mount a raid on the foodstore at the hub. Such a cut-and-grab raid may take only 12–15 seconds to complete and prey items up to several hundred times as heavy as the thieves can be spirited away, although this takes longer. The *Nephila* host is not completely devoid of countermeasures, and reacts to the presence of *Argyrodes* near the hub by doing a rush-job on the next new insect arrival, thus starving the thieves of the time needed to make a successful raid.

The effects of such constant poaching are at the least annoying when only two or three *Argyrodes* are present, but can be positively disastrous when 45 are gathered in a single web, every one of them adept at avoiding any (rare) attempts at eviction by their host. *Nephila clavipes* reacts to a heavy parasite load by moving its web, although this only buys a few days of respite before a new crowd of freeloaders piles in.

A. antipodiana is rather unusual in being able to build its own small web, as well being an uninvited guest of *Araneus pustulosa*. The *Argyrodes* is not very good at coping with prey in its own web, often not wrapping it well enough to prevent its escape, presumably because it is used to dealing with prey professionally packaged by its host.

In a number of instances, dewdrop spiders have been seen eating their hosts' webs, probably as a response to hard times, for silk is rich in proteins, and webs are regularly eaten and recycled by many spiders.

A FREE RIDE AND A FREE MEAL

The tiny mite-like spider *Curimagua bayano* (Symphytognathidae) has a very strange relationship with the large *Diplura* sp. mygalomorph spider, whose burrows it shares in Panama. *C. bayano* rides around on the host just behind its head, creeping down its impressively large chelicerae to suck up some of the abundant salivary juices which the host pours onto prey as it is comprehensively mashed into a pulp. The minuscule rider has poorly developed mouthparts incapable of killing and digesting even small prey, making it totally dependent on its host to provide a regular supply of liquid food. Some *Curimagua* species are free-living, constructing minute webs with an incredibly fine mesh which probably nets a supply of pollen and fungus spores from the air.

In its intimate physical association with a much larger host, *C. bayano* is similar to some jackal flies (Milichiidae) which assemble on a spider's body and wait to share in its food. *Nephila* and *Argiope* seem to be the most attractive hosts for these flies, which also accompany crab-spiders, as well as predatory insects. As many as eight tiny milichiids can assemble on the huge abdomen of a *Nephila* spider. They are remarkably sure-footed, being able to sit tight throughout the vigorous prey-wrapping procedures carried out by the host.

Two jackal flies (Milichiidae) perched on the back of an **Argiope flavipalpis** female, waiting for prey to arrive in a Ugandan rainforest.

webs of the agelenid *Agelenopsis pennsylvanica*. The spiders completely ignore the bug's presence as it wanders easily around the web, feeding on tiny flotsam, such as aphids, which are of no interest to the spiders.

SOCIAL SPIDERS

Of the 35,000 or so known species of spiders in the world, only some 40 or so species in 16 families are known to exhibit some kind of aggregating behaviour or group living. These families are: Dictynidae, Amaurobiidae, Oecobiidae, Uloboridae, Pholcidae, Scytodidae, Desidae, Eresidae, Araneidae, Theridiidae, Agelenidae, Dipluridae, Oxyopidae, Thomisidae, Sparassidae and Lycosidae. None of these is truly social in the manner exhibited by ants and termites, and many wasps and bees. Unlike in these highly social insects, spiders never exhibit a reproductive division of labour, nor the evolution of different castes suited for specific tasks within the nest.

Even so, the degree of communality seen in spiders does show considerable variation, although even its very existence may even depend on environmental condi-

Some dewdrop spiders mainly specialize in filching any prey items too small for the host to bother with. Similar habits are known in some *Mysmenopsis* spiders in *Diplura* webs, as well as by several mirid bugs, including *Ranzovius contubernalis* in the USA. This bug inhabits the space webs of the subsocial theridiid *Anelosimus studiosus*, and the sheet

tions. Thus females of *Philoponella oweni* in Arizona build their webs in interconnected groups when suitable protected crevice habitats are in short supply and prey is abundant; yet they lead solitary lifestyles when the situation is reversed. The invariably communal societies of interconnected orbwebs in *P. republicana* from South America are very

The quantity of prey per web which can be intercepted by this mass of interconnected orb-webs of the sheet orb-weaver **Metepeira labyrinthea** (Araneidae) above a stream in the Chilean Andes is probably greater than a lone web could attain.

(*Below*) The interconnected orb-webs of the communal-territorial **Metabus gravidus** (Araneidae) from Costa Rica.

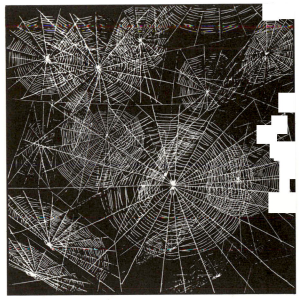

simple, and there is little or no cooperation between neighbours. Even when they gang up to subdue a large insect, only one of their number will win the fight to claim its corpse.

Metabus gravidus (Araneidae) in Costa Rica has arrived at a similar level of communality in large colonies suspended over rainforest rivers. Each spider makes and lives off its own web, but may have to surrender it to a neighbour after a brief fight. Even males mount successful takeovers of female-owned webs and defend them as their own. The advantages of living together probably lie in the greater chance of a large cluster of webs intercepting more prey per web than single webs alone could accomplish. This probably also applies to the social spitting spider *Scytodes fusca* from Australia, the only known social scytodid. It too lives in web-clusters, containing up to 50 females, sometimes with their young; the males are banished to the silk connecting the individual webs. Neighbours tolerate one another only as long as territorial web-rights are respected – trespassers can expect the web's owner to let fly with jets of sticky silk.

By contrast, the uloborid *Philoponella republicana* from South America establishes central roosts where clusters of spiders spend much of their time in amicable togetherness, emerging at dawn to build their individual orb-webs. Large insects are usually handled cooperatively. Some spiders will be hard at it, applying the silk wrapping (uloborids

The huge mass of interconnected webs of the dome-web spider **Cyrtophora citricola** (Araneidae) can extend for hundreds of metres, covering the vegetation. These are in Uganda.

(*Opposite above*) An individual dome-web spider **Cyrtophora citricola**. These seem to ignore the hundreds of **Leucaje** sp. (Tetragnathidae) spiders (*opposite below*) which build their neat horizontal orb-webs within the huge colonies.

SQUATTERS' RIGHTS

Most colonies of social spiders are host to a variety of squatters which scrounge a living. In Australia and Sri Lanka several species of *Olios* huntsman spiders (Sparassidae) regularly invade the webs of social spiders, namely the amaurobiid *Phryganoporus* (*Budumna*) *candida* in Australia and *Stegodyphus sarisinorum* in Sri Lanka. Both of these build sticky sheet-webs which the *Olios* seem to have difficulty in negotiating, moving as though ploughing through deep snow and keeping going only through sheer brute strength. If possible, the *Olios* uses the numerous leaves and twigs which permeate the silk as stepping-stones to make life easier. The invaders feed only on insects trapped in the webs, build their own nest-webs within the all-encompassing structure and seem largely immune to retaliation by the owners. *P. candida* also suffers the incursions of *Simaetha paetula* and *S. thoracica*, two unusual jumping spiders. These often place their nests within the fabric of the social webs, and scavenge prey from around the periphery, thus as far as possible avoiding contact with the sticky silk.

In India, the tiny cribellate spider *Uloburus ferokus* spends its life within the sheet-webs of *Stegodyphus sarasinorum*, making a living by feeding on tiny prey, such as aphids, which the host spider normally ignores.

Several species of social spiders have domestic relationships with moth larvae. These crawl around the nests unmolested, feeding on prey residues, and do not adhere to the sticky silk in cribellar nests. Such relationships only seem to develop with social spiders with long-lasting webs, which often develop into virtual junk-heaps of mealtime leftovers. The nests of *P. candidus* in Queensland become veritable menageries, full of booklice, thrips, ants, mites, wasps, lacewings and mirid bugs (both predacious on the spiders' eggs), several kinds of beetles and a miscellany of spiders, some of which are kleptoparasites while others are predators on their hosts. The caterpillars of several kinds of oecophorid moth occasionally reach plague proportions, ravaging the nest structure, although in lesser numbers they could play a beneficial role in scavenging decaying food remnants and empty egg-sacs. The spiders leave the caterpillars strictly alone, wary of a repugnant defensive secretion which they can emit when molested. The gnaphosid spider, *Lampona fasciata*, is frequent in the nest areas and preys on its host, while large numbers of dewdrop spiders are invariably present.

The large communal nests of *Anelosimus eximius* can contain uninvited guests from as many as 12 different families of spiders. Most communal sheet-type webs probably contain similarly high levels of commensals and parasites.

---

have no poison glands), while others neatly fold protruding legs and wings out of the way; still others will be pouring on digestive enzymes. Yet once the prey is securely trussed, the team spirit dissolves into a free-for-all over possession of the corpse, with the outcome usually ending with a single claimant. However, when the prey is large, there is usually plenty left over for some of the claimant's former allies to take their share. Among the araneid orb-weavers, only *Eriophora bistriata* is known to cooperate both in prey capture and then in feeding.

One of the great potential advantages of the social life is the ability to gang up on larger prey too much of a handful for a single spider. This means subduing the strongly territorial tendencies still evident in the above spiders and declaration of the whole web as a free circulation zone. This advantageous state of affairs has arisen in a number of spiders. A *Tapinillus* lynx spider from Ecuador is unusual both in constructing a web and in being social. As with most social spiders, the colonies are long-lived and very stable. Large prey is handled communally, with the captors taking the first sitting, after which the juveniles are allowed to join in the feast. Most importantly, cannibalistic tendencies have been completely subdued, even under starvation conditions, a most vital advance for true social harmony.

A major step upwards in social organization of day-to-day activities, involving frequent physical contact between adults, cooperative construction of both nests and webs, and group prey capture and feeding activities has been taken in the families Eresidae, Agelenidae, Dictynidae and Theridiidae. These all build sheet- or tangle webs rather than orbs. This is relevant to social development, as sheets and tangles lend themselves to joint artisanship, while an orb-web can really only be efficiently constructed by the spider which first started it.

Stegodyphus sarasinorum (Eresidae) from India shows a highly developed sense of teamwork. 'Pilot spiders' with empty bellies are stationed on the web (instead of resting in lairs) awaiting the arrival of prey. If something too large to handle comes along, they recruit helpers by tapping and pulling the web in a coded message to 'come quickly'. A mass of spiders soon congregates, peppering the prey with bites and pouring on liberal quantities of digestive secretions. They then all crowd cosily together to suck up the resulting nutritious broth. At no point is the prey wrapped in silk, unlike in most web-building spiders. During the day, when large clusters of guzzling spiders would attract sharp-eyed enemies such as crows, the spiders manhandle the corpse down into the nest, but at night they feed where it lies. Any member of the commune is allowed to partake of its share, regardless of whether or not it assisted in the slaughter. Distasteful chemically defended prey, such as blister beetles and stinkbugs, are dumped as soon as they arrive.

In *Stegodyphus mimosarum* from Africa, social *entente cordiale* is less complete. Spiders which played truant during prey capture are turned back when feeding gets underway, leading to ugly fights as the truants try to gatecrash the feast. Recruitment displays are also absent, and each spider acts with complete self-interest by trying to claim the prey for itself and smuggle it back to its own retreat.

Mallos gregalis (Dictynidae) from Mexico builds massive communal webs containing up to 20,000 individuals. The sticky sheet-web, penetrated below by a complex warren of resting and nursery tunnels, is a communal effort, and plays a vital role in keeping the peace. It does this by enhancing the vibrations made by flies (almost the sole prey), eliciting a team attack, while damping the movements made by individual spiders. This eliminates chance cannibalistic attacks due to mistaken identity. The frenzied buzzing of a trapped fly brings up to 30 spiders at the double. These overwhelm the prey by sheer numbers, without either wrapping it in silk or using the lengthy venomous bites seen in most spiders. This is probably important in preventing 'accidental' wrapping or biting of compatriots during the mêlée surrounding a victim. Once the battle is won, the colony's weaker members, such as tiny spiderlings, are allowed to come and sup on the corpse, already predigested for them by the copious outpourings of the massed adults.

The fact that the huge webs of *M. gregalis* normally attract swarms of houseflies and bluebottles, but little else, seems to be no mere coincidence. In fact the webs are huge garbage dumps, containing innumerable prey remains which are incorporated into the webbing, rather than being fastidiously discarded as in other social spiders. In addition, *M. gregalis* does not drain its prey completely dry. The nest is thereby converted into a huge smelly 'bait' for muscoid flies, attracted to special symbiotic yeasts which thrive on the numerous corpses. The expected growth of meat-spoiling bacteria does not materialize, probably because of some inhibiting factor injected by the spiders during feeding, which favours the growth of yeasts over bacteria.

05 Continuing the Line

PREPARING FOR COURTSHIP

Male spiders are often much smaller than the females, so with far less growing to do, the males often mature a long way ahead of any prospective sexual partners. This situation can be extreme, as in males of *Mastophora cornigera* and *Ordgarius magnificus*, which are said to be already mature upon emerging from the egg-sac. Males of *M. dizzydeani* and *M. hutchinsoni* only require one or two moults to reach adulthood. Such precociousness is not surprising, given that adult male body length in these species is usually less than 2mm, while a female can go up to 20mm, needing many weeks and numerous moults to attain her sexual readiness. Even when males and females are of approximately equal size, the males still tend to be more precocious and mature first, probably because the more rapidly a male can enter the highly competitive sexual marathon, the better his chances of coming out a winner.

LOCATING THE FEMALE

The task of tracking down a female is probably much easier than it seems to us. In wolf spiders (Lycosidae) and their like, chemoreceptors on the front legs of the males respond to recently deposited female silk (e.g. drag-lines) impregnated with her sexual pheromones. This scent rapidly decays and disappears under the influence of rain and dew. This saves males the trouble of needlessly following trails which are days old among the maze of fresher lines which criss-cross most habitats. Male

SPERM INDUCTION

The only arachnids which possess a penis for the direct introduction of sperm into the female are harvestman (Opiliones). Spiders, like mites, whip-scorpions and all the rest, must accomplish this basic act in a surprisingly roundabout way. Just after he has matured, the male has to carry out the strange act of sperm induction. In most spiders this happens before the male sets off on his sexual quest, and without any need for stimulation through a female's proximity. Linyphiids are an exception, in which it is chemical contact with the female's web which stimulates sperm induction, although in *Mynoglenes* the start of courtship precedes sperm induction. In *Lepthyphantes leprosus*, the male engages in several hours of 'practice' pseudocopulation before he actually charges his palps and gets down to mating for real.

Sperm induction involves transferring semen from the genitalia situated on the rear underside of the abdomen, into the palps sited at the front of the spider, below the head. The complexity of these organs in many spiders, and their actual mechanism of functioning, have been described in Chapter 01. Although some male spiders could theoretically effect a direct transfer from genitals to palp, in practice this is always accomplished via an intermediary artifice, the sperm-web. At its simplest, as in pholcids, just a single line, stretched between the male's outstretched front legs, is held directly across the genital opening. The semen is then picked up from the web in the chelicerae and then transferred to the palps.

A rather more complex miniature web is typical of most spiders, including araneids. In *Araneus diadematus*, the male deposits a blob of semen on the upper surface of a rectangular sperm-web suspended between a few blades of grass. He then dips his palps into the liquid directly from the upper surface; in other species the situation is reversed, absorption taking place through the underside of the web. Prior to dipping his palps in the semen, the male usually chews them, an action which by wetting them possibly eases the absorption of the liquid semen.

SPERM INDUCTION

A male nursery-web spider **Pisaura mirabilis** charging his palps with sperm from some silken lines held between his third pair of legs.

Sperm induction in most spiders usually takes some 10–15 minutes. However, in most mygalomorphs it is a much more lengthy process, taking up to three hours. It involves the construction of an extensive sheet-web two-thirds the size of the male's body. He then lies on the web while leaning over to absorb sperm from the underside.

Duly charged with sperm and ready for sexual action, the adult male sets off in search of a mate. For most web-building spiders, this marks the beginning of a lengthy period of fasting. Once he has forsaken his juvenile web, the wandering suitor will not make another. Despite much exhausting searching out of females, the male will generally not feed, relying for his continued stamina on reserves of fat stored during his growing-up stage. Although most individuals now dedicate themselves unreservedly to the sexual matter in hand, there are exceptions. For example, in tropical America, males of four species of orb-web builders were seen evicting spiders from their webs and using them to catch prey. Roaming males may also grab the chance to snap up any insect which offers itself as a sitting duck. The tiny males of *Nephila* and *Argiope* often take advantage of their temporary residence in a female's web to snatch a meal or two.

91

wolf spiders will also occasionally take a wrong turning and follow male drag-lines and those of the wrong species, but get it right most of the time. Even the empty substrate where a female has recently rested will elicit male courtship behaviour. This need not necessarily be on a solid surface. In the American fishing spider, *Dolomedes triton*, the female's pheromones dissolve into the water and are detected by the males. These pheromones in themselves are sufficient to spark off a bout of courtship behaviour.

Web-building spiders seem to face greater problems. A tiny male *Argiope* with his short legs, not really built for cross-country walking, may have to discover the location of widely scattered female webs hidden away among a forest of trees and bushes. Yet every female web seems to have one or two resident males in position near the hub. How have they managed to do it? It seems that the females themselves are responsible for advertising the location of their webs by releasing guidance pheromones into the air, rather in the manner of female moths. The tiny male spiders can then move in reasonably accurately towards a female's airborne beacon, without having to hang around for ages in the hope of stumbling across some female silk.

Newly-moulted adult virgins may muster a considerable retinue of males, so why are the webs of older adult females nearby bereft of male companionship? The answer lies in female fickleness. For example, virgin females of *Cyrtophora cicatrosa* (Araneidae) advertise for a mate by discharging a pheromone which the males can detect a metre or more away. A few days after her first mating, the female switches off her emissions and changes her attitude towards suitors. The first arrival during her pheromonal 'personal column' stage will have received a warm welcome, but late-comers are given a hostile reception and driven viciously from the web.

In some other spiders, the females label the webs themselves with pheromones. A web's relatively huge surface area makes it a very efficient long-range broadcasting device. A female of the sierra dome spider (*Linyphia litigosa*) from the USA will start to incorporate a 'come hither' pheromone on her web if, despite having been 'available' for

SPERM PRIORITY

Much of the in-fighting exhibited by male spiders is dictated by the compulsion to be the first suitor to inseminate a female. This applies especially to entelegyne species, in which the females' sperm-storage organs are of the so-called 'conduit' type, having separate sperm pathways for entry from the male and exit to the eggs. In such a system, sperm from the first mate is thought to head the queue to its final goal – the eggs – on a first-in, first-out basis, regardless of the presence of additional sperm from subsequent matings. In practical terms, this means that a female's first mate will fertilize all, or most, of her eggs. However, there is other evidence contradicting this most comprehensively, revealing a second-male fertilization rate of over 60 per cent – higher than in the first male! Nevertheless in general, first-male priority probably operates in most entelegyne species.

This first-male sperm priority is responsible for a great deal of unbridled rivalry between males. It also stimulates a form of guarding behaviour called the 'suitor phenomenon', in which males seek to thwart their sexual competitors by moving in with immature females and guarding them until their final moult. The guardian can therefore be sure of being the first male to inseminate the newly adult female. Any future sexual liaisons that the female may make are irrelevant. Any subsequent suitors are much too late, and are wasting their time in a virtually futile exercise, which might earn paternity of a handful of offspring at the most. The assumption that entelegyne spiders would show first-male sperm priority was (it was thought) amply confirmed by a study of cohabitation in 161 species of spiders. Of these, only seven had cul-de-sac spermathecae, apparent vindication of the theory.

Familiar orb-web genera with 'conduit' spermathecal design which have been studied for first-male sperm precedence include: *Leucaje, Gasteracantha, Nephila* and *Argiope* among the Araneidae; *Phidippus* among the Salticidae; and *Frontinella* and *Linyphia* in the Linyphiidae. Haplogyne females with cul-de-sac spermathecal design are not generally guarded when subadult, because sperm is not allocated to

SPERM PRIORITY – DOES THE FIRST MATE ALWAYS WIN?

fertilization on a first-in-first-out basis. These are therefore far more attractive as adults. In some (perhaps most) cases a single mating will provide all the sperm needed by a female to fertilize a succession of egg batches. The theridiid *Achaearanea wau* can store sperm for up to 80 days, although the viability of the eggs decreases markedly as time progresses. *Paraplectanoides crassipes* (Araneidae) from Australia can store sperm for as long as six years and still produce egg batches with almost 100 per cent fertility.

The suitor phenomenon impels the early-maturing males of many species to move in with a female as much as a week or two before her final moult. At this stage, the male lodger might even be larger than his unwilling hostess, enabling him to force entry and settle himself in despite her best efforts to expel him. Another advantage of being present at the female's final moult is the ease with which mating can then take place. The newly-moulted virgin is weak and supple, and probably particularly receptive to her lodger's advances. Evidence for cohabitation is proving to be extremely common in spiders; cohabitation is probably more important in smoothing spiders' often turbulent sexual relationships than had earlier been thought.

A bank orb-weaver **Araneus (Larinioides) cornutus** male cohabiting with an immature female in England.

several days since becoming adult, she is nevertheless still a virgin. Although such a possibility is slim in a dense population, it could happen where the habitat is less favourable, and webs more sparsely distributed. When a male arrives, the first thing he does is to pull the web down and wrap it tightly into a bundle. This apparent act of senseless vandalism does in fact have a deadly serious motive. By vastly reducing the surface area available for the evaporation and transmission of the female's pheromone, the male has effectively blanked-out the female's advertisement. This is an essential first move, because the first male to respond must try and suppress any competition, both for reasons of sperm priority (*see* box, pages 92–3) and for his own welfare. If a rival shows up, then there will probably be a no-holds-barred fight for the female, with possible injury or death the price of losing. Unfortunately for the female, the destruction of her web incurs costs in terms of protein lost, a particularly serious problem for linyphiids which, unlike most spiders, are not able to recycle their silk by eating it.

Sometimes females seem to make their pheromonal broadcasts while actually moulting, although this could be an unintentional release of normal chemicals involved in the moulting process, which nevertheless alerts males tuned into it. One of the authors has observed a male *Enoplognatha ovata* (Theridiidae) mating with a rather shaky female hanging below her recently shed skin, while four other males 'kicked their heels' on the web's periphery. The fact that no fewer than five males had arrived for the important last moult in a species whose webs are widely scattered seems significant.

PATTERNS OF COURTSHIP

THE SUITOR PHENOMENON AND THE KAMIKAZE MALE

With spiders, it is generally probably true to say that the type of courtship methods employed exploit the same senses which are most vital in prey capture. Thus sharp-sighted hunters such as jumping spiders and wolf spiders tend towards visually-based courtship. Web-builders harness the web itself, which is equally efficient at transmitting either vibrations from prey or from a courting male. Short-sighted hunters often use no courtship at all, and probably depend on scent and touch for adequate recognition between the sexes.

Some form of precopulatory courtship is often essential because in many spiders the female has to adopt a special 'submissive posture', without which the male cannot properly insert his palpal organs. Full female compliance is therefore usually essential. The reception enjoyed by her suitor seems to vary, depending on how near to egg-laying she may be, and how many previous suitors she has already accepted.

Virgin females probably tend to be willing participants in sexual relationships, while a few days before laying their eggs they become highly intolerant of further attempts at seduction. In a study of the American crab-spider *Misumenoides formosipes*, virgin females fended off suitors on less than ten per cent of occasions, while in once-mated females, this rose to nearly 50 per cent. In hunting spiders recalcitrant females can exploit their mobility to make themselves scarce when confronted by yet another pushy male signalling his amorous intentions. Web-builders stay put and shake the web vigorously in an unmistakable 'get lost' message to the male. If he fails to take the hint and keeps on coming, he will probably be savagely attacked.

Even the most violently hostile reception may not be enough to repel a male driven to gamble on a final last-gasp mating before the female lays her eggs. These 'last fling' males may dispense with their usual caution and fall back on 'kamikaze' tactics, forcing their attentions on the females. There is little to be lost by such a devil-may-care attitude. Once all the females have laid their eggs, the surviving males have nothing to gain through becoming celibate geriatrics. Going out on a final note of sexual triumph would therefore make perfect sense.

The risks generally run by male spiders during their reproductive endeavours have probably been greatly overstressed. Sexual relations are probably good most of the time, often excellent, and it is

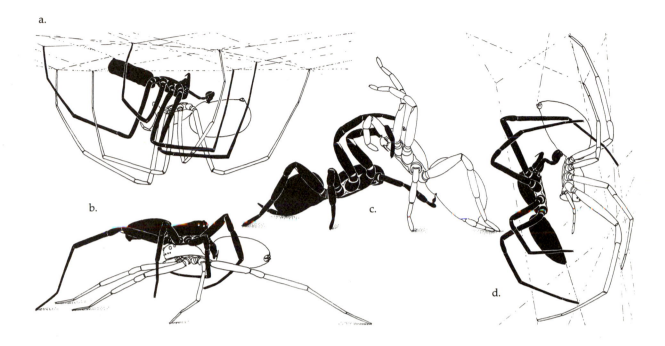

The mating position of various spider families. Although there are many variations on a theme, they can be simplified into four basic types, exemplified by the following (the males are in solid black):

a. Linyphiidae, which mate beneath the sheet-web.
b. Lycosidae which mate on the ground or on leaves etc., the female often running around for hours unencumbered by the male's presence.
c. Tarantulas which also mate on a solid substrate.
d. Clubionidae (**Cheiracanthium**) hang from threads.

usually only males who push their luck at the last moment who run really serious risks of suffering a premature death. And, as mentioned above, such 'kamikaze' males are dispensable anyway. There are exceptions to the 'good relations' rule, as explained below, but even some of these are in the best interest of the males.

MYGALOMORPHS: COURTSHIP IN THE SHORT-SIGHTED HUNTERS

The most static of all spiders, at least in the female sex, are the burrow-living mygalomorphs such as trapdoor and purse-web spiders. The females may lay batches of eggs regularly throughout their lives. They receive regular visits from males, who forsake the cosy security of their own burrows and brave the hostile world above ground in their quest for females. Male tarantulas, as in most of these spiders, respond automatically to the pheromone-laden silk surrounding female burrows. *Aphonopelma chalcodes* from the USA taps out a greeting on the threshold of the female's burrow, whereupon she pops quickly out. If her mood is responsive, she adopts what at first sight seems to be an aggressive posture, tilted back on her hind legs, her front legs held upwards and her fangs bared. Strangely enough, first impressions are misleading, for this is not the signal for the male to retreat, but

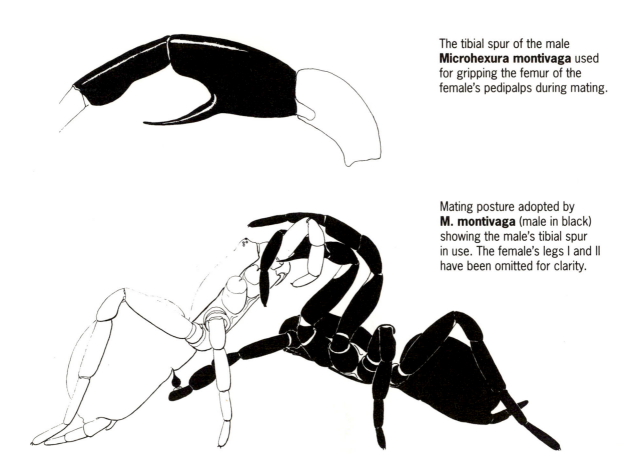

The tibial spur of the male **Microhexura montivaga** used for gripping the femur of the female's pedipalps during mating.

Mating posture adopted by **M. montivaga** (male in black) showing the male's tibial spur in use. The female's legs I and II have been omitted for clarity.

to advance confidently. The female is in fact baring her fangs specifically to enable the male to grasp them with a special prong on his forelegs (*see* illustration); her tilted stance is also essential in enabling him to creep beneath her and insert his palps, easing her back even further as he pushes forwards. If she fails to adopt the necessary stance immediately, the male taps her gently with his legs until she does. A closely similar train of events has been observed in most other theraphosids studied. Many mygalomorph males also perform a preliminary body-jerking or quivering display. In some of the other families, the male's tibial prong grips the female on her pedipalps, chelicerae, or front pairs of legs, rather than the fangs.

For the male *Atypus* purse-web spider, the main problem to be surmounted is to gain entry to the female's sealed silken tube without being mistaken for prey and eaten. He avoids this because his delicately-probing front legs with their hyper-sensitive chemoreceptors instantly recognize the female's silken purse at the merest touch. He can therefore stop dead before he has clambered over the purse by mistake and received a surprise pair of fangs through his belly. Standing safely to one side he can strike up a rapid drumming against the silk with his palps and legs. Now, should the female within be of a mind to make a meal of her visitor, as popular myth would suggest is normal habit for female spiders, she will never have a better chance to cash in on her invisibility to have a stab at running him through with her long fangs. In reality, she does nothing of the sort. If copulation is not currently on her agenda, she very sociably lets him know by briskly plucking at the silk. The mere absence of such a response is his signal to soften the silk with a blob of saliva and then tear his way inside. Once in the narrow confines of the female's burrow, she again has him at her mercy, yet sexual relations tend to go smoothly and copulation follows satisfactorily with the female's back pressed up against the walls of her tube. It is worth stressing here that the female's disinclination to act the role of *femme fatale* in order to nab an easy meal is common in spiders, as is the female's habit of giving the male plenty of warning when he is not wanted.

COURTSHIP IN CRAB-SPIDERS

In crab-spiders (Thomisidae), the male is usually a midget beside the bulky female, who is normally also a different colour. In *Epicadus heterogaster* from Brazil, the huge knobbly white female is probably over 100 times as heavy as the tiny dark-brown male.

His diminutive stature is significant for the male in two ways. Firstly, locating the very scattered females involves so much walking that they lend a hand by broadcasting a female pheromone, either from the body or from the silk which is laid down thinly across the substrate. Secondly, the male's small size seems to be an important factor in ensuring harmonious relationships between the sexes. A plump female *Misumena* or *Thomisus* waiting quietly on a flower will quickly dispatch an insect of superior size and power, yet they appear to be completely unaware of the presence of a tiny male. Indeed, he can walk straight in and without so much as a glimmer of courtship clamber up on to the female's body and walk around all over her, easing himself beneath her enormous bulk to insert his palps at will. The most that the male does as a concession to courtship is to drum on the female's abdomen and perhaps give her a few gentle bites. However, it is also possible

The minute brown **Epicadus heterogaster** male (Thomisidae) is just visible beneath the huge white body of the female in a Brazilian rainforest.

A male European flower spider **Misumena vatia** walking around unmolested on the body of the female.

that as the male clambers up the leaf or stem of the female's plant, he announces his arrival by vibrating the plant in a species-specific message. Such a subtle means of communication would be very difficult for an observer to detect. At any point it would be easy for the female to turn on the male and grab him, but she does not. If a male's advances are unwelcome, she lets him know by raising her front legs in an offensive stance. If he still comes forward, she reinforces her message by vibrating her body.

Females of the North American *Misumenoides formosipes* habitually sit on flowers. When they reach their last juvenile instar, they become highly attractive to the males, who guard them until they become adult. Virgin females are in short supply, so with every unattached male in hot pursuit they are highly valued by their guardians. If necessary they will fight to the death to protect their property, and the loser's corpse provides a useful victory feast. Males on guard-duty also tend to have an advantage during combat through being better supplied with liquid energy in the form of nectar. Males of this species are perhaps unusual in devoting many hours to lapping up energy-giving nectar from flowers, and feeding on protein-rich pollen (which would be externally digested, being too large to swallow whole). Water is the usual exclusive tipple of male spiders.

A hard-pressed male can escape from a tricky situation during combat with a rival, or in the occasional rough-and-tumble with a female (she is up to 50 times his size), by shedding one or more of his legs and hobbling off as fast as his remaining legs will allow. Late in the season it is common to see just about any male spiders minus one or more legs, probably through similar reasons. Once a female *M. formosipes* has been inseminated, her sexual 'share price' collapses, and she is of little future interest to males in increasing their reproductive investment. The operation of first-male sperm priority is the reason for this sudden decline in popularity.

THE SEXUAL ACT IN *CLUBIONA*

Clubiona spp. are mostly smallish brown spiders which generally spend the day in silken cells under stones or leaves, emerging at night to hunt. Males probably have to rely on a rather hit-or-miss method of finding females, basically by stumbling across them. Once found, a female is too precious to lose, so with a total lack of finesse the male grabs her and hangs on tightly. A female will rarely protest unduly at this treatment, and allows the male to climb on her back so that he can insert a palp from one side. Mating takes some considerable time, and the author has several times seen a female of *C. terrestris* running around among grass with a male clinging to her back, thoroughly engrossed in his two-hour mating session.

Clubionid females often run around for hours with the male *in copula*. This is a pair of ant-mimicking **Myrmecium** sp. from Trinidad, looking just like an ant carrying a dead nest-mate, a common sight. Indeed, this is exactly what the photographer first thought they were.

VISUAL COURTSHIP IN WOLF SPIDERS

Courtship in the common *Pardosa* (wolf spiders) is probably more easy to observe than in any other spider. It often takes place in some conspicuous spot, such as a rock, log or on a leaf, and the males are so persistent that they plug away with almost constant courtship throughout the day, regardless of the level of reception they receive. As in many spiders, the male will initiate courtship merely upon contact with pheromone-impregnated female silk, and will continue to perform to a chemical ghost for some time after the female has decamped through lack of interest. The male's repertoire is highly visual, employing semaphoring and shivering movements of the conspicuous palps and legs. A signalling male moves rather in the manner of a clockwork toy as he gradually inches towards the female. The males will sometimes press ahead with courtship directed at females of the wrong species, but the females are more discriminating and never respond to such approaches. Males also perform dominance displays after copulating and in contact with rival males, strutting around on stilted legs in a stereotyped fashion.

In sedentary burrow-living wolf spiders, the male can take advantage of a sub-adult female's housebound state by becoming consort in residence until she makes her final moult. This is the normal state of affairs in *Geolycosa turricola* from the USA. The male's courtship is unusual, for a lycosid, in lacking any palp-waving or abdomen-vibrating component.

SOUND AND VIBRATIONS: COURTSHIP IN HUNTING SPIDERS

The fact that male spiders can generate sound has long been known. Sound production is currently known from 26 families and involves one of two methods:

♦ STRIDULATION (THE RUBBING OF ONE
   BODY PART AGAINST ANOTHER)
♦ PERCUSSION (DRUMMING AGAINST
   THE SUBSTRATE).

Stridulatory mechanisms have evolved separately on several occasions in different families of spiders, with at least eight kinds now being recognized, as defined by the relative body parts which are called into play.

In the highly arboreal European buzzing spider (*Anyphaena accentuata*), the male beats a rapid tattoo against a leaf with his abdomen, producing a sound which is clearly audible to the human ear. The males often carry out courtship on top of the female's nest, comprised of a tuft of newly opened oak leaves bound together with silk. He sits and taps alternately with each palp, while simultaneously vibrating his abdomen. No sound is audible, but presumably the female is well aware of the knocking on her roof, and of its source. After a few minutes, she comes rushing out and grapples with the male, in what at first sight seems like a rebuff. However, shortly after she returns inside, the male follows her with every sign of confidence and remains inside, presumably to mate. It therefore seems that the earlier grappling session could be a confirmation of interest by the female, rather than rejection. Females of *Araneus (Larinioides) cornutus* also grapple shortly before adopting the mating posture.

By drumming on a fallen dead leaf, the Australian salticid *Saitis michaelseni* produces a grasshopper-like buzzing which can be heard several metres away. The male first makes a visual presentation to the female, introducing himself by gently performing some vertical salutes with his white-tipped front legs. Only then does he move to the other side of her leaf, positions himself above her and launches into his serenade. His 'song' is generated by a brace of files at the rear of the cephalothorax, rubbing against a stubble of short hairs at the front of the abdomen (similar mechanisms are known from a variety of Clubionidae, Gnaphosidae, Hahniidae and Theridiidae). By vigorously waggling his abdomen up and down, a loud buzzing results, greatly amplified by the dead-leaf platform on which he performs. In the final act of his solo recital he adds a dash of straight percussion by rapping his front legs against the leaf.

Sound production is found in several North American wolf spiders. Indeed, reports of 'drumming' in *Lycosa gulosa* go back nearly a 100 years.

A male buzzing spider **Anyphaena accentuata** drumming on the female's nest under some oak leaves in an English woodland.

This is hardly surprising, considering that a male of this species bashing away on a dead leaf can be heard clearly up to 6m away. Sound-producers are usually partially or wholly active at night, when visual communication would not be very effective.

By 'squatting low' and pedalling with his palps one at a time, *Lycosa rabida* creates friction between a file on the tibia of the palp and a scraper on its opposing tarsus. The volume of stridulation which results is boosted via contact between bunches of

COMMUNICATION BY RIPPLES

The fisher spider (*Dolomedes triton*) uses water as its medium of courtship transmissions. The female's legs are constantly monitoring surface ripples in order to distinguish those caused by falling leaves from those generated by potential prey. The male therefore, performs leg jerks which engender pulses of ripples unlike those from any other cause. He combines these with leg- and palp-waving displays, thus ensuring not only that the female is aware of his presence, but also that he is not mistaken for prey and attacked.

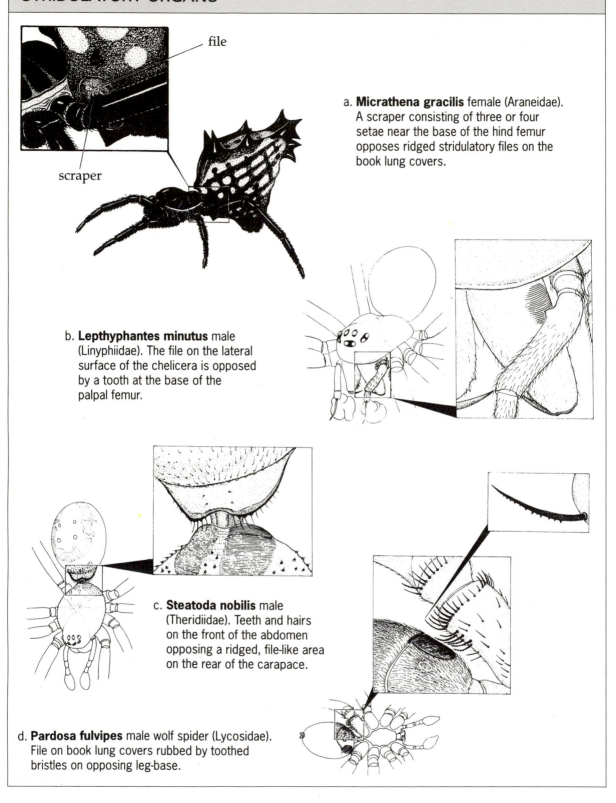

a. **Micrathena gracilis** female (Araneidae). A scraper consisting of three or four setae near the base of the hind femur opposes ridged stridulatory files on the book lung covers.

b. **Lepthyphantes minutus** male (Linyphiidae). The file on the lateral surface of the chelicera is opposed by a tooth at the base of the palpal femur.

c. **Steatoda nobilis** male (Theridiidae). Teeth and hairs on the front of the abdomen opposing a ridged, file-like area on the rear of the carapace.

d. **Pardosa fulvipes** male wolf spider (Lycosidae). File on book lung covers rubbed by toothed bristles on opposing leg-base.

non-slip spines on the palpal tip and a dead leaf on the forest floor, which acts as a natural loudspeaker. (Male *Phidippus mystaceus,* jumping spiders, produce a 'trill' using similar substrate-coupling palpal spines, although the stridulatory organs on the palps are differently arranged.) After a bout of pure percussion, the male *L. rabida* sticks out one of his front legs and performs a few gentle taps, accompanying these with abdominal vibrations and more palpal drumming. This song-and-dance medley constitutes a courtship sequence, after which the male lapses into inactivity. This is the female's cue to show that she has been an attentive audience, and she replies to his overtures with some leg waves, taking a promising step or two forwards as she does so. Only after the female advances towards the male and actually touches him will copulation follow. Interestingly enough, during daylight hours females will agree to mate without any of the acoustic signals at all, but at night, when this species is also active, the acoustic element alone is enough to bring in an audience.

It seems that these spiders can actually detect airborne sounds, probably via the sensitive trichobothria and slit sensillae on their legs, but females respond better to vibrations perceived via the substrate. Males also 'drum' in dominance contests with rival males, but use a different pattern of sounds in this context. The actual act of copulation takes around an hour, and its imminent end is signalled when the female starts to get fidgety. Duly warned, the male suddenly clamps his chelicerae around his mate's carapace and gives her a powerful pinch before jumping off. She is left in a somewhat limp and deflated condition, but she recovers from her rough treatment a few minutes later.

Substrate-coupled drumming is the rule in several American wolf spiders, including *L. gulosa, L. aspersa* and *L. carolinensis.* However, in a number of European species pure percussion seems to be used, without the stridulatory addition. Thus, in *Hygrolycosa rubrofasciata,* the underside of the abdomen bears a shiny plate which is used to strike dry leaves.

In two closely related North American wolf spiders, *Schizocosa rovneri* and *S. ocreata,* a similar method of sound production seems to be the key component in preventing accidental hybridization between this pair of closely related species. As usual, it is the males who are short on discrimination, as their courtship repertoire can be automatically triggered by contact with females of either species. Fortunately, the females can adequately distinguish between the idiosyncratic displays performed by their respective males, whose physical appearance is very similar. However, the tibia of the male *S. ocreata* is uniquely adorned with a tuft of black bristles. These are prominently flaunted as the male struts around the female, tapping with his front legs and jerking his body from side to side in something of a swagger. He backs up this spectacle by stridulating with simultaneous palpal movements. The female responds both to his 'signature tune' and his visual set piece, but it seems to be the leg-tuft adornments in the latter which make all the difference.

By contrast, the *S. rovneri* male, bereft of showy tufts which can be flourished on parade, stays his ground and places his trust in sound. Threading his abdomen through his legs, often simultaneously beating it against the substrate, he bursts out with a spasm of palpal pedalling. This produces a stridulation easily perceived by humans and comprised of a series of pulses at 4.5 second intervals. The two males thus produce entirely different acoustic signatures, not so very different in context from those familiarly exemplified by grasshoppers, crickets, frogs and birds. The female *S. rovneri* will indicate her readiness to mate merely upon hearing her suitor's serenade, but *S. ocreata* females are not satisfied with mere song alone and must receive the full visual pageant as well. Not surprisingly, in another species, the strictly nocturnal *S. mccooki* sound is the exclusive medium and there is no visual display. This species is unusual in that the males do not respond chemotactically to female silk, but only to contact with the female herself.

In *Heteropoda venatoria* from Florida the faint buzzing hum produced by the males derives from contact between the substrate and adhesive tarsal hairs on the vibrating legs, without the assistance of a stridulatory organ. The large solitary *Cupiennius* wandering spiders (Ctenidae) which are such a feature of the rainforests of Costa Rica communicate their intentions through vibrating the broad shiny leaves of the bromeliad and heliconia plants on which they spend much of their time. Males kick off their vibratory repertoire when they contact female silk, and females respond with their own vibrations. Unfortunately, rival males are wont to home in on these duets as a cue to the location of a prospective mate. They are likely to engage in bouts of ritualized vibratory 'contests' with the courting male, something which is not of indifferent interest to the female, who by her vibrations, encourages male competitions which are likely to provide her with the fittest mate.

BRIDAL BONDAGE

Bridal binding with a silken veil has long been known in some crab spiders (Thomisidae), but has recently been observed in a number of additional families. The most familiar user of this device is the diminutive male of the European *Xysticus cristatus* and related species. After a brief tussle upon first meeting her mate to be, the female remains surprisingly passive while the male makes circuit after circuit upon her body, laying down a skein of silk which envelops her head, cephalothorax and legs. While doing the rounds, he gently strokes her with his legs, reinforcing her compliant 'mood', which is essential to the next step. With the veil securely in place, the male has to heave the female's abdomen upwards from the rear, in order to insert himself head-first beneath it and insert his palps. Repeated palpal insertions can take as much as 90 minutes, during which time the female remains immobile and does not endeavour to remove her silken handcuffs. The fact that the female *could* break free at any time is evident from the relative ease with which she finally shrugs off her bonds when the male has departed.

The next example of bridal veil construction comes in the American wolf spider, *Pisaurina mira* (Pisauridae). The male locates the female by following her drag-line, touching it repeatedly with his palps. After just a brief interplay of legs, the sum total of apparent courtship, the female steps off the leaf and drops a short distance on her drag-line. The male follows her down likewise, by which time the female is in a trance-like state and can be manipulated at will. Her legs are tightly clasped to her sides, neatly arranged to receive the silk pinions which the male now trails around them, spinning her round like a top. After reinforcing her drag-line with his own, he boards her and inserts his palps. As in *Xysticus* the female is able to shrug off her bonds with little trouble, once the male has departed. The whole scenario is unusual on two counts, firstly for the bridal veil, and secondly for the aerial copulation which is seldom seen in hunting spiders.

Another pisaurid, *Ancylometes bogotensis*, has also yielded the secrets of its bondage-style sexual behaviour. Once again, courtship is sparse and the female again facilitates the male's tying operations by first hunching her legs, although she does this while still lying on the substrate. Once she is trussed up (and the male makes a really thorough job of this), he tilts her over to one side so that he can mate. After some 10–15 minutes, he departs, leaving the female to loosen the ties and free her legs of the clinging silk. Unlike in the species already described, this is not the work of a few seconds, but a painstaking process which can take some two to three hours.

A *modus operandi* with remarkable similarities to that seen in *Pisaurina mira*, but this time in a lynx spider (Oxyopidae), has been observed by one of the authors in Uganda (illustrated opposite). Large numbers of females sit around on top of leaves and on the broad blades of a large grass. The male approaches the female from the rear, but makes his ascent up the underside of the leaf. Vibrations generated by his movements must surely be felt by the female, yet she does not react as she would to approaching prey, so presumably he has some way of letting her know who he is. After tapping the leaf directly beneath her with his legs, he moves round on to her side of the leaf, but just behind her. Edging closer, he tickles her gently with his front legs, whereupon a receptive female turns and walks off

An **Oxyopes** male stroking the female in courtship in Uganda.

(*Bottom left*) The male twirls the female and wraps her in silk.

(*Bottom right*) The female has seized the male and pierced him with her fangs killing him almost instantly.

the edge of the leaf and hangs suspended with clenched legs. After following her down, the male wraps her in silk, both by twirling her around on her thread, and by running in rapid circles over her body, trailing silk behind him. This takes several minutes, after which he attempts to insert a palp. It was at this juncture that things went horribly wrong in the episodes observed by one of the the authors. Either the female simply sprung out of her bonds and shinned back up her drag-line to the leaf, or she embraced the male as he inserted his palp and sank her fangs into him, upon which he seemed to deflate abruptly, suffering apparently instantaneous death.

Observations over the next few days showed why the males were having such little success. Females started to build their maternity nests everywhere. The mating attempts must all therefore have been last-ditch 'kamikaze' affairs. Most of the males had at least one palp missing, presumably from earlier matings. In light of this, it is all the more surprising that the females should have shown any positive response to the males' courtship overtures.

In the two pisaurids and the oxyopid, the males are little inferior in stature to the females. In all but *A. bogotensis*, the female is perfectly able to free herself from her 'bonds' at any juncture. The real function of the 'bridal veil' therefore remains obscure. In *Xysticus*, it may be important in anchoring the female down, keeping her firmly in place when the male lifts her abdomen. However, one feature which is common to all these spiders is the simplicity of the courtship. The 'bridal' silk, impregnated with male pheromones, is placed (significantly) in contact with the female's legs, just where her contact chemoreceptors are situated. By enswathing the female in his pheromone-soaked silk for the duration of the mating process, the male could be compensating for the lack of extended courtship. The female may thus receive a constant chemical reinforcement of her mate's identity, which allied to his movements on her body, prevents her from prematurely breaking out of her submissive trance (*see also* silk-laying in *Argiope* and *Nephila*, pages 120–2). However, this must be considered as pure conjecture at present.

'Bungee-jump' copulation is also seen in at least two other lynx spiders, the European *Oxyopes heterophthalmus* and the American green lynx spider (*Peucetia viridans*), but without the added refinement of the bridal veil. In *P. viridans*, the couple may drop off the leaf several times for repeated sessions of copulation, palpal insertion each time being a lightning-quick lunge lasting only a fraction of a second. The male will then wander off in search of a new mate, having ensured that the female he just left will never mate again, by blocking access to her genitalia with a plug. This consists of a hard blackish substance which is probably dried semen. Similar 'chastity belts' are also applied by males in other families, although it may be part of the male's palp which breaks off inside the epigyne and forms the plug.

COURTSHIP IN JUMPING SPIDERS

Male jumping spiders are among the most brilliantly coloured of all spiders, often rivalling jewel beetles or butterflies in their combinations of scintillatingly bright colours. The females are usually drab and often quite unlike the males in appearance. In fact they often resemble a different species, and indeed in the past have sometimes been described as such – or even as different genera! As with many birds and lizards, the male jumping spider's resplendent livery has evolved in a sexual context. The females are presumed to be 'impressed' by handsome suitors who show off their finery during quite complex courtship displays.

The males' colours are often associated with specific bodily adornments, such as tufts of hairs or scales situated on the front legs, palps, face or abdomen. The mechanics of the male's exhibitionism are usually designed to parade such adornments to maximum advantage. Legs, palps and abdomen may all be waved in species-specific sequences during complicated routines.

The male cannot, however, always rely on being able to stage-manage his show on an ideal platform such as a leaf or log, where his twirling and prancing can be best appreciated. The females spend

A male **Helpis minitabunda** jumping spider (Salticidae) in attendance upon a female in her silken nest in a forest in Queensland, Australia.

much of their time in their nests, from where they cannot witness events on the outside. The male's response is to tailor his approach to the circumstances. Thus, the American *Phidippus johnsoni* responds to a female in the open with his full dance routine, consisting of to-and-fro eight-stepping, zig-zag waltzing to right and left and seductive gesturing with his front legs. An adult female ensconced inside her nest elicits a quite different tactic. Ostentation is now replaced by the male probing and vibrating the silk of the nest with his legs and chelicerae. A responsive female allows the male to come inside and they mate. A penultimate instar female elicits the same style of vibrating courtship, but this time the male adds his own

silken living quarters to the nest and cohabits with the female until she moults. Such cohabitation is common in the Australian *Portia fimbriata*, but is unusual in often involving sub-adult males, who may remain in residence for up to eight weeks.

As female nests are often long-lived, they often attract the attention of more than one male, leading to conflict. In salticids this is often highly ritualized, thus deciding a winner without the risks inherent in battle. The males of some ant-mimicking jumping spiders, such as *Myrmarachne lupata* from Australia and *M. plataleoides* from Asia, have taken such ritual contests to the extreme by developing grotesquely elongated chelicerae and fangs (about five times longer than in the females).

THE WEDDING-PRESENT SPIDER

Dance-fly males (Empididae) are well known for their habit of presenting their mates with nuptial gifts; bittacid hanging flies (Mecoptera) do likewise. Yet of all the 35,000 known species of spiders around the world, just one has adopted similar habits. Fortunately, this paradigm among spiders is the familiar nursery-web spider (*Pisaura mirabilis*), which happens to be extremely common near the authors' home in Cornwall, England. In fact, up to 14 basking females per square metre can be found in May and June on low vegetation (mostly nettles) alongside a slow-moving lowland stream nearby. Being frequently privy to the fascinating sexual protocols of this species has not therefore presented much difficulty.

Before setting off on his nuptial quest, the male must first catch an insect, destined to play a key role as his 'wedding gift' . In Cornwall, this gift often comprises a male assassin fly (*Empis tessellata*), which ironically enough is busy presenting its own females with nuptial gifts at this time of year. With his gift to hand, the male *P. mirabilis* now does something which marks a significant departure from his procedure with normal prey. This, as with all wolf spiders, is left unwrapped. By contrast, prey destined for presentation to his mate is gift-wrapped in a dense swathe of very shiny white silk, finishing up roughly the shape of a ball.

The male wraps his 'gift' in silk before setting off in search of a female.

The male in classic courtship pose, presenting the 'gift' to the female.

During his search for a mate, the male assumes an unusual robot-like jerky manner. He can detect a female who is out of his direct line of sight, so pheromonal communication is presumably involved. He is also behaviourally very flexible when faced with an awkward situation, such as a female in a less than ideally accessible position. Under ideal conditions, with the female basking on a large leaf, he will make a frontal approach, his shiny white gift proffered prominently in his chelicerae. Stopping just short, he takes up a bizarre stance with his abdomen pointed vertically down at the leaf, and his long legs bent upwards at a peculiar angle. To ensure that the female is able to scrutinize the gift without impediment, he keeps his large palps stowed well out of the way to either side. A receptive female responds by creeping forwards, only to find that the male leans backwards, holding the gift just out of her reach. Finally, she manages to claim it in her chelicerae, although it is still not hers to

continued overleaf

continued

keep, for the male still maintains a silken security line between the gift and his spinnerets. Once the female is preoccupied with her gift, the male can occupy himself with mating, which takes an hour or more, during which the inflation of the palpal bulb can be clearly seen. Now and again the male takes a meal-break, joining the female in her quiet sucking on his gift before going back to the task in hand.

The males also rise to the challenge of approaching a female in a more tricky situation. This most often happens when the female's leaf is too small to allow a frontal approach, often compounded by the fact that she is heavily gravid and unlikely to be in a very responsive mood. It is essential somehow to gain her interest first, and the male does this by peering up over the edge of her leaf while gently tugging it. To add visual appeal, he waves his palps around in an attention-grabbing way. His reluctance to barge right in is based not on fear of lethal retaliation but fear that the female will rush off before she has glimpsed his trump-card – the gift. In practice, females seldom even stand their ground, let alone attack, but prefer to duck out of the male's sight as soon as he arrives and hide. But the males have single-track minds and persevere, never giving up, even when they have to spend long periods sitting in front of an impassive female, tantalizingly jerking the gift in a bid to kindle some spark of interest.

The mating act with the inflated palpal bulb clearly visible.

Dealing with a difficult situation. This male is tugging the edge of a nettle leaf in order to gain the attention of a heavily gravid female. She eventually ran off.

None of the above squares very well with the common notion that nuptial gifts are safety devices intended to placate the predatory females. First, the males are just as large as the females, and rather more agile. Secondly, aggressive responses by the females are extremely rare. In experimental conditions, the gift itself caused cannibalism during fights over ownership, with either sex ending up eating the other. Even when males and females are artificially cooped up together for a few days after mating, no cannibalism occurs, despite the abnormality of such a situation.

It is likely that the gift actually serves a dual function. The first may be analogous to the bridal veil. In the absence of the complex courtship seen in most wolf spiders, the gift may function as a 'badge of identity'. If not, why bother to wrap it in so much silk? Secondly, it serves the male's interests to present the biggest possible gift, which his mate will then turn into eggs. Well-fed females grow bigger, produce more eggs and are ready to lay them sooner than females on an inadequate diet. Early egg-laying also helps to reduce depredations by a *Trychosis* wasp, which attacks the egg-sacs at increasing rates as the season progresses. Any helping hand the male can give to his mate must be worthwhile, given that fewer than 10 per cent of females actually survive to the stage of hatching their offspring.

Continuing the Line

In *M. lupata* the two 'duellists' stand face to face, spread their chelicerae widely and unsheath their huge caliper-like fangs. As they close for the clinch, it looks as though a fatality is inevitable, with the fangs deployed like lances. In fact all they are doing is getting close enough to compare the relative lengths of one another's chelicerae. It seems that in this species, size really is important! One of the contestants might fold his fang along the outer side of his opponent's chelicerae, or they may even engage in a brief cheliceral lock, but that is as far as it goes. The loser gives way gracefully and retires, while the winner does not try to press home his advantage by launching a sneak attack on his retreating opponent.

The development of such grotesquely enlarged 'fighting equipment' has had two unusual consequences for *M. lupata* and *M. plataleoides*. First, the size of their chelicerae prevents the male from

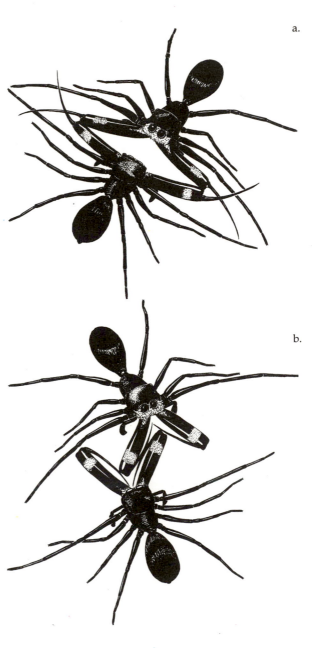

a.

b.

The huge projecting chelicerae of the male spear-jawed jumper **Myrmarachne plataleoides** (Salticidae) prevent him from feeding in the normal fashion. This male was loitering around close to a nest of **Oecophylla smaragdina** red weaver ants in a forest in Nepal.

Myrmarachne lupata males in ritualistic display.

a. the males push their widely-gaping chelicerae together in an 'embrace'.
b. the two males engage in a ritualistic 'bite' with fangs safely stowed out of the way, using the chelicerae to grip the opponent.

adopting the normal salticid copulatory stance above the female, so he has to stand beside her. Secondly, the fangs lack a venom duct, probably because of the infeasibility of pushing venom at adequate pressure up such a distance. The males cannot therefore dispatch their prey quickly through lethal injection, but have to skewer them kebab-style on their fangs.

COURTSHIP IN WEB-BUILDING SPIDERS

A web is not just a trap – it is also a signalling device. If the occupant is a female, then her web will faithfully convey to her not only the characteristic random vibrations of struggling prey, but also the more regular transmissions created deliberately by a courting male. The sense of sight plays the same zero role in governing sexual relations as it does in prey capture. However, the chemotactic sense is probably important, enabling the male to recognize silk of the correct females.

Analysing the vibratory signals employed by male spiders in webs is not easy, so little concrete information is available on precisely how the web reacts to the male's courtship scenario of tweakings, palpal drumming and whole-body vibrations. However, a detailed analysis is available for several European amaurobiids which build extensive sheet webs of densely woven silk. Important detailed differences were found in the information communicated by three species of *Amaurobius*, namely *A. similis, A. fenestralis* and *A. ferox*.

Males of the *A. similis* will initiate courtship merely upon contacting the empty web of their own females, but are immune to web silk of the other two. Courtship mainly involves vigorous bouts of palpal web-drumming, generating a signal with a mean frequency of 4.1 Hz. Males of *A. fenestralis* produce two signal types. First, a brisk tattoo beaten with legs and palps, giving an irregular signal; secondly, vibrations of the abdomen producing a mean frequency of 150 Hz. Lastly, *A. ferox* males are unstimulated by female web silk and need the presence of the female herself before striking up courtship. His repertoire of four distinct signals uses palpal followed by abdominal vibrations (4.60 Hz and 68 Hz), the latter starting at a higher frequency and gradually declining. Then come individual taps with the palps and lower frequency abdominal vibrations at 47 Hz. The differences in these procedures enable the females to distinguish their own males, and to tell them apart from a struggling prey with its random vibrations. Thus, the females never seem to react to a male's signal with predatory instincts.

Males of *Tegenaria parietina* may use a special abdominal vibration not only in courtship, but also to defuse female aggression during long cohabiting sessions lasting many months. Despite sharing the web, each spider catches its own prey, but they do sometimes sleep together in the tube retreat. The male is most likely to employ his abdominal vibrations when the female suddenly moves, as when prey arrives. When this happens, it probably sets in train an automatic sequence of behaviours leading to attack upon any nearby object. As the male is the nearest of these, he would receive the brunt of any accidental attack, so he seems to be reminding the female of who he is. During courtship, the male also pulls the web upwards and then lets it go with a kind of twang. The sudden release of tension sends a very brief signal of 15 Hz to the female in her retreat. Rapid palpal drumming represents the final overture when the two finally come face to face.

Contact with female silk causes the male of *Coelotes terrestris* to do the shakes, quivering his whole body to produce copious signals of 12 Hz, which cover his forward advance. Upon meeting the female, he pummels her with his front legs, whereupon she collapses into the hunched-legged submissive posture seen in many female spiders.

In late July, the large sheet-webs of the European *Agelena labyrinthica* are reaching the end of their useful life, for their owners will soon desert them in order to lay their eggs. Look carefully, and you may find that each web is occupied by a male, flinging himself at the web's occupant in a reckless style of courtship to which he would never have resorted a few weeks earlier. But with egg-laying now so close, 'kamikaze' tactics are now the only way of

A mating pair of grassland funnel-weavers **Agelena labyrinthica** (Agelenidae) in England at the mouth of the female's funnel to one side of her large sheet web. The female is in a state of catalepsy.

obtaining a last-minute mating. So the male dispenses with finesse and plunges straight across the silken mat, confronting the aggressive-stanced female in the mouth of her lair. Being only fractionally inferior in size, the male can afford to be quite insistent, and he may even intimidate her to the point of forcing her to retreat back down the silken funnel (although the occasional sight of males shooting across the webs and off the edge, as if jet-propelled, also indicates that the females are not always so easily browbeaten).

Agelena females have a spermatheca of conduit-design, presumed to be linked to first-male sperm precedence, so just what these suicidal males were trying to gain is a puzzle. Perhaps, like in *A. limbata*

from Japan, the first male does not have such a complete monopoly after all, leaving everything to play for right up to the moment the females lay their eggs. In this species, the second male to mate was found to sire an average of some 62 percent of the offspring, a glittering prize indeed and well worth dying for to obtain. A worthwhile proportion of the females (about 30 per cent) plays along by showing a willingness to mate more than once. The males attempt to stymie future competitors by blocking the epigyne with a palpal secretion. However, some males are better than others at making a good job of this. Poorly-made plugs can be levered off by the next male to come along, leaving the epigyne open. A full-blown genital plug is

COURTSHIP, COHABITATION AND GENTLEMANLY BEHAVIOUR IN PHOLCIDS

Courtship in the cosmopolitan rafter spider (*Pholcus phalangioides*) is extremely basic. The male merely emits faint tremors with his abdomen as he creeps towards the female and clasps her in a spindly embrace. It seems that such Spartan introductions are sufficient for the female's needs, and she quietly submits to some three hours of copulation. The male then leaves her and ambles off to seek further conquests, visiting as many females as possible during his lifespan.

Such male promiscuity is not typical of all pholcids. In a trio of *Modismus* spp. and a *Blechroscelis* from Colombia the males are dedicated house-husbands during long periods of cohabitation in females' webs. They carry out housework such as repairing the web when it is damaged by heavy rain and removing bits of leaf and other rubbish which becomes trapped. Such domestic situations are eagerly sought and are the subject of fierce fights between rival males. When an insect becomes trapped, it is often attacked by the male, who may initially drive the female away if she tries to step in for a share. However, all she has to do to change his attitude is 'beg' for the spoils by vibrating her abdomen and two front pairs of legs, upon which the male gracefully steps aside for her to feed. It seems that such self-denying behaviour is common among cohabiting males, who as a result feed less often than males leading the bachelor life.

therefore the only foolproof method of snookering the competition. First males to mate do still gain a flying start because the majority of females will only mate once.

In the similar American species *Agelenopsis aperta*, the females only mate once, as do the majority of the males. Virgin females probably attract their one and only mate by emitting a pheromone. Emission commences just after the final moult and gradually increases until insemination takes place, after which the pheromone is switched off.

BLACK WIDOWS AND OTHER THERIDIIDS

Stridulatory organs are common in this family, being used to send vibratory messages through the rather scrappy space-web built by the female. The stridulatory mechanism consists of a cluster of tiny teeth situated at the base of the abdomen, rubbing against files at the opposing apex of the cephalothorax. Just bobbing the abdomen up and down operates the mechanism. Different kinds of web vibrations are also caused by movements of the legs, palps and abdomen. In many species, courtship is designed to tempt the female to move on to a special mating thread which the male has previously constructed in her web. Many araneids do likewise.

The *Latrodectus* widow spiders, including the notorious black widow (*L. mactans*), have earned their name from the female's supposed penchant for making a meal of her mate as a grand finale to his copulatory performance. There are few observations which could confirm whether or not this is normal practice under natural conditions, but there are compelling reasons for assuming that it ought to be. During the male's first mating, he parts with the tip of his palpal embolus. This both terminates his brief sexual career and prevents the female from mating again, thus ensuring that his single act of copulation has not been wasted. Given this pair of circumstances, euthanasia is now probably the best option, especially if at the same time it can posthumously boost his reproductive success. The best way of accomplishing this is to donate his body to his mate, thereby directly enabling her to convert him into eggs.

NUPTIAL FEEDING ON MALE BODY-FLUIDS

In a number of spiders, the female apparently feeds upon fluids oozing from special structures on the male's body. It has long been known that in males of *Argyrodes*, the cephalothorax is often crowned with two substantial knobs, one behind the other. Only recently has their precise role been worked out, in the New Zealand *A. antipodeana*. Upon first meeting, the male and female clasp one another's front legs and force them out to the sides. Now the female feels with her palps on the male's head, trying to locate the furrow marking a narrow gap between the knobs. This furrow is bathed in a liquid, presumed to be a pheromone, derived from the branching hairs which cover the foremost knob. The female's chelicerae lie within the furrow during copulation. Even when the male takes a break from palpal insertions, the female stays in the groove, whose pheromonal secretions presumably function to stimulate the female sexually and keep her correctly positioned.

The heads of some male linyphiids are even more bizarrely ornamented, often, like in *Argyrodes*, with rounded knobs above the eyes, associated with lateral grooves. In *Hypomma bituberculatum* from Europe, the male's courtship advances are greeted by a sudden lunge by the female, her fangs gaping widely with apparent homicidal intent. Rather unexpectedly, the male stays his ground and hugs his sides. As the female closes in, she slips her chelicerae deftly around his protruding head-turret, so that her fangs glide smoothly into the associated grooves on either side. With this clip-fit slickly established, they are ready to mate. In many species the zone beside the grooves bears

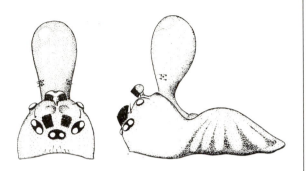

The strange lobed head of the male **Mitrager noordami** from Java is typical of many erigonine males (Linyphiidae).

a stubble of extremely fine hairs moistened with a secretion, and it is upon this that the female presumably sups during mating. In some species the female may even dribble saliva on to the male's head, and then slurp it back up, presumably now fortified with a good dose of dissolved male pheromones.

In *Baryphyma pratense* from Europe, the male offers not a taste of pheromone, but a more nutritious helping of his own blood. As soon as the female's chelicerae fasten on his head-grooves, a large blob of chrome-yellow blood suddenly bulges forth, upon which the female dines as they copulate. The sacrifice of such a comparatively large volume of blood apparently does not inconvenience the males, as proved by their capacity to mate again a mere 24 hours later.

In the western black widow (*Latrodectus hesperus*) from North America, the male drops some tempting hints that he is 'available' for consumption by only moving casually away from his mate after copulation. He then kicks his heels tantalizingly close by, almost egging the female on to have a go. A day or so later his shrivelled husk will be his only remaining testimony to his self-sacrificing investment in his offspring. This carefree behaviour only starts once his vital single act of mating has been successfully pulled off, in huge contrast to his opening gambit. Then he just must not make an error, so he carefully follows the formula laid down, vibrating his abdomen, tapping the web rhythmically with his palps and throwing fine silk both upon the web and upon the female herself. When the female responds with a murderous charge, he is ready for it and drops off on his safety thread. However, like all male spiders, he will not take 'no' for an answer, so he keeps on trying, cutting some of the female's web-lines to narrow down her field of operations and make it more and more difficult for her to elude him.

Fortunately for the males, life is not always so frustrating. Some females can hardly wait to get on with it, and may even encourage the male to get a move on by giving enticing body jerks and abdomen waggles.

THE ORB-WEB AS SEXUAL ARENA

A characteristic of many orb-web spiders, particularly in *Araneus, Argiope, Nephila, Gasteracantha* and *Micrathena* is the amazingly small size of the male compared with the female. This can have either positive or negative effects on the degree of courtship demanded of him, and his prospects even of short-term survival. The males often compound their nuptial difficulties by having to coax the female off her familiar web silk and onto a special mating thread which the male will have prepared earlier. This will either be positioned in a gap cut out of the female's web beside the hub, or off to one side. Once she has been enticed to the correct spot, the female must also be encouraged to adopt a specific head-down posture, failing which the male cannot creep beneath her to insert his palps. Finally, it is probable that the male's courtship also triggers internal changes within the female, producing essential temporary modifications to the structure of the epigyne which facilitate palpal insertion.

Some courtship procedures also seem designed to exhaust the female's predatory tendencies. In *Scoloderus cordatus* from the USA, the male first attaches a horizontal mating thread to the female's web and then strikes up the usual silk-strumming routine. This is conventional enough, but as soon as the female touches his thread, the male quickly turns his back on her, hitches the line to his spinnerets, severs it near his mouth and thereby converts his body into a bridge. As the female now strives to move along the line, the male merely pays out a ream of silk from his spinnerets, leaving the female treadmilling on the spot. This goes on until the female tires and stops tugging, whereupon the male turns around and again tempts her with his strumming. During several such sessions, the male gradually creeps close enough to caress the female, after which they may mate. Cannibalism upon the males seems to be exceedingly rare, while the latter will help themselves to prey morsels trapped in the female's web. Similar 'treadmill' courtship is seen in *Isoxya*.

Much has been made of the thankless task supposedly facing male *Araneus* in their prolonged and seemingly perilous courtship of the bulky females. However, it seems likely that females of many *Araneus* spp. most often enjoy a very brief period of adult virginity, being mated by a cohabiting consort shortly after their last moult. The agonizingly protracted and hazardous courtships seen later in the season are generally directed at heavily gravid females who will certainly not be virgins. Given this, it is hardly surprising that late-arriving suitors are greeted with a hostile response.

Even without cohabitation, some females just seem to be naturally amenable to the male's demands. In *Araneus (Larinioides) cornutus* the female often comes hurrying down as soon as the male starts signalling his presence. Several bouts of full-blooded sparring between the female and the male (half her size) then follow, during which it may be the female who drops off on her safety line when the going gets too rough. Yet a few moments later she is helpfully adopting the required drooping posture, allowing the male to make several rather swift jabs with his palps. Sparring matches seem to be a regular part of courtship, and the females will comply with repeated demands from the same male and copulate over and over again, with no sign of aggression.

The tiny male of *Araneus pallidus* suffers a different fate. He will certainly end up mortally impaled on his mate's fangs, yet without such an outcome

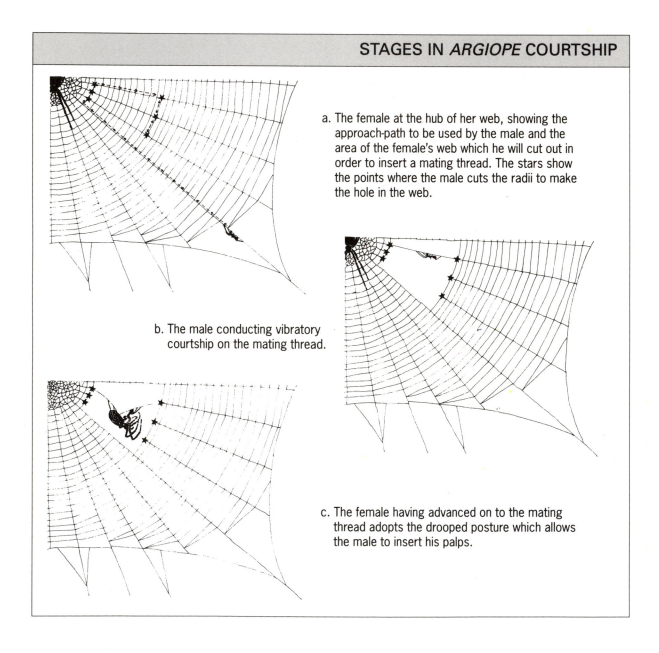

STAGES IN *ARGIOPE* COURTSHIP

a. The female at the hub of her web, showing the approach-path to be used by the male and the area of the female's web which he will cut out in order to insert a mating thread. The stars show the points where the male cuts the radii to make the hole in the web.

b. The male conducting vibratory courtship on the mating thread.

c. The female having advanced on to the mating thread adopts the drooped posture which allows the male to insert his palps.

his nuptial efforts will be a failure. Because he is a real midget, he cannot clamber across the gap between the web and the female's openly proffered underside. Instead, he is obliged to hurl himself in her direction and hope to latch hold securely with a single palp. With no handholds on the female's smooth underside, he now flops backwards and is suspended rather insecurely by one palp, directly in front of the female's jaws. From this point onwards, however, success is assured. The female fixes him safely in place with her jaws and proceeds to convert him into an empty husk,

This European female bank orb-weaver **Araneus (Larinioides) cornutus** has adopted the special posture which allows the smaller male to insert his palps. She responded rapidly several times to the male's courtship and permitted several acts of copulation.

The courtship procedure as conducted in many genera of araneids, including **Gasteracantha**, **Micrathena** and **Eriophora**.

a. The male first attaches a mating-thread between an exterior anchor-point and the female's web (ends indicated by stars). He then conducts vibratory courtship to entice her onto the thread.
b. The female advances onto the thread, adopts the drooped posture and they mate.

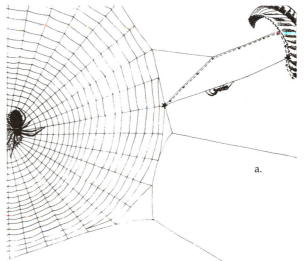

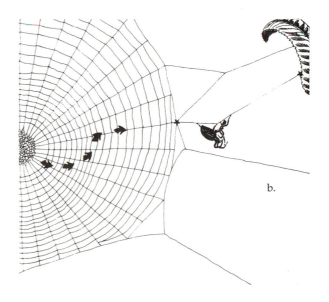

but not before the essential act of insemination has been accomplished.

The scenario in *Cyrtophora cicatrosa* is remarkably similar, except that the Liliputian males are incredibly incompetent at jumping across onto the female's body. They usually have to make several (up to 20) stabs at it before the female can finally pin them in place.

In *Argiope*, the male is a pygmy compared with his mate, and it seems that it is this very smallness which allows him to share her web for some considerable time. He is also able to share her food with no retaliation and also participates in illicit

This lobed argiope **Argiope lobata** female (Araneidae) in South Africa is playing host to a tiny male lodger visible just behind her.

meals alongside kleptoparasitic *Argyrodes* which have pilfered food from the female. Quite often, two or three males may be present, vying with one another for the prime position on the opposite side of the hub to the female. Courtship is usually vibratory and the male often spends a protracted period walking around on the female's body. Astoundingly enough, males have been observed parading around on females of the wrong species, yet without being punished for their mistake.

In *Argiope aemula*, the male lays down a skein of very fine silk in his wanderings to and fro across the female's body. This very open-meshed application is much too flimsy to constitute the kind of bridal veil seen in other spiders, but may serve the presumed same purpose of transferring mood-altering pheromones via the silk. In most species of *Argiope*, the females start to wrap the male during mating, and he may or may not tear himself free in time, often with the loss of just a palp or a leg or two. The fact that such maimed males can still conduct a successful vibratory courtship, despite a deficit of web-plucking legs, indicates that vibratory courtship is probably not a high-precision exercise.

The fact of being in copulation with a male does not prevent a female from rushing off to deal with an insect, forcing her mate to disengage in a hurry and leap to safety. Sometimes she leaves behind a male already wrapped and ready for

EUNUCH PROTECTORS

In another araneid, *Herennia ornatissima*, from Asia the tiny almost ant-like males also make a considerable sojourn in the female's ladder-web, strung close to the bark of a tree or a vertical rock. In common with many araneids in which the males are extremely small, courtship is very basic, and includes some laying down of fine silk over the female. The act of copulation seems to inflict such severe damage on the male's palps that they can never be used again, so he bites them off and suspends them in the female's web. As females of this species are inherently promiscuous, the little eunuch now commits the rest of his remaining life to protecting his reproductive investment by guarding the female. He becomes an inconspicuous chaperone up in one corner of the web, always ready to come down and do battle against any male intent on reaching the female. His allotted task is a tough one, for up to seven males may be resident on the web at any one time. Resident eunuchs are also prevalent in the webs of *Nephilengys cruentata* from West Africa, presumably for similar reasons.

The tiny male ornate orb-weaver **Herennia ornatissima** (Araneidae) from Malaysia, visible at top-right, is guarding the large female against sexual incursions by rival males.

consumption, upon which a resident male may nip in and steal the corpse of his erstwhile sexual rival.

COURTSHIP IN *NEPHILA*

The huge golden webs made by *Nephila* are a common sight in the tropics. There exists a vast disparity in size between the sexes, such that a gravid female *N. maculata* may weigh several hundred times as much as the male. Using mere body length as a yardstick, the comparison is less impressive, with females being some eight times longer than the males.

The actual size of the male can have a significant impact on how much courtship (if any) he needs to perform and whether or not he will be allowed free rein to take up temporary abode in the female's web. In the common New World *N. clavipes*, the tiny male has unrestricted freedom of movement within the female's web, and is also granted *carte blanche* to walk over her body and mate whenever he likes. His greatest worry is over attacks by rival males, rather than from the female. Males tend to congregate on the females' webs, and fight for a desirable position just above the hub, close to the female. 'Peripheral males' who have been exiled to the web's outer support area regularly make challenges against the 'hub male'. These often fizzle out almost at the start, when the 'hub male' shakes his body and plucks the web forcibly with his legs, sending the pretender packing without the need for combat. When a challenge is carried through, there is a brief but violent burst of grappling and biting before one of the contestants gives way and retires. The bachelor band of 'peripheral males' get on quite well together, and it is only the 'hub male' who is subject to their constant sniping. If he loses his title, he joins them in amicable neutrality.

The position of 'hub male' is so intently sought after for two reasons. First, 'hub males' are super-studs who gain practically all the matings. Secondly, they are better placed to pinch some of the prey which the female has hung at the hub. Also, despite living cheek by jowl with the female, they are no more likely to be killed than the 'peripheral males'. Such killings are rare anyway, and seldom in a sexual context. Most 'peripheral males' are born losers, never likely to unseat a 'hub male' and therefore doomed to a life of celibacy.

In the giant wood spider, *N. maculata*, the male spends days criss-crossing the female's huge body with a dense but very fine mesh of silk, all carried out with no risk of retaliation. As already suggested, when enough pheromone-laden silk has been accumulated, it may trigger sexual receptivity in the female. However, males will also snatch a chance mating with a newly-moulted female, or one who is busy feeding.

In *Nephila edulis* from Australia, the male seizes his chance when an arriving insect hangs struggling in the female's web. The male simply lacks any kind of courtship, so must synchronize his approach with the female's meal time, when her predatory instincts are being fully satisfied. As he makes his approach, the male regularly plucks the web, as if gauging the female's appetite for her meal. Only if she continues to feed will he cautiously crawl over her and insert a palp. He is much larger than most *Nephila* males, thus increasing the risk of attack. However, his agility and alertness usually keep him safe.

Golden orb-weavers **Nephila clavipes** in an Argentinian rainforest. The hub-male is walking around on the huge female's body (she is feeding on a large cicada) while a rival male begins to mount a challenge from the periphery at top-right.

MATE-GUARDING IN THE LINYPHIIDAE

Much of the male behaviour in linyphiids is motivated by the first-male sperm precedence which has been proven in some species and probably operates in the majority. The first act of a newly matured male *Linyphia triangularis* is to make a beeline for a sub-adult female's web, where he takes up residence. Quickly establishing who is

MATE-GUARDING IN *METELLINA SEGMENTATA*

In this extremely common European species, males usually cohabit for a day or two with females. There is a high turnover of consorts, although few of them manage to mate with more than one female. A male will only try his luck when the female is busy biting or wrapping an insect. He is about her size, but has longer front legs, with which he reaches around the insect to tickle the female. She often retreats back to her lair, rather than stay to feed and thereby suffer the male's insistent courtship, making this a particularly long drawn-out affair. The male obstinately refuses to give up, and will repeatedly try to rekindle the female's interest by enticingly jerking the prey.

When he does finally manage to sidle around the prey and creep over the female, he still has to construct a nuptial thread onto which he must coax her. Battles over the right to remain as consort are frequent, often leading to the death of one of the contenders. When this happens, the loser's corpse will either provide the next meal for the victor, or better still, will serve nicely as the essential trigger for his next bout of courtship.

A male common orb-weaver **Metellina (Meta) segmentata** (right) courting a female over the body of a cranefly (Tipulidae) in an English forest.

Upon moving into the female's web, the male **Linyphia triangularis** (right) soon takes command.

boss, he soon monopolizes the majority of the web's catch of prey. Just after the female's final moult, he begins his courtship.

As in most linyphiids, courtship consists of three separate phases. First, the male engages in a series of pseudocopulations using empty palps. Then he carries out sperm induction, ready for the final phase when he again copulates, but this time for real. The start of sperm induction can be a critical juncture, for this is the cue used by any rival males, quietly waiting on the web's periphery, to start getting involved. A small male who has lost out in challenges to the consort can now make good his losses. By barging in and disrupting the consort's sex-life, it may be possible to harry him from the web before consummation takes place, leaving the field clear for his smaller and now victorious rival. Such 'spoiling' tactics are beautifully refined, with the 'spoiler' timing his intrusion to perfection, probably alerted by recognizable vibrations caused by sperm-web construction.

Defeated males of the American bowl and doily spider (*Frontinella pyramitela*) fall back on a far less rewarding 'last call' tactic. As a dominant male retires after a successful mating session, his smaller rival creeps in and adds his own modicum of sperm to the supply residing in the female's spermatheca. His chances of siring any offspring are however remote, given the first-male sperm precedence in this species, so the futility of his actions is obvious. However, interference with copulation is also 'on call', especially when several males are resident in the web.

The consort often remains in the female's web for some time after mating, which is strange, given the lack of need to stay and guard paternity. The promise of food is a more likely reason, as the hanger-on steals a large proportion of the female's prey, putting on weight which will give him a fighting edge over other males. The downside of this 'cuckoo' behaviour is the impact on the female's food intake and therefore the weight gain in her eggs (fertilized by the unwanted boarder). However, this may be offset by the 50 per cent reduction in predation against the females by marauding mimetids and theridiids. In shared webs, their aggressive mimicry is just as liable to lure the male to his death as the female.

Frontinella pyramitela males use a session of pseudocopulation to judge whether or not the female is a virgin. In another North American species, the sierra dome spider, *Linyphia litigiosa*, a newly-moulted adult virgin will notify her change of reproductive status to her consort. Rather than always giving him the cold shoulder whenever they meet, she now actively seeks out his company. Once she has mated, she strums the web to any subsequent suitor to inform him of her loss of virginity.

Egg-laying and Parental Care

The sex life of the male spider is dominated by a kiss-and-run attitude. Apart from possible guard duty to protect his paternity, he will take no further part in the development of his progeny, other than supplying the sperm. By contrast, once even the first batch of sperm lies safe within her spermathecae, the female has merely reached another stage on the long and perilous road leading to the safe production of her spiderlings. She will probably have to waste precious energy fighting off droves of persistent suitors, although she may be able to recover some of her expenses by occasionally making a meal of them. Finally, however, she will have to make a break with her past life and find a secure place to build her egg-sac.

The number of eggs is often directly related to the size of the mother. Thus, just four tiny eggs cocooned in a fluffy globe less than 1mm in diameter in the tiny *Curimagua bayano*, and up to 1,200 in some giant species of *Nephila*, with each individual egg being larger than the entire *C. bayano* egg-sac. In some tiny spiders, such as *Telema* spp. (Telemidae) and *Atrophonysia intertidalis* (Barychelidae) only a single egg is normally laid in each cocoon. The female of *Tetrablemma deccanensis* measures some 1.15mm in length, and produces a single egg around 0.4mm in diameter – not far short of half the diameter of the female! What happens after egg-laying varies enormously from species to species. Some lay just a single batch and then die.

The egg-sac of the giant wood spider **Nephila maculata** contains more than a thousand eggs, making quite a sight when the golden babies emerge in this Sri Lankan forest.

125

Others lay multiple batches over a period of time, leaving each one to its own devices. The mother has done all she can for them by selecting a safe place and protecting them with silk, and sometimes camouflage or even armour. For example, many species of two-tailed spiders (*Hersilia*) prise off flakes of bark and lichens with their chelicerae and use them to disguise the broad silk sheet covering the flattened egg mass, while the European *Agroeca brunnea* attaches her white bell-shaped egg-sac to a stem and then covers it with a hard shell of mud, carried up from below in the chelicerae. Some theraphosids incorporate urticating hairs into their egg-sacs. These are scraped off the sides of the abdomen, using the back legs, and probably help to repel incursions by the larvae of parasitic flies.

The habit of remaining with the eggs is very common in female spiders. In some species,

(*Above*) A female two-tailed spider **Hersilia caudata** (Hersiliidae) on a tree in a forest in the Gambia. She is guarding two very flattened egg-sacs. The lowermost has already been thoroughly camouflaged with bits of bark, while the uppermost has yet to receive its full covering.

A female **Verrucosa** sp. (Araneidae) guarding her egg-sac under a leaf in a Costa Rican rainforest.

the female sits astride or beside one or more egg-sacs, while in others she carries the egg-sac around with her at all times. This intimate association between mother and egg-sac can be very prolonged – as much as 11 weeks in some large theraphosids, during which the egg-sac is vigorously defended. The number of spiders which then go one step further and help their tiny offspring to weather their first few days or weeks of life is, however, vastly smaller. The ultimate act of maternal philanthropy, found in a number of species, is for the female to bequeath her corpse to her brood as a growth-boosting funeral bonanza.

THE EGG-LAYING PROCEDURE

Most spiders lay their eggs under cover of darkness. *Nephila edulis* from Australia moves off her large web onto a nearby bush and lays down a webbing of yellow and white silk beneath a protective canopy of leaves. She then adds a soft bed of fine yellow silk upon which she deposits her eggs, forcing them upwards against the mat with a bobbing action which counteracts gravity. As they emerge they are covered with a sticky mucous coating which cements them to the silk. She then covers everything in a further blanket of yellow silk wound round and round the leaves and egg mass, so that the finished article measures some 4cm across. Although conspicuous at first against the vegetation, the silk covering soon undergoes a colour change to green, when it is much harder to detect. Each female lays a single egg batch (although other members of the genus lay several, e.g. *N. senegalensis* in Africa which produces a lifetime output of some 4,500 eggs in four batches) and then deserts it for the two to three months needed for the eggs to hatch.

In many temperate-zone spiders, the egg-sac has to withstand the rigours of winter, placing an extra emphasis on its structural integrity and location, so that the spiderlings have a chance of making it safely through to spring. Like many spiderlings, those of *Nephila* remain crowded together for two

A **Myrmecium** sp. spider (Clubionidae) fastening her egg-sac to a leaf in rainforest in Costa Rica. When it was finished, she left it, and a few days later the whitish silk had turned to a dark camouflaged bluish-green.

127

EGG-LAYING AND PARENTAL CARE IN WOLF SPIDERS

The most eye-catching egg-sacs are those carried around by the wolf spiders. The maternal behaviours exhibited by *Pardosa lapidicina* from North America are probably mirrored by most of the genus. The female starts off by fashioning a silken platform between two suitably raised objects. This provides the base for a slightly lens-shaped silken mat which takes about 30 minutes to complete. This acts as a cradle for her 50 or so eggs, dropped into place from an arched posture. The next step – covering the eggs – is performed at a feverish pace. She begins by looping silk across the mass, then stitches a flatter layer of silk on top in another 30 minutes of intense application. She then uses her palps and chelicerae to cut and prise the structure free from its guy-lines and holds it in her third pair of legs. Now she can begin the final task of moulding the egg-sac into a shape suitable for carrying around. She does this by rotating it, while using her chelicerae to turn down the seam to one side, tacking it in place with silk from her spinnerets. It now ceases to resemble a fried egg and becomes the rather flattened sphere typical of the genus. Her final task is to attach the carrying handle. Holding the sac in her palps and third pair of legs, she bends her body forwards and upwards to touch the spinnerets to the sac's surface and attach a miniature button of silk. This remains tied to the spinnerets by a short sheaf of threads. Some ten minutes later she unhitches the sac and turns it over, covering its surface with a colourless liquid dribbled from her mouth. The function of this fluid is unknown, but it is likely to have an antibacterial or fungicidal effect.

A female wolf spider is strongly possessive of her egg-sac and will fiercely repel any intruder which tries to steal it, including enemies from which she would normally flee. As the sac is linked to her spinnerets out of the way at the rear, she is free to continue hunting and feeding during her prolonged stint of carrying it around. During this period she devotes much of her time to selecting the optimum microclimate for speedy development of her young. In practical terms, this usually means plenty of time spent basking on logs, stones or leaves.

*A host of **Pardosa prativaga** spiderlings pour forth from the egg-sac and assemble on their mother's back.*

This is particularly important after a period of damp cool weather, when fungal infection of the sac could be a problem.

The only time the female voluntarily disconnects the sac from its fastenings is for periodical examination. She turns it over and over in her legs and strokes its surface with her palpi and chelicerae. In this way she can probably monitor what is going on inside, whether the offspring are thriving, and when they are about to hatch. Recent observations on the European *Pardosa hortensis* indicate that the female may actually open the sac quite regularly and feed the offspring with saliva, repairing the sac with fresh silk each time. This may be the reason why egg-sacs separated from the mother yield far fewer viable offspring than normal sacs. The female's ability to feel the pulse of the egg-sac's inner workings from an exterior examination is evident from the way in which artificially unmated females will discard their barren sac after a day or so.

The nursery-web spider **Pisaura mirabilis** carries her egg-sac speared on the points of her fangs.

About 12 hours before the young are due to emerge they become very active inside the sac. This restless movement is presumably detected by their mother, for she unhitches the sac and tears a perforation around the seam with her chelicerae and palps. With this essential operation complete (the young will die within their prison if their mother fails in her duty) she reattaches the sac. Soon afterwards a torrent of tiny spiderlings begins to stream out and assemble on their mother's back, in the manner typical of the Lycosidae (and Trechaleidae). The stimulus for this regimented conduct seems to be the special knobbed hairs which cover the assembly areas of the female's abdomen. These act as physical signposts for the emerging offspring, and also function as holdfasts, enabling them to cling on when the mother has to beat a hasty retreat through a dense tangle of vegetation. However, all is not lost if a few young are dislodged, for they can reboard via their mother's legs, tracing their return path by following the silken lines which she always belays behind her. They ride around thus for a week or more, remaining inactive except when their mother somehow indicates that water is nearby, when they dismount to drink. They are quite safe when moving around near their mother, as during this stage (the second instar) she will not attack either her own spiderlings or those belonging to another female. The offspring do not feed while on their mother's back, but survive on the remains of the egg-yolk, before eventually moulting and dispersing, when they lose their immunity to attack by the females.

Pisaurids also carry their egg-sacs around, but neatly if inconveniently speared on the tips of the female's fangs, leaving her unable to feed. Nor do the young assemble on their mothers' backs, which therefore lack the special knobbed-hair 'baby-grabs'. Instead, pisaurids generally build a silken tent in which to place the egg-sac just before hatching. The mother then stands guard over the offspring for a while until they disperse.

to three weeks in a succession of communal webs, before finally dispersing to build webs of their own.

Bolas-spider egg-sacs come in a variety of shapes and sizes, and may be quite spectacular, attracting attention to the presence of the spider in an area. The outer envelope is extremely tough and durable, and depending on the species, the shape goes from spherical to pear-shaped or even udder-like. Surface texture can be smooth or decorated with points, scallops and other protuberances. The appearance is often highly cryptic, and the sac may resemble dry berries, galls, or the buds of plants. Females normally produce more than a single egg-sac over a lifetime, and the eventual total output of eggs can be prodigious – up to 9,000 in *Mastophora dizzydeani* from Colombia. Producing an egg-sac is a major investment for any spider, as it may represent quite a substantial percentage of the female body weight. This runs to 70 per cent or more in some species, so it is not surprising that females guarding their egg-sacs often have a distinctly shrunken appearance.

The sacs themselves do not always contain a full complement of fertile eggs. Often a percentage will be inviable and fail to hatch. Examples are known from at least six families (Clubionidae, Gnaphosidae, Uloboridae, Theridiidae, Thomisidae and Salticidae) in which the healthy spiderlings profit from these unhatched eggs as a source of food. This usually happens during the first instar (i.e. before the first true moult) but in some theridiids, such as *Achaearanea wau*, the habit is carried through to the second instar. In the jumping spiders, *Cyrba* and *Portia*, spiderlings not only feed on inviable eggs, but also cannibalize their healthily developing brothers and sisters.

The importance which such larval cannibalism may attain has been demonstrated in a most peculiar way in *Achaearanea tepidariorum*, a cosmopolitan theridiid around man's habitations. Spiderlings within the egg-sac do not normally resort to cannibalism, but do so when the eggs are attacked by a tiny *Baeus* sp. parasitic wasp (Scelionidae). The wasp has to penetrate the sac in order to lay its eggs, and as it burrows through a mass of spiderlings, it provokes a backlash from the occupants which eventually rebound upon one another, leading to cannibalism. Upon hatching, and during the vitally important second instar dispersal stage, spiderlings with a cannibalistic history show a significantly higher survival rate than those without.

MAKING A NEST

Pisaurids are but one of many examples of spiders which build some kind of maternity nest in which to guard the eggs. The one use to which all jumping spiders still put silk is of this type. Copious amounts of silk are employed to bind together leaves or twigs (two species of *Thiania* fasten the leaves together with robust silken rivets), or form a cell beneath stones or tree-bark. Some species place their egg cocoons on a leaf, then enclose them in a silken tube in which the female sits, provided with escape exits at either end. Some unusual variations occur. Thus, adult females of *Hypaeus cucullatus* from Costa Rica build a flattened nest out in the open on the underside of a large leaf. The nest is made entirely of a particularly tough brand of silk, and in view of its exposed nature, it is reinforced with a substantial silken brace, built either at right angles to the nest or across it at an angle.

In *Pellenes nigrociliatus*, the female builds her nest inside snail shells which she suspends from vegetation on silken lines. *Portia fimbriata* from Australia nests in a suspended leaf. Marauding females often mount raids on such nests, driving away the occupant, eating the eggs and replacing them with their own batch built over the ruins of the old one. A *Euryattus* sp. from Australia gradually hauls a rolled-up leaf into an aerial position (up to 1m above the ground) on a series of strong composite support lines. This comprises a complicated and well-planned operation, with the spider obviously relying heavily on its excellent eyesight to survey the area of operations beforehand. Up to seven very flattened papery egg-sacs are then placed in the nest.

Several lynx spiders from Africa cut off a green living leaf and suspend it in a network of silken lines. The female fills the space in the partly curled-over

PAY-OFFS FOR PARENTAL CARE IN THE GREEN LYNX SPIDER

So many female spiders from different families stay behind to guard their egg-sacs that it is automatically taken for granted that this must be the best action to take. Such a view should not be taken for granted, however. For example, instead of staying to guard her eggs, a female could in theory perhaps gain greater reproductive returns by deserting them. She could then use the extra time to feed herself up and lay a new egg batch, or perhaps several more.

A cost-benefit analysis of maternal behaviour has been carried out on the green lynx spider, *Peucetia viridans*. The female fastens her rather knobbly egg-sac to a leaf with an array of silken

A green lynx spider **Peucetia viridans** (Oxyopidae) stands guard on her egg-sac on a columnar cactus in Mexico.

guy-lines. She is steadfast in its defence, doing her best to drive off enemies such as jumping spiders and females of her own species, who will kill her if they can and then eat both mother and eggs. However, the most omnipresent threat comes from ants. Lone scouts can easily be picked off one at a time, but with a massed attack, the female has to change her tactics. Cutting all but one or two of the guy-lines, she retreats on to the egg sac, now suspended in mid-air where the ants will find it difficult to follow. However, faced by repeated invasions, the female opts for actually moving the egg-sac to a safer place. Rather than just picking it up in her chelicerae and trotting off, as would be expected, she uses a curiously clumsy procedure, alternately attaching and detaching tow-lines so that the sac is dragged along bit by bit.

When hatching is imminent, the female spins a canopy over the sac, tilts it over somewhat and tears an opening in one side. Although this behaviour promotes overall survival in the brood, it is not absolutely vital. Unlike in lycosids and pisaurids, the young can force an exit if they have to. The offspring rarely feed before scattering, and when they do it is merely a matter of pushing in to eat alongside their mother, rather than being provided specifically with food. The pay-off for the female after six to eight weeks of devoted attention is a higher rate of survival for her egg-sacs compared with unguarded ones, which suffer very heavily from damage by ants and bad weather.

An **Oxyopes** sp. female lynx spider in a Ugandan rainforest is still standing on guard when her babies hatch in the suspended-leaf nest she has made.

nest construction. She builds a conspicuous white wholly silken nest out in the open among grass or leaves. Within the nest, there is a labyrinth of tunnels in which the spider lays her eggs and guards them. The investment in silk is considerable, representing bodily material which could alternatively have been converted into eggs, so the advantages of building such a massive and complex structure must be substantial. It may be designed to baffle parasites and other enemies by making the eggs difficult to find, leading them instead into an ambush by the guarding female.

THE MOTHERCARE SPIDER AND OTHERS

In some species, the mother actively participates in securing food for her offspring. Females of *Ixeuticus martius* and *I. robustus* (Desidae) from New Zealand perform the slaughtering process, but then leave the prey to the exclusive attentions of their offspring. In the communal-territorial spider *Scytodes fusca* from Queensland, the mother hauls prey back to the nest as food for her offspring; she herself eats all her own meals out on the web. The female of *Achaearanea riparia* actually announces to her waiting brood that an insect she has subdued is prepared and ready for consumption. She communicates this by stroking the web in a characteristic manner, bringing the hungry mob rushing down to the feast. By contrast, if some threat should materialize while the offspring are crowded vulnerably around their meal, the mother urgently plucks the web in a totally different way. This alarm causes the offspring to stop feeding in a hurry and dash back up to the relative safety of the silken retreat.

In a very small but fascinating selection of spiders, the female not only stays with her brood, but actually feeds them mouth to mouth as do birds. One of these, the European mothercare spider *Theridion sisyphium* is so common that it is relatively easy to watch the entertaining domestic arrangements in action. The female spends large amounts

leaf with her egg-sac, then stands guard over the exposed part on top of the nest. For the first few days the brownish female is conspicuous on the green leaf, which itself looks rather out of place. Then as the leaf gradually withers and turns brown, it merely resembles a fallen leaf whose fall was arrested by the web, while the brown female is now virtually invisible. She is still there when her young hatch, but whether she provides them with any care is unknown.

The European *Agelena labyrinthica* is exceptionally extravagant and inventive in her use of silk in of time hanging immobile in her web. Suddenly the untidy pack of youngsters which has been hanging around restlessly in one corner of the web will come tumbling down through the silk towards her. Forming a huddle around one or more of her legs, they begin to give them a good shaking. This is their way of begging for food. She often responds rather testily by kicking out hard and sending them flying, but hunger drives them back for another go and eventually she relents. She must give some signal,

A mothercare spider **Theridion sisyphium** feeds alongside her brood on a hoverfly in an English woodland.

for suddenly, in dribs and drabs, the youngsters leave their hustling and gather around their mother's mouth to drink a liquid oozing from it. In fact, their first meal after hatching will come from the same source, which remains the chief diet for a while. The liquid itself is highly nutritious, being comprised of predigested insects mixed with cells derived from the mother's gut-lining.

With such heavy daily demands made on her bodily reserves, the mother soon becomes shrunken if prey is short. During the first few days, any prey which does arrive is killed by the mother and then bitten all over and 'marinated' in her digestive juices. This tenderizing process makes the prey accessible to the tiny spiderlings with their weak jaws. However, as the days pass, the spiderlings rapidly gain in strength on their wholesome liquid diet and can soon join in to subdue prey, making their own small contribution of fine silk as the insect strives to disentangle itself from the web. Mother and brood then share the feast together. Boosted by such a nourishing diet, the growth of the offspring is rapid and they moult in just a week, much faster than in species whose offspring have to fend for themselves.

In at least five genera in three families, the female finally donates her corpse to her offspring. In fact, in some *Stegodyphus* (Eresidae) the female, old age fast coming on and her brood growing rapidly, makes advance preparations for her final sacrifice. Nothing is visible from the outside, but inside she is gradually starting to break down her own substance, transforming herself into a handy liquid broth, to be decanted by her offspring from within the unbroken packaging. In fact, all she is doing is stepping up her earlier contribution to its logical limit. She too has raised her brood on regurgitated fluids, and now instead of auto-digesting just the gut walls, she goes the whole hog and dissolves the whole body contents.

COMPLEX MATERNAL CARE IN SOCIAL SPIDERS

As would be expected, some advanced forms of maternal care are quite widespread in social spiders. Complex maternal care can only really develop if the occupants of a nest get on reasonably well with one another. Levels of tolerance vary widely, such that adults of *Achaearanea wau* rarely even come within touching distance of one another, while at the other extreme *Eriophora bistriata* forms substantial resting masses of closely-packed adults huddled amicably together.

The African *Stegodyphus sarisinorum* exhibits a high degree of sociality. Cannibalism is strictly ruled out, otherwise social disintegration could set in. However, it seems that within the silken nests which riddle the colony, the juveniles break the 'no cannibalism' taboo and regularly dine on their mothers once they have reached such an advanced state of senility as to be virtually the walking dead. Not only that, but it seems that the spiderlings may even cross the parental barrier and feed randomly on any moribund female who happens to be available. It seems that such potentially disruptive behaviour is actually encouraged by the females involved. With advancing senility, they probably give some kind of signal which overrules the normal refusal to cannibalize healthy individuals. (Normally even starved colony members cannot be induced to feed on a healthy nest mate.) Indeed, some of the geriatric females seem to invite participation in cannibalistic mealtimes by joining self-service body shops which make it easy for broods from different parents to feed unselectively, not just on mother, but on any of the corpses.

A very small number of social spiders have reached the acme of social development by progressing to a division of labour, if only in a very basic form. In *Anelosimus eximius*, females will regurgitate food to any and all spiderlings, not just their own. The thousands of spiders which throng the extensive webs are not only derived from several different generations, they also have specific tasks which they undertake within the colony – two significant points in common with the social wasps. Web repair and sanitation is a routine daily job for adult females and juveniles of the third instar and beyond. However, the latter are mainly called up in huge quantities to serve as emergency extras when disaster hits the web, calling for major repairs, such as a large animal blundering through. Attacks by enemies, especially spider-hunting wasps are countered jointly, a great benefit of social life. Custodial responsibility for the egg-sacs is shared out among a succession of females. As with most social spiders, the males take a far less active role, although in the African *Agelena consociata*, with a similarly high social attainment, the males do work for a living. In this highly developed species, even egg-laying has become a communal affair within a nursery chamber, where even juveniles share the babysitting work with the adults. Crèches full of small spiderlings are the focal point for frequent visits by females, bringing in prey items or offering mouth-to-mouth feeding.

In *Phryganoporus (Badumna) candidus*, the females also dole out food willy-nilly to any spiderlings, regardless of parentage. Take this away, and the first instar spiderlings have a poor chance of survival.

COLONY-FOUNDING IN SOCIAL SPIDERS

One characteristic of most social spider colonies, especially those of the sheet-web type, is their extreme longevity. It is also common to find numerous colonies interconnected, forming a huge spider metropolis which may stretch for hundreds of metres, although, strictly speaking, each colony within such a hook-up is separately organized. The founding of new colonies varies from species to species, and can be surprisingly difficult. Indeed, in *Agelena consociata*, there does not even seem to *be* any mechanism for emigration from the old colony. Just how this species spreads is

therefore something of a mystery, unless accidental transmission to new sites by large animals is the operative process. In *Anelosimus eximius*, individual females sometimes leave the nest and attempt to set up home by themselves Their success rates are hopelessly low and colony spread seems to proceed mainly via simple extension of the boundaries into the 'suburbs'. In *Phryganoporus candidus*, the majority of the sub-adult females leave home at quite an early stage to go it alone. The males remain at home until they mature and then migrate in search of females.

In the highly social *Achaearanea wau*, emigration to found a new colony takes place in a well-organized manner not unlike that of swarm-founding polistine wasps. Under cover of darkness, work parties of adult females gradually extend a broad loosely-woven silken highway (up to 1m wide and several metres long) away from the parent colony to the planned development site. Over the next night or two, a proportion of the nest's adult and juvenile females (plus the occasional adult male) strike out along the highway, forming temporary resting bivouacs under leaves, and finally being back in the prey-catching business with fresh webs some two days after leaving home. The highway remains in place but deserted for a few days before falling apart. The scarcity of male emigrants is not important, given that most of the migrating females have sperm-filled spermatheca. The new colony also probably acts as a magnet for wandering Romeos from other colonies. Just why the sudden break-out happens is unknown, but kleptoparasitic pressures (e.g. *Argyrodes*, dewdrop spiders) may be to blame. When these become too blighting to bear, the spiders will first try and starve them out by discontinuing repairs to the web. They might even destroy it completely and retire to their retreats. Thus denied their supply of free food, the kleptoparasites have little choice but to move out in search of richer pickings.

In a large communal web a female **Cyrtophora cicatrosa** (Araneidae) stands guard beneath her egg-sacs in India as a stream of babies pours forth.

07 Defensive Behaviours

Although spiders are themselves predators, they also suffer from the disadvantage of being small and (in general) tasty, which means that a great many larger predators are going to be after them. Enemies of spiders range from other spiders (probably the major predators) to parasitic wasps and mantispids, hunting wasps, assassin bugs, scorpions, centipedes, bandicoots, possums, mice, shrews, monkeys, lizards, frogs and a wide assortment of birds. In response to such a Noah's ark of foes, spiders have evolved an assortment of survival strategies.

AVOIDING THE PREDATOR

Trapdoor spiders would seem to be among the most secure of domestic residents, protected from view by a sturdily built and almost invisible door. Nevertheless, they are not immune to invasion. In Australia bandicoots will dig them out, a level of overkill which the spider is helpless to prevent. Smaller predators, especially hunting wasps, but also large centipedes and scorpions, are more easily fooled or deterred. Gaining entry is the

first obstacle, for trapdoor spiders are very good at locking and bolting the snugly-fitting door by hanging on tightly with the jaws and legs, making it difficult to prize open from the outside. If the enemy still manages to gain entry, other diversionary

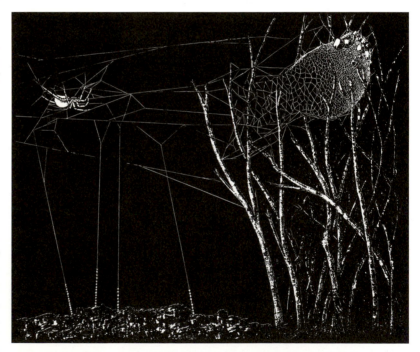

The web of **Latrodectus revivensis** with upper right, the nest whose upper section is liberally adorned with debris, the lower section being virtually an open meshwork; the capture platform where the spider is shown; and the perpendicular capture threads bearing sticky globules at their lowermost ends near the ground. Under cover of nightfall the spider emerges from her nest and rests beneath the capture platform to keep tabs on the sticky threads.

tactics may come into play. In the Australian *Stan-wellia nebulosa*, a cavity hollowed out of the vertical burrow wall contains a strategically balanced pebble. The spider hurriedly pulls this into place behind it on its retreat downwards, effectively blocking entry. In *Cyclocosmia truncata* from North America, the spider's own flattened and highly armoured rear-end makes a close fit for the burrow and thereby serves this same blocking purpose. *Lampropodus iridescens* from Australia seeks to fool the intruder by hiding inside a side-shaft part-way down the burrow, closing a secondary trapdoor behind it. A number of spiders from several different families build a forked burrow, with one fork serving as an escape route should an enemy enter down the other.

Web-building spiders, salticids and many others spend much of their time inside silken nests or retreats which provide some measure of concealment and protection. These are often constructed between two leaves, or under stones and bark. Sometimes the lair itself may be camouflaged. Most *Latrodectus* widow spiders build their lairs on or near the ground, under stones or bushes. However, *Latrodectus revivensis* from Israel's Negev Desert builds a web consisting of a series of sticky-tipped threads hanging vertically downwards and anchored to stones on the ground. To one side, and sited well up above the ground, there is a substantial dome-like lair. This is decorated with all kinds of handy detritus, such as beetle skeletons, rabbit droppings, snail shells, seeds, leaves and bits of twig. The nest of *L. pallidus* from the same area is similar. These nests serve to keep the spider cool during the hot desert summers, while also giving protection from visually hunting predators such as shrikes.

The inclusion of debris within the web as a camouflaging device is not uncommon. It is typical of many species of *Cyclosa*, which incorporate debris-laden stabilimental lines or spirals within their webs. In the spiral type, the spider sits more or less in the centre on a mass of insect remains and other rubbish. The other type consists of a rubbish-laden vertical line with a gap left in the middle in which the spider makes a perfect and wonderfully invisible fit. Like all web-builders, if touched the spider leaps to safety on its drag-line.

A **Cyclosa** sp. (Araneidae) sits in the gap in her linear stabilimentum in a Venezuelan forest.

THE BARRIER-WEB IN *NEPHILA CLAVIPES*

The addition of a tangled barrier web on one or both sides of the main orb is seen in a number of araneid genera, including *Argiope*, *Leucauge* and *Nephila*. In *N. clavipes*, the barrier-webs are sited either side of the spider as it sits on the hub. The mesh size employed does little to hinder the inward progress of the spider's main prey, which is rather small. However, the barrier-webs certainly do constitute an effective barrier to the spider's enemies, such as giant pseudostigmatid damselflies and birds, which are confounded by the barrier webs in their attempts to grab the spider. Whereas the spider remains at the hub during such attacks, the arrival of a proficient web-walker such as a parasitic wasp causes the spider to drop to the ground.

This is a common escape ploy used by many families of spiders. While on the ground most species clasp their legs to their sides, rather resembling a tiny clot of earth and therefore very hard to detect among the clutter of soil debris. As it drops, the spider trails its drag-line, an essential safeguard for guiding the spider back to its web or nest full of eggs once the danger is past.

CAMOUFLAGED SPIDERS

Many spiders sit completely exposed in the open, relying on camouflage for protection. A number of species in *Mastophora*, *Poltys*, *Dolophones* and *Caerostris* resemble bumps on branches where a twig has broken off. Some species actually resemble twigs, or blend into bark, such as (*Hersilia* spp.) two-tailed spiders and lichen spiders (*Pandercetes*), which are only obvious when they move. The latter bear hair-fringes along the sides of the body and legs which eliminate the spider's shadow, and the spider also sits close to the bark. However, if touched the spider instantly races around the opposite side of the trunk, moving with such a swift and well-oiled motion that it seems to disappear from in front of one's eyes. It then freezes and is amazingly difficult to pick out again. It will play cat and mouse like this for some time. Speckled spiders such as *Arctosa perita* live on sandy ground. *Portia* jumping spiders look like mobile flecks of dead leaf, while *Arachnura* scorpion spiders (Araneidae) seem just like a leaf caught in a web. The tropical American crab-spiders of the genus *Onocolus*

This large **Eriophora transmarina** looks just like one more bump on a knobbly branch as she sits beside her web in Australia.

resemble bits of dead leaf stranded on vegetation, while many tropical *Eriophora* and *Verrucosa* (Araneidae) sit on leaves where they resemble natural brown blotches or fallen dead leaves.

A number of crab-spiders, particularly *Phrynarachne*, along with some South American species of *Verrucosa* and *Micrathena* (Araneidae) resemble bird droppings, on the basis that nothing large and dangerous goes out looking for bird droppings to add to the menu! Some spiders can even

It takes considerable expertise to spot this lichen spider **Pandercetes gracilis** (Sparassidae) so beautifully does she blend into the bark of a tree in an Australian forest.

(Below) **Arctosa perita** is common on sand-dunes in England where it is difficult to spot unless it moves.

139

The crab spider **Phrynarachne tuberosa** from Nepal is a remarkable mimic of a bird-dropping. Note how the front legs are held against the body on one side and away from the body on the other, thus destroying the spider's give-away bilateral symmetry. The sepsid fly on the right appears to be attracted to the spider, perhaps because of a scent it releases mimicking that of a genuine dropping.

(*Below*) A yellow flower spider **Misumena vatia** female on a ragwort **Senecio jacobaea** flower in England.

change colour so that they can switch backgrounds, or continue to blend into one which has been uncontrollably modified. In the flower spider (*Misumena vatia*), the colour change (which occurs only in adult females) is reversible, from yellow to white and back again, depending on the flower colour chosen by the spider. The yellow colour gradually suffuses the spider as a yellow carotenoid pigment slowly migrates from the intestine to the outer cuticle. Merely by reversing the process, the spider reverts to white.

Similar abilities are also found in some of the rather flattened bark-inhabiting species of *Trechalea* (wolf spiders) from South America. On a dark-brown trunk the spider will also be dark brown, and so will blend in very nicely. If the spider then moves to a pale grey trunk, it will have switched to its new background colour within 30 minutes. This ability is particularly useful in a *Trechalea* species which inhabits the Brazilian *campo cerrado*, a savannah-like habitat of open grasslands and dense scrubby woodland. Bush-fires are naturally frequent, leaving in their wake a forest of singed but quite healthy trees and bushes. Any *Trechalea* spiders inhabiting trunks which avoided the flames are still brown; those on slightly charred trunks are brown speckled with black; those on thoroughly charcoaled trunks will be black. The grasshoppers which share the spiders' habitat show a similar ability, known as fire melanism. Incidentally, when *T. manauensis* which inhabits Brazil's

The melanic form of a **Trechalea** sp. spider after a fire in the Brazilian *campo cerrado*.

flooded *varzea* forests is attacked, it dives down into the water and swims to safety, remaining submerged for up to 15 minutes, surrounded by a plastron of air sticking to its body hairs.

SPIDERS AS ANTS

Ants are among the most abundant and conspicuous of invertebrates, yet they are food for only a very small band of specialists. Ants are rejected on sight by most visually-hunting predators such as birds, and after a brief touch by non-visual predators such as most spiders and predatory insects. Several factors seem to make ants undesirable as food, namely their frequent ability to sting, tough exterior, powerful jaws, chemical sprays, foul taste and dangerously large numbers. With ants thus being virtually immune to attack by generalist predators, it is not surprising that a variety of spiders have acquired this immunity second-hand by becoming superbly convincing mimics.

Ant-mimicry is found in several spider families, including the Theridiidae, Araneidae, Thomisidae, Zodariidae, Eresidae and Gnaphosidae, but most notably in the Clubionidae and Salticidae. In a few instances, as in the salticid *Cosmophasis*, the mimics also feed on ants. However, it is unlikely that their ant-like appearance is much help in this, as ants live in a world of scent and touch rather than vision. In general, spiders mimic ants to gain protection from sharp-eyed predators such as birds and spider-hunting wasps. The importance of fooling the latter can be seen from a census of *Sceliphron* mud-dauber wasp nests in Central Africa. These nests were crammed with spiders from many families, including nearly 200 specimens of salticids, yet not one of these was an ant-mimicking *Myrmarachne*, of which two species were common in the area.

It is not much good looking amazingly ant-like and then blowing your cover by behaving completely out of character. Thus, one of the prime constituents of ant-mimicry in spiders, which makes a huge contribution to the difficulty of distinguishing spider from ant, is the mimic's realistic manner of moving. Ants run in a noticeably zig-zag start–stop manner, their antennae incessantly quivering. These mannerisms are faithfully copied by their spider-mimics. Having no antennae, the spiders cope beautifully by waving their spare pair of front legs around instead, leaving six legs to walk on, just like an ant. Such behaviour is not really so remarkable,

SOME ANT-MIMICKING SPIDERS AND THEIR LIKELY ANT MODEL

SPIDER	ANT	LOCATION
Mazax pax (Clubionidae)	*Ectatomma ruidum*	Panama
Myrmecium bifasciatum (Clubionidae) (yellow morph)	*Megalomyrmex modestus*	Brazil
M. bifasciatum (black morph)	*Camponotus femoratus*	Brazil
Martella furva (Salticidae)	*Camponotus brevis*	Panama
Synemosyna americana (Salticidae)	*Pseudomyrmex boopis*	Panama
Sphecotypus niger (Salticidae)	*Pachycondyla villosa*	Brazil
Aphantochilus rogersi (Thomisidae)	*Zacryptocerus pusillus*	Brazil
Myrmarachne foenisex (Salticidae)	*Oecophylla longinoda*	Ghana
M. elongata (Salticidae)	*Tetraponera anthracina*	Ghana
Anatea formicaria (Theridiidae)	*Chelaner croceiventre*	New Caledonia

The remarkable similarity between the lateral silhouettes of an **Aphantochilus** sp. spider (above) and its cephalotine ant model from South America.

*The clubionid **Zuniga magna** (top) from Brazil's Atlantic coast rainforests mimics ants such as this **Pachycondyla** sp. (bottom).*

close encounters, as the ants are always belligerent. *Myrmarachne* jumping spiders (with more than 160 species, the richest genus of ant-mimics) are adept at keeping clear of their models, using their superior eyesight to dodge out of sight beneath a leaf, or drop on a silken line as soon as they spot an ant coming too close for comfort. In many cases, the spider's faithful mimicry of the specific ant model is quite remarkable. *Pachycondyla obscuricornis* is a large forest-floor ant from Panama, entirely black save for bright yellow tips to the antennae. Its clubionid spider-mimic, *Castianeira memnonia*, is also black, but has yellow tips to its front legs. In many clubionids and salticids, the juvenile instars mimic one species of ant, the adult female a different species and the adult male yet another. The clubionid *Castianeira rica* mimics about five classes of ant models in the Costa Rican rainforest where ants of many types abound.

The remarkable jumping spider *Diolenius minotaurus* from New Guinea resembles one of the *Crematogaster* ants which constantly wags its cocked 'tail' (i.e. the gaster) in the air as it walks. The spider does likewise, and also bears upon the top of the cephalothorax a strange bifurcate 'horn' which rather resembles (at least to the authors' eyes) the upward-pointing open jaws of the ant in its threat posture. Several salticids (e.g. *Padilla* spp., some *Allococalodes* and *Cocalodes*, *Thorellia ensifera*) have forward-projecting 'horns' of various types whose function is unknown, but is almost certainly sexual rather than defensive.

given that many spiders wave their front legs around anyway, as it is on these that the chemo receptors are mounted. Incidentally, the ant-mimicking salticid genus *Peckhamia* is an exception, waving its second pair of legs.

The spiders often live at close quarters to the specific species of ant which they mimic, but do not prey on it. They have to watch their step during

143

Micrathena schreibersi (Araneidae) flaunting her warningly coloured underside in a Brazilian rainforest.

extravagantly spiny outgrowths which embellish the carapace make these spiders difficult to manipulate in the mouth and swallow, buying plenty of time for their nauseating taste to sink home. Being tough, such treatment is less likely to damage these spiders than most. The majority of species are decked out in bright colours, especially combinations of yellow, red and black, something which is otherwise rare in orb-web spiders. These are probably warning colours, easy visual memory-prods designed to remind a predator not to bother next time. Birds often play safe anyway, avoiding any unusual-looking colourful objects on principle. When approached closely or even touched, some thorn-spiders do not drop from the web, but stilt up high on their legs away from the web, hold the abdomen out at right angles to the orb to expose the garishly-marked underside, and bob intimidatingly up and down.

MIMICS OF MUTILLID WASPS

Ants are not the only unpleasant hymenopterous insects mimicked by spiders. Mutillid wasps are greatly feared for their excruciatingly painful sting, with the result that the majority of species are warningly coloured. The wingless females are often seen running round restlessly on the ground or on vegetation. They are mimicked by a number of salticids and clubionids, and in Uganda the mutillid *Glossotilla liopyga* is mimicked both by a *Graptartia* sp. drassid and an undescribed species of salticid.

Some spiders use colour in quite a different way. There is considerable evidence to indicate that the *Gasteracantha* and *Micrathena* thorn-spiders are unpalatable to many predators and are quickly rejected after a brief taste-by-touch investigation. Indeed, some spiders manifest symptoms of extreme distress after merely contacting a *Gasteracantha*. The

ACTIVE DEFENCE

The reaction of many web-building spiders to the perceived proximity of an enemy is to pump rapidly up and down so that the body becomes a blur. For example, *Vespula* species social wasps will try and pluck *Araneus* spiders out of their webs, but are unable to gain purchase on the spider when it is pumping. The bigger the spider, the more likely it is to respond by pumping rather than dropping, when confronted by a predator such as a hummingbird. These not only attack spiders in their webs, but also filch egg masses and trapped insects. A number of species of pholcids, such as *Pholcus phalangioides*, *Psilochorus sphaeroides* and *Smeringopus pallidus* whirl the body on their long hyperflexible legs, rather like doing the 'twist', so that it becomes a blur. Whirling is a very effective countermeasure against web-invading jumping spiders.

Spiders which react to threat by employing first-strike defences or becoming aggressive are relatively rare. Many large tarantulas (Theraphosidae) from the New World (but not for some strange reason from the Old World) can propel a shower of urticating barbed hairs into an enemy's face. Their method of propulsion is the back legs, which are vibrated rapidly downwards against the dense pelt on the top of the abdomen. The base of each hair is abruptly narrowed, making it easily detached. The hairs have an agonizing effect when targeted in the eyes, and also cause severe itching and inflammation on exposed skin and respiratory tract. Young coatimundis in tropical America, unversed in the tricks played by these spiders, will attack, kill and eat them upon their first ever meeting. Next time, the pain of that first encounter well remembered, the coati turns up its nose and looks for easier prey. The large *Theraphosa leblondi* can actually warn off an enemy by producing a sibilant snake-like hissing sound. This emanates from special hooked hairs on its legs, which are briskly rubbed together.

The black widow spider, *Latrodectus mactans*, uses a specific defense against its normal run of small predators, such as mice. When closely menaced, as by a small damp snout sniffing inquiringly, the spider pulls from its spinnerets strands of highly viscous silk, holding it as a protective net in its outspread legs. The spider will lunge at its opponent, spreading the sticky web over its face, a tactic which has proved effective against *Peromyscus* mice. These do not seem to mind the web's taste, but do object to having a sticky mess gumming up their highly sensitive noses. Many *Latrodectus* spp. are particularly vulnerable to predation by mice, because they both share the same kind of retreats, in dark places under stones, logs or floorboards.

Large trapdoor spiders, theraphosids and other well-built types caught cold out in the open tilt back defensively when threatened and raise their front legs, exposing the long fangs to look as intimidating as possible. Some do not wait for the threat to materialize, but attack first, jumping at the enemy and biting. This can be a very dangerous tactic when the species involved is highly venomous, such as a Sydney funnel-web *Atrax robustus* or Brazilian wandering spider (*Phoneutria* sp.). The green lynx spider, *Peucetia viridans* improves on this by imitating a spitting cobra and spits venom into the face of its adversary, thus avoiding the perilously close contact necessary with biting. The venom is bitter-tasting, has an irritant effect upon the human eye and can interfere with vision for up to two days. The venom is ejected directly from the tips of the fangs and can attain a range of 20cm.

There is one deadly enemy against which the spiders have few answers – the spider-hunting wasps. The mere hint of one of these fearless hunters making its approach is enough to make most spiders desert their post in blind panic. Burrow-living spiders are at special risk, for if cornered within the nest, they seem to lose the will to fight, and simply give in and accept their doom. Contact with such a wasp is one of the few things which will force one of these highly sedentary spiders to quit its burrow. Once outside, the spider has a fighting chance, for it seems to sense that if it stays still and hides, the wasp may be unable to find it. This is because, like many male spiders, it is probably chemocontact with the silk around the spider's burrow that alerts the wasp to its location. Bereft of that chemical

A spider-hunting wasp makes heavy work of hauling the paralysed body of an **Araneus** sp. spider in a rainforest beside the massive Iguacu Falls in Argentina.

(*Right*) The bright yellow larva of a parasitic wasp is clearly visible attached to the abdomen of this golden orb weaver **Nephila clavipes** female in a rainforest in Argentina.

clue, the wasp may spend many minutes frantically searching in ever increasing circles around a spider which saves its life by remaining still.

With parasitic wasps and mantispids, the problem seems to be one of detection – the spiders often simply do not see them coming. This is hardly surprising when the enemy concerned is the tiny larva of a mantispid, many of which develop inside spider egg-sacs. Some mantispid larvae cannot penetrate completed sacs, so wait around until a spider passes by and jump on board. While the larva is waiting for the spider (if female) to produce its egg-sac, it will feed on its blood.

08 Spider Ecology

As in insects, spiders have comprehensively colonized most terrestrial environments. These range from the macro habitat, such as rainforests, marshes, grasslands and mountainsides, to minihabitats such as the nests of birds, ants or termites, mole burrows and caves, as well as man-made environments such as houses and mine-shafts. The ant-guests are particularly interesting, as to survive unmolested alongside their fierce hosts, they have probably learned the ant's tactile language, as well as acquiring the vital chemical nest scent. A small *Continusa* sp. salticid from Costa Rica seems to have a definitely symbiotic relationship with its *Tapinoma melanocephalum* ant host in its fragile nests. These are built from debris and placed on the underside of the leaves of rainforest trees. The spiders are very

The glasshouse spider **Achaearanea tepidariorum** (Theridiidae) is a cosmopolitan species found in and around man's habitations. This female is guarding her egg-sac in the author's glasshouse.

A **Pardosa purbeckensis** wolf spider (Lycosidae) with her egg-sac in an English saltmarsh.

faithful to their adopted homes, always returning after an excursion and usually accompanying the ants when they move home. The rather weak and defenceless ants seem to benefit from the spiders' presence, producing stronger colonies than when spiders are absent. Vigilance against parasites and enemies by the sharp-eyed lodgers could possibly be the reason.

There are important differences between the distributions of major spider families in the tropical and temperate zones. Thus, the Linyphiidae is the preponderant family in most temperate regions, both in terms of number of individuals and number of species. In contrast, these mainly tiny spiders are scarce in tropical areas, especially in rainforests, where spiders tend to be large or very large. Thus the myriad dew-spangled linyphiid hammock-webs, forming a sparkling mantle across an English meadow, and so very much a part of the European or American countryside, have no counterpart in the tropics.

The one major habitat which neither insects nor spiders have really managed to crack is the sea. Also, unlike in insects, spiders have scarcely colonized the freshwater environment. This is because no spider has developed the ability to 'breathe' underwater using a gill or via diffusion, as has happened with numerous insects, particularly in their larval stages. The best that most spiders can manage is to spend a few hours temporarily submerged, breathing air from a plastron trapped on the dense surface pile. This is the survival technique used by spiders which are periodically submerged, such as the European wolf spider, *Pardosa purbeckensis*, which is flooded out every time the tide sweeps across its saltmarsh home. The spiders can survive under water for as long as ten hours, far more than is needed before the tide again recedes.

The remarkable and unique European water spider, *Argyroneta aquatica*, has developed a far more high-tech approach, which enables it to live a comfortable underwater life on a permanent basis – it constructs a diving-bell. This starts off as an arched silken roof between the stems of water plants. While putting this in place, the spider breathes via the plastron of air trapped on her body. However, to stock her chamber with air she needs larger supplies, which she gathers in a special way. Rising upwards, she sticks her behind out through the surface film, forms her legs into a kind of basket and then flips downwards, having enfolded a bubble of air between her legs and abdomen. With her third pair of legs occupied in holding her bubble, which therefore trails somewhat behind her, she powers her way back down to her home, swimming with her other three pairs of legs. Alternatively, she will walk down the stems of nearby plants. She enters her nest head-first from below, upon which the air bubble bobs naturally upwards, to be trapped by the silken ceiling. Several trips are necessary for fully stocking the chamber with air, but the spider is then ready to carry out her entire life from within her aquatic home. She will leap out to pounce upon prey, but also hunts actively in the water at night. All feeding takes place in the diving-bell, as does mating and egg-laying. However, a regular food supply is not essential, as the water spider has about half the metabolic rate of any other species of spider so far studied.

During winter, the water spider remains submerged and may even become frozen in a block of ice, sometimes inside an empty snail shell which often does duty as winter quarters. When frozen thus, the spider has lost its air bubble and is completely encapsulated by the ice. After gentle thawing out, most spiders are usually found to be alive and perfectly healthy, quickly resuming normal activity. However, it should be remembered that temperatures within the ice are often far higher than out on the exposed land, where the thermometer can dip below −30°C.

Winter is always a hazardous time for any temperate spiders. Although most species overwinter as eggs, many survive as sub-adults or adults by hiding away in the less extreme conditions found under tufts of grass or peeling bark. Salticids often form small overwintering congregations, consisting of numerous individual winter nests clustered beneath the bark of a tree or rocks on the ground, sometimes with spiders from other families. However, even in relatively protected situations, a prolonged bout of severe weather can send temperatures plunging way below freezing for long periods. In order to survive such extremes, some spiders have been found to exhibit tissue freezing-points as low as −34°C. Interestingly enough, this freezing point is often lower in winter than in summer, indicating an adaptation to declining temperatures as winter tightens its grip. Once the tissues actually freeze, the spider dies, unlike some insects which can survive extended periods of freezing of their tissues. Glycerol is one of the substances which act as antifreeze in spiders, helping to tide them through the winter.

One of the most extreme environments imaginable is a wave-pounded rocky seashore, yet even here spiders have not found the problems of maintaining life to be insurmountable. *Desis marina* (Desidae) inhabits rocky shores in New Zealand, where it builds its silk-lined air-retaining nests in rock cavities, and in the tunnellings created by limpets and chitons within large seaweed holdfasts. A number of other *Desis* species live in similar habitats throughout the Indo-Pacific region. *Desis marina* may have to endure up to three weeks of total submergence beneath the raging sea. The female stays on hand to guard her eggs, which will not hatch without her presence. The eggs take around two months to hatch, and the spiderlings then remain at home for a further two months. This is a long developmental period for a spider, and as the female also produces a succession of egg masses, she is tied to the nest for as long as five months. Such lengthy enforced imprisonment is the price dictated by the low sea temperatures of this harsh environment.

The seashore is not the only extreme environment successfully colonized by spiders. Jumping spiders have been found on the upper slopes of Mount Everest at an altitude of over 6,500m. They were all species of *Euophrys*, a genus of some 130 species with a wide ecological reach, including woodlands. One of the species from Everest bears the highly descriptive name *omnisuperstes*, which literally means 'standing above all'. The spiders, which lack any obvious physical adaptations to their difficult habitat, live on a diet of small flies and springtails. The whole small community depends on vegetation blown up onto the barren heights from lower down where plant growth is possible. The insects make a living from the rotting vegetation itself, and the fungi which help in its decay. The spiders then form the topmost link in a very simple food chain. Strangely enough, feeding and sexual activity are easily possible whenever the sun is shining, because ground temperatures at over 5,000m are then superior to those lower down the mountain.

Small northern island-only groups, such as the Faroes, surrounded by the ever-cold waters of the North Atlantic also represent a tough environment for spiders. In total, only some 70 species manage to glean a living in this mountainous and treeless gale-lashed habitat. Most of these are tiny linyphiids, and many are also rare or local, only occurring on one of the islands. The preponderance of linyphiids, and the fact that some species are quite common, has a twofold explanation. First, linyphiids are suitably adapted for living in the meagre shelter provided by rocks, stones and tussock grass. Secondly, except for a few which have been accidentally transported to the islands by man, the rest of the spider fauna will have reached the Faroes by ballooning (*see* box opposite). Linyphiids balloon mostly as adults, especially as mated females, who can soon establish a thriving colony in their new homeland. Other inhabitants of the Faroes, such as wolf spiders, crab-spiders and clubionids only take to the air as juveniles. This greatly reduces the likelihood that spiders of both sexes will happen to land on the same small island, grow successfully to adulthood and then happen to meet one another. These families are therefore poorly represented and mostly very restricted in distribution.

Where conditions are more favourable, however, such as in the tropics, families other than the linyphiids may be more successful in becoming quickly established. For example, less than 50 years after the cataclysmic explosion destroyed the tropical island of Krakatoa, more than 90 species of spiders from several families had become established via ballooning.

In deserts, it is not cold or strong winds which are the enemy, but drought. Compared with insects, spiders have had relatively little success in colonizing arid environments. Those species which do occur are often burrowers, taking refuge during the hottest periods below ground, where temperatures remain almost unchanged throughout the year. In the world's driest desert, the Atacama-Sechura of northern Chile and southern Peru, spiders are conspicuously absent from huge areas for year after year when no rains come. The only clue to their presence lies in the occasional sight of a broad-mouthed silk-lined burrow leading down into otherwise bare ground. No doubt the mygalomorph insulated in its nest beneath is in a state of long-term torpor. This suspended animation will only be broken when rain returns (perhaps after five or six years). Then both the short-lived wild flowers and the insects which feed on them, and in their turn feed the spiders, will also be woken from their long dormancy by the rain. Life only exists throughout the drought in tiny oases of green, marking a salt-water seepage in which salt tolerant plants thrive lushly. Here even web-builders such as araneids can eke out an existence in small numbers, whatever the state of the rainfall.

The Namib Desert along the western coast of Southern Africa is another of the world's drier deserts, noted for the vast expanses of huge sand-dunes and glistening quartzite plains. Few spiders are visible above ground, but secure below the shifting sands it is a different story. Here, insulated from heat, drought and enemies lurks a variety of spiders, including three large species of huntsman spiders. Where these inhabit the same area, they tend to be restricted to certain specific mini-environments, thereby minimizing the degree of competition for the meagre food supply offered by this hostile place. Whereas the white lady spider, *Leucorchestris arenicola*, inhabits the lowermost slopes of

EIGHT-LEGGED AERONAUTS

Being wingless, it might be thought that the ability of spiders to spread and colonize distant regions would be greatly inferior to that shown by the insects, so many of which are winged. However, any comparison between mobility in insects and spiders is not all in the former's favour – they just do things differently. Spiders may indeed lack wings, but they are by no means earthbound. Whereas all insects take to the air as adults (there are no winged larval stages), spiders mostly do it in their very early juvenile stages. The exceptions are those which remain tiny throughout their lives, such as most linyphiids, which tend to wait for adulthood before taking to the skies.

Spiders do not so much fly as balloon. The lift is not provided by a gas-filled bag but by long skeins of their own very light silk. Ballooning behaviour can occur in just about any spiders, even those with restricted habitats such as the water spider (*Argyroneta aquatica*) and purse-web spider (*Atypus affinis*). Ballooning most often takes place under certain favourable weather conditions of warm clear days and light winds. The actual mechanics of the operation varies somewhat between mygalomorph and araneomorph spiders. The mygalomorphs seem to have a rather limited ability as aeronauts, which may explain why they often appear in dense but scattered clusters. The spiderlings migrate from the maternal burrow to a high point, such as a tree stump, and then simply jump off on their dragLines. If things go well, the breeze eases the bungee-jumper away from the stump, gradually lifting the tiny spider up towards the horizontal as more and more silk is pulled out behind it. Eventually the guy-line becomes so long that it fractures near its connection to the launch-point, and the spider drifts off on the breeze. The dragline can attain a length of 6m before it finally breaks free from its attachment.

The procedure in araneomorph spiders is quite different. The spider runs to some high point, stands with its face to the wind, tilts its abdomen upwards and emits a thread of extremely fine silk. How this first starter-thread gets going is unknown, as normally silk is pulled not squirted from the spinnerets. Be that as it may, once the thread is on its way relatively little air movement is required to pull out more silk, until eventually the line is long enough to whip the spider off its feet and haul it skywards. Certain spots seem to be very favourable for this process. Thus, when one of the authors was attempting to photograph the linyphiid *Erigone atra* ballooning off the apex of a shed roof, a fresh supply of individuals was constantly coming in to land. These would then all quickly scamper up to exactly the same place on the roof, tilt up their abdomens and they were off, just a minute or two after arrival.

The constant comings and goings on this small roof probably exemplifies the relatively short-distance movements which are generally typical of ballooning. However, long-distance flights triggered by thermals or strong winds happen often enough for the rapid colonization of distant islands, as already noted, and for the occurrence of spider aeronauts at altitudes above 6,000m.

Silken lines can also be initiated in a similar way as spanning lines for orb-webs. The topmost line of an orb-web is the support for all subsequent construction, so has to be securely in place right from the start. One way to bridge the gap is to carry the line across, but drifting it across on the air is probably more common, especially when it can be several metres long. In a *Caerostris* web (Araneidae) measured in Madagascar, the spanning-line bridged a river and was approximately 5m long, supporting a huge orb.

Even when no water intervenes, walking a gap is seldom practical, so drift-lines take over. The spider launches such a line much as in ballooning. Although very thin, the drift-line can support the weight of the spider as it pulls it taught and then crosses, trailing behind a thicker line to reinforce the original. A second method of initiating these spanning-lines is to drop on a drag-line. Just below the top of this, and therefore not carrying any weight, is attached a second line. This 'spare' line eventually becomes caught by the wind, which reels out more silk from the spinnerets until eventually the billowing line is long enough to catch hold of some distant object.

the dunes, where the sand is more compacted and stable, *Carparachne aureoflava* prefers the upper, steeper less-stable slopes. A similar preference for different areas of the dunes is also shown by many of the spider's prey insects, so that they share less than 50 per cent of their prey species in common. Such partitioning of resources is essential in an environment in which much of the animal life ultimately depends on a detritus-based eco-system, with the detritus being blown in from outside.

For the huntsman spiders, being large and powerful are assets in enabling them to tackle virtually anything which comes along, including the tough-shelled tenebrionid beetles which are such a prominent feature of the Namib, as well as geckoes and scorpions. Even so, each spider only manages to catch an average of ten decent-sized prey per year, weighing around two-and-a-half times as much as the spider itself. Compare this with the situation in a similar-sized wolf spider in one of the Australian deserts, where annual dietary income would be some four times greater. In really tough times, the Namib spiders may have to fast for more than four months, when turning to cannibalism may be the only short-term answer.

Even in more favourable habitats, circumstances may dictate that a spider should not remain in the same area throughout the year. For example, when the summer's baking sun makes the lava flows in the southwestern USA too hot for comfort, the resident *Agelenopsis aperta* funnel-web spiders move out to the relatively moderate conditions offered by the nearby grasslands. Even within the lava bed habitat, one spider may earn a better living than its

An **Agelenopsis aperta** female (Agelenidae) in typical desert habitat in Arizona.

near neighbours. Thus, a prime web site will be blessed with shade, flowering plants which will attract insects, and a litter-covered ground surface which will not reflect too much burning heat up into the web. This combination will deliver to the owner an offspring output (which is what *really* matters) more than a dozen times greater than a web in less advantageous surroundings. Top real estate is hard to come by and must be fought for, as the spiders occur at densities at, or near, the maximum attainable for the area.

In cooler northern Europe, wolf spiders (*Pardosa lugubris*) migrate away from the woodlands where they have nurtured their brood, and into more open areas nearby, leaving behind the spiderlings to glean a living on the shady woodland floor. In the tropics, *Nephila maculata* adults prefer to rig up their huge webs along trails and in tree-fall clearings in the forest, whereas the juveniles prefer the open spaces to be found in neighbouring cleared grasslands. This enormous spider breeds continuously throughout the year, at least in truly tropical areas such as New Guinea and Malaysia. Its relative *Nephila clavipes* in the Americas is commonest in the tropical zones, but also occurs in temperate habitats, where its life-cycle is tied to the seasons. In the southeastern USA, development to adulthood takes place during the summer, then eggs (usually two clutches per female) are laid in the fall when all the adults die. This leaves the tiny second-instar spiderlings to pass the winter inside the egg-sacs, from which they emerge the following spring. In tropical Panama, the same species manages to fit in two such complete reproductive cycles per year, coinciding with twin peaks in prey abundance, occasioned by rainfall rather than temperature.

In any habitat, tropical or temperate, there are always specialists which are restricted to a certain micro-habitat, but are not too fussy about where that occurs. Thus (*Hersilia* spp.) two-tailed spiders in the tropics are restricted to living exteriorly on tree trunks, but these can be deep inside gloomy rainforests and on sun-drenched isolated trees along roadsides. It seems that it is the tree that is important, its position less so. The wolf spider

The araneid **Alpaida tabula** is one of many spiders which spend their lives on tree trunks. Unlike many, this species from Peru is not cryptically patterned, and both visually and ecologically it parallels **Herennia ornatissima** from tropical Asia.

(*Arctosa perita*) in Europe is generally an inhabitant of coastal dunes, where it is often seen running about on the extensive areas of bare sand. It is also found inland on heathlands, but prefers those which have had large areas of bare ground recently created by a wild-fire. Within a few years, as the vegetation recovers, *A. perita* retreats to artificially cleared firebreaks around the heathland edge.

Interestingly enough, spoil-tips resulting from man's mining operations also provide suitable bare ground, and have also been colonized by this spider. Specimens from the dark heathland soils and coal-spattered spoil-tips are much darker than those on the sand-dunes, presumably as a result of natural selection favouring individuals which best match their local background. A number of other bare-ground spiders are also quick to colonize heathland laid bare by fire, presumably arriving as a result of migratory ballooning, and then gradually declining as the vegetation recovers.

RELATIONSHIPS WITH MAN

The relationship between spiders and mankind has been an ambiguous one over the centuries. On the one hand, many people have a baseless fear and loathing of spiders, stemming solely from their creepy appearance. On the other hand, spiders are admired for their perceived beneficial role in controlling insects, and in many countries it is considered bad luck to kill a spider.

Fortunately, there has always been a small but dedicated band of spider enthusiasts, committed to devoting their lives to unravelling the mysteries of spider life histories. Until quite recently, the majority of these earnest researchers and observers were amateurs, giving generously of their spare time. One of the greatest names in spider history, responsible for discovering and describing a huge number of new species of spiders worldwide, was a clergyman, the Reverend O.P. Pickard-Cambridge. Spiders were his passion, the church his calling. Another great seeker after truths was W.S. Bristowe. His researches and writings inspired so many of today's enthusiasts (including both of the authors), yet by profession he was an industrialist. Bristowe was really the first person to delve deeply into the domestic life of spiders, especially their extraordinary sexual habits.

Today, things have moved on. Now we do not merely want to know what spiders actually *do*, but *why* they do it. And why they do one thing, and not another; and would the other really be best after all? Such complex investigations are generally beyond the scope of the amateur, as they often require the full facilities of a university science department. A good sounding in mathematics is also necessary for the statistical analysis of results, as these often underpin the final conclusions. The nature of the investigation upon which some of the information mentioned earlier in this book was based, might therefore be of interest.

Take, for example, the information about development in the nursery-web spider, *Pisaura mirabilis*. How do we *know* that well-fed females mature earlier, lay more eggs and therefore benefit from the extra meal derived from the male's nuptial gift? The painstaking piece of research which established this information was carried out in southern England by two Americans. One, Professor Randy Thornhill from the University of New Mexico at Albuquerque, is an authority on nuptial gift presentation in insects, and the cost-benefit analysis thereof. To extend his studies to the only species of spider with similar habits, he had to come to Europe. His co-researcher was Professor Steven Austad, a foremost expert on spider behaviour and physiology from Harvard University.

For 24 days during 1984 these two scientists captured, measured (various body parameters), marked (with hobby paint) and released (where they were captured) every adult *P. mirabilis* in their 2,000m² study site. This involved marking 189 females. Later on, all nursery webs were marked with plastic flags as they appeared, noting the presence of a guarding female and number of spiderlings which had emerged from the egg-sac; also any parasites if they had emerged instead. During 1985 20 penultimate instar females were also captured and reared in a laboratory. Here they were randomly separated into two batches and given different feeding regimes to assess the effect of food intake on the timing of egg production and egg weight. These females were mated with randomly selected males and the feeding regime maintained. The date of egg-laying and the number of eggs were then noted.

Results in 1984 (after statistical analysis) indicated that marked females which died before producing egg-sacs were significantly (by mathematical definition) smaller than those which survived gestation. So during 1985, in order to try and assess at which point females suffer mortality, the researchers made measurements of females at three different points. First, carrying egg-sacs containing just eggs; secondly, carrying egg-sacs containing second instar spiderlings; and thirdly, guarding spiderlings on a nest. After being subjected to statistical analysis, the whole project yielded a variety of results which indicated the contribution made by the male in feeding the female.

Sometimes researchers seek to confirm the 'obvious'. It had long been known that female *Theridion sisyphium* regurgitate food to their young. But 'knowing' is not good enough for the scientists. It has to be proven beyond all doubt. So two German researchers, Kullmann and Kloft, fed the female spiders with flies which had themselves been fed with a fluid containing a radioactive isotope. The spiders then in turn became radioactive. After the spiderlings had apparently fed from their mother's mouth, they were now checked and also found to be radioactive, therefore proving that they had undoubtedly taken up fluid from their mother.

VENOMOUS SPIDERS

Spiders seldom go out of their way to be aggressive and attack us humans. Most spider bites result from accidental contact with venomous species, either because they have moved into our homes or outhouses or because they live amongst vegetation through which we might be walking. The black widow spider, *Latrodactus mactans*, the most dangerous of the American species is, for example, very retiring and will drop out of its web at the slightest disturbance. One of the authors has first-hand experience of this, for on a recent trip to the USA he found his first black widow with prey. He failed, however, to obtain his sought after photograph of this event, for each time he approached the web, camera at the ready, she dropped to the ground below the web, only to reappear and recommence feeding a few minutes later. Following several repetitions of this behaviour, the photographer gave up.

There are at least two spiders, however, with highly toxic venoms and who are not scared when cornered and will attack man if threatened. These are the Australian mygalomorph funnel-web spiders of the genus *Atrax* and the ctenid Brazilian wandering spider, *Phoneutria nigriventer*, which can grow up to 12cm across the legs. Both types of spider come into contact with man in or around his home and require treating with the greatest respect.

The reason why spiders are venomous is quite obvious. They often catch prey considerably bigger than themselves and which could be a physical threat to them. An injection which will bring about an almost instantaneous paralysis of the prey is therefore of great advantage to the spider. Thus the venom of many spiders, for example the black widow just discussed or the Sydney funnel-web spider, is neurotoxic, i.e. it blocks nerve impulses passing to the muscles bringing about almost instant paralysis. As a result, when these species bite humans, the discomfort, including muscle cramps and difficulty in breathing are due to paralysis of the various muscles, even though the amount of poison injected is very small. When, however, you consider that black widow venom is reckoned to be 15 times more potent than rattlesnake venom, it is a good thing that her venom load is very small. Adults seldom die from the effects of the bite of a spider injecting neurotoxic venom, unless they have a weak heart, though children, being of smaller stature, are more likely to die.

Some spiders inject a slower acting, necrotic venom into their prey. This has the effect of slowing it down and at the same time starting the process of digesting the prey internally. One group of such spiders, the brown spiders of the family Loxoscelidae, unfortunately sometimes bite man by accident, with unpleasant results. At the site of the bite, the venom causes local tissue damage followed by ulceration which can be quite severe, causing deep lesions in the tissues which take weeks or even months to heal.

This picture shows how easy it would be for a person to be accidentally bitten by a spider. This North American female black widow **Latrodactus mactans** (Theridiidae), with her familiar red hourglass marking, has built her web beneath a table on the veranda where a family occasionally sits and eats. As it happens, the family was aware of and not at all worried by her presence.

In extreme cases, gangrene also develops, causing further damage and in some cases the result can be the death of the person bitten.

SPIDERS AS PETS

Despite what has just been discussed in the previous section, it has become fashionable in recent years to keep spiders, especially mygalomorph tarantulas, as pets. Like most fads in pet-keeping, this is something of a two-edged sword. It has helped to increase the interest in, and awareness of, a group of extremely interesting animals which usually get a bad press. On the other hand, in order to fulfill people's requirement for exotic species there has been overcollecting in the wild, with a consequent undesirable reduction in numbers of certain species, the Mexican red-kneed spider for example. Happily, however, this and other species can now be bred quite successfully in captivity so that this pressure on wild populations has decreased somewhat.

The interest in spiders as pets is, however, still in its infancy and it will probably be a long time before most people react to a furry spider with the same delight that they would a furry kitten!

GLOSSARY OF BIOLOGICAL TERMS

Book lungs   Gas exchange organs found in the abdomen of many, but not all, families of spiders.

Carapace   The strong, chitinous plate covering the cephalothorax (*see* below).

Cephalothorax   The single structure formed by the fusing together of the head and thorax in spiders.

Chelicerae   The more technical term for the spider's jaws.

Cribellum   A specialized structure found in a number of spider families which produces multi-stranded hackled band silk.

Egg-sac   Silken structure in which the female spider encloses her eggs.

Fang   Second joint of a chelicera (*see* above) which is needle sharp and through which the venom is injected into the prey.

Lair   Structure or area away from the main web, but connected to the latter by a silken thread, in which the spider may spend all or part of the day awaiting the arrival of prey.

Pedipalps (or palps)   Jointed head appendages resembling the legs but bearing sensory organs. In male spiders the terminal segment is modified for mating.

Pheromone   Chemical substance produced externally to attract a spider of the opposite sex or, in some special cases, to attract prey.

Spinnerets   Structures on the underside of the abdomen in both male and female spiders from which silk is extruded.

Tarantula   Strictly speaking the European wolf spider *Lycosa tarantula*, but now generally used to describe the large, hairy mygalomorph spiders often kept as pets.

INDEX

Tudor Children

Haydn Middleton

www.heinemann.co.uk/library
Visit our website to find out more information about **Heinemann Library** books.

To order:
 Phone 44 (0) 1865 888066
 Send a fax to 44 (0) 1865 314091
 Visit the Heinemann Bookshop at www.heinemann.co.uk/library to browse our catalogue and order online.

First published in Great Britain by Heinemann Library, Halley Court, Jordan Hill, Oxford OX2 8EJ, part of Harcourt Education.

Heinemann is a registered trademark of Harcourt Education Ltd.

Editorial: Lucy Thunder and Helen Cox
Design: Jo Hinton-Malivoire, Richard Parker and
    Tinstar Design Limited (www.tinstar.co.uk)
Illustrations: Tokay Interactive Ltd
Picture Research: Rebecca Sodergren
Production: Séverine Ribierre

Originated by Ambassador Litho Ltd
Printed in Hong Kong, China
    by Wing King Tong

ISBN 0 431 14616 0
07 06 05 04 03
10 9 8 7 6 5 4 3 2 1

British Library Cataloguing in Publication Data
Middleton, Haydn
    Tudor Children. – (People in the past)
    305.2'3'0942'09031
A full catalogue record for this book is available from the British Library.

Acknowledgements
The publishers would like to thank the following for permission to reproduce photographs:

AKG p**16**; Art Archive/Victoria and Albert Museum/Sally Chappell p**6**; ATP p**25**; Bridgeman Art Archive/Christies p**23b**; Bridgeman Art Library pp**19**, **26**, **28**, **32**, **37**; English Heritage/National Monuments Record p**30**; Fotomas Index pp**29**, **31**; Hulton Getty pp**9**, **24**; Mary Evans Picture Library pp**7**, **15**, **21**; Museum of London pp**13**, **36**; National Portrait Gallery, pp**33**, **38**; National Trust Photographic Library pp**23a** (John Hammond), **34–5** (W H Rendell); Reproduction by kind permission of Viscount De L'Isle, from his private collection at Penshurst Place p**41**; Robert Erbe p**27**; The Royal Collection 2000/Her Royal Majesty Queen Elizabeth II pp**10**, **14**; Tate Picture Library p**12**; Shakespeare Centre Library p**43**; Woodmansterne Ltd p**17**.

Cover photograph of three Tudor children reproduced with permission of Bridgeman Art Library.

The publishers would like to thank Rebecca Vickers for her assistance with the preparation of this book.

Every effort has been made to contact copyright holders of any material reproduced in this book. Any omissions will be rectified in subsequent printings if notice is given to the publishers.

Contents

Words appearing in the text in bold, **like this**, are explained in the Glossary.

The Tudor world

Five hundred years ago the world was a very different place. Europeans were only just realizing that America existed, and they had no idea about Australia. Meanwhile, the mighty **Ottoman Turks** were threatening to conquer the whole of Europe itself. And England (including the Principality of Wales) and Scotland were separate kingdoms, each with its own royal family.

From 1485 to 1603 the Tudor family ruled over England. We now call that period 'Tudor times'. The men, women and children who lived then we call 'Tudor people'. Some of these people were very rich. Many more were extremely poor. In this book you can find out what life was like for the children of both sorts of people.

There were only five Tudor **monarchs**, and the last three were all children of Henry VIII. Henry himself was the son of the first Tudor, Henry VII.

A world unlike ours

The everyday world of Tudor people – rich and poor alike – was not much like ours. About half the number of children born died before their first birthday. Yet the number of people kept rising fast. Maybe half the population was under 20 years of age.

The majority of Tudor people lived in country villages, not in cities, although there *were* big cities, like London, Bristol and Norwich, in Tudor times.

The Tudor family
The Tudor family ruled England and Wales from 1485 until 1603:
King Henry VII (king from 1485 to 1509)
King Henry VIII (king from 1509 to 1547)
King Edward VI (king from 1547 to 1553)
Queen Mary I (queen from 1553 to 1558)
Queen Elizabeth I (queen from 1558 to 1603)

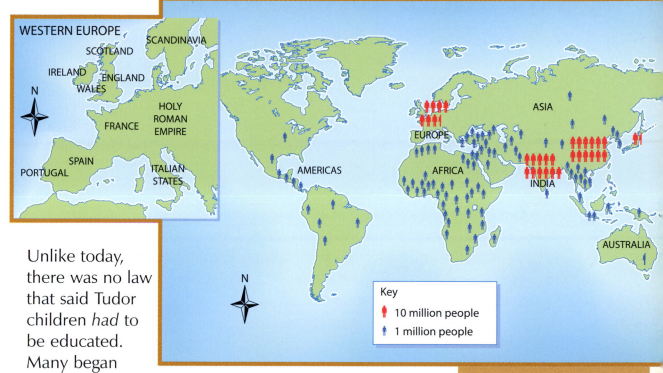

WESTERN EUROPE

SCANDINAVIA
SCOTLAND
IRELAND
ENGLAND
WALES
N
HOLY
ROMAN
FRANCE
EMPIRE
SPAIN
PORTUGAL
ITALIAN
STATES

EUROPE
ASIA
AMERICAS
AFRICA
INDIA
AUSTRALIA

N

Key

🔴 10 million people

🔵 1 million people

Unlike today, there was no law that said Tudor children *had* to be educated. Many began work very young. Their choice of jobs was much more limited than it is now. Most boys followed in their fathers' footsteps and did farm work of some kind. Girls were expected simply to marry, then look after their own families and maybe make cloth in their homes.

As you will find in this book, we know more about the rich than the poor, since more records about them have survived. But we can still use lots of clues to find out how poor children lived.

This map gives a rough idea of the size of the world's **population** in early Tudor times. There were far more people living in Europe and Asia than in the rest of the world, and hardly any in America. Europe was split into different countries, some of which are shown here.

Tudor money note

In this book, Tudor sums of money are shown in pounds (£), shillings (s) and pennies (d). There were 12d in a shilling, and 20s in a pound – which was worth a lot more then! Most people earned less than £10 in a whole year, and you could go to the theatre for a single penny.

The Tudor household

What is a typical British family like today? That is hard to answer. It all depends on how rich or poor the family is, where it lives, how many people are in it, and so on. It is just as hard to say what a typical Tudor family was like. Tudor families came in all shapes and sizes. Some lived in palaces. Others were so poor, they had to sleep under hedges.

In certain Tudor homes, not all the people were related to one another. Some of them were servants. Other non-relatives could be young **apprentices** or just children 'on loan' from other families (see pages 18 to 19). The family plus everyone else made up what was called the 'household'.

Domestic discipline

The person in charge of the entire household was the head of the family. Almost always, this was a man. He had great power. 'He is the highest in the family …,' wrote William Gouge in his book *Domesticall Duties*. 'He is like a king in his own home.'

The family of a wealthy Tudor man, Thomas More. Richer families tended to be bigger than poorer ones, partly because the rich could afford to have more children. In their spacious homes, they were also more likely to have more distant relatives living with them.

'The family that prays together, stays together,' is an old saying. This Tudor father is explaining a religious point to his family.

Tudor fathers – helped by their wives – expected to be obeyed by the children around them. Tudor books on child-rearing made it clear that 'a youth is just an untamed beast'. The most popular book of all, the Bible, also said: 'If you **smite** him with the rod, you shall deliver his soul from Hell.'

As England changed from a **Catholic** into a **Protestant** country, many parents took such words more seriously than before, and sometimes inflicted severe beatings on children. So did some Tudor teachers. They believed it was their duty to drive 'sinfulness' out of the young. Then, by learning obedience and discipline, children would grow into good, God-fearing adults.

Household sizes

In 1599 a **census** was taken at Ealing, near London. There were 404 people living in 85 households. This meant that four to five people probably lived in each one. In richer households there tended to be more people, including servants and more distant relatives. Some members of these families were grandparents – but only a minority of men and women lived that long. Like today, most families consisted of just two generations under one roof: parents and children. These are called 'nuclear' families.

Hazards of childbirth

On 13 October 1564, a newborn baby was christened in the **parish** church of Morebath, a tiny Devon village. We can read his name – Christopher Goodman – in the parish register of **baptisms**, deaths and marriages. We also read that another child was born that day – Christopher's twin. This child did not survive. The **midwife christened** it 'Creature'.

Maybe she gave it this odd name after only its head appeared. So she might not yet have known if it was a boy or a girl. But she had no time to wait. People believed that christening saved a dying child's soul from hell. It also meant that 'Creature' could then be given a Christian burial in a churchyard. Eight days later there was another funeral at Morebath – that of the mother of baby Christopher and 'Creature'.

A brood of children

Such sad stories were quite common in Tudor times. Childbirth could be highly dangerous for baby and mother alike. There were no hospital births, no antiseptics for operations, and very little medicine to ease the pain.

It was seen as a wife's role to have a brood of children and so most mothers had more children than today. After marrying in their mid-twenties, they could look forward to about fifteen years of having children and rearing them.

Napier's casebook

Richard Napier was a doctor and **astrologer**. In his casebook he recorded details about the patients he treated. These included John Flesher, whose wife died in childbirth, and then the baby died, too. As a result, wrote Napier, Flesher was 'very sorrowful and apt to weep; and at other times very angry.' He also described the misery of many mothers whose children had died. After Ellen Craftes' child was crushed by a door 'her head, heart and stomach became ill, her eyes dimmed with grief that she cannot see well.'

Poorer mothers breast-fed their babies. Whilst breast-feeding, they were unlikely to become pregnant again. So in poorer families there could be gaps of two years or more between births. A mother might then have five to seven children in all. Many of these died at birth or in childhood. Some parents in early Tudor times gave more than one of their children the same name. They did not seem to worry that this might cause confusion. The modern historian Lawrence Stone wrote that perhaps they accepted that one would die before growing up. The Timewell family, which also lived in Morebath, had three sons – all named John!

A German picture from 1513 showing a woman about to give birth. The person kneeling in front of her is a midwife. Births took place at home, not in hospitals.

A son and heir

People today are free to decide who gets their property after they die. They write legal documents called 'wills', to make clear who should receive what. A parent might divide everything up equally between his or her children. Or they might leave all their goods and money to someone else entirely. Many Tudor people made wills too, but in wealthy families almost all the property went to the eldest son. This system was called 'primogeniture' – from the Latin words meaning 'first-born'.

King Henry VIII is shown here with his third wife, Jane Seymour – mother of his only surviving, **legitimate** son, Prince Edward.

Rich Tudor parents were therefore keen to have a boy baby as soon as possible. He would be the male 'heir' to the family fortune. (And unlike a daughter, he would carry on the family name, since a Tudor woman had to take her husband's name when she married.) Ideally, rich parents wanted *two* sons. Then if the first died during childhood, his brother could become the new heir. In this way, there would be 'an heir and a spare'!

Family tensions

There was another reason why some Tudor parents preferred boy babies to girls. Girls could turn out to be much more expensive. When a daughter got married, her parents had to give some money to the father of the man she was to marry (the groom). This sum was called a 'marriage portion' or a 'dowry'. In return, the groom's family agreed to support the girl if the groom died before she did.

So money did not buy happiness for all the children in rich families. Younger sons often had to make their own way in the world; they might become soldiers or merchants or make a career in the church. Daughters depended on making 'a good marriage'. Often the younger brothers envied the eldest son, who was going to inherit so much.

Things were less complicated in poorer families. Although they had less property, many parents made sure in their wills that *all* their children received a share.

Only men can rule?

A king passed on to his eldest son not just his property but the crown as well. (Until Tudor times, people generally thought that a woman could not possibly rule the country.) King Henry VIII was so desperate to have a healthy male 'heir and a spare' that he got married six times. Only one of his wives, Jane Seymour, gave birth to a son who survived, Edward. He was crowned king after his father in 1547, but died six years later with no son of his own to take over. Then England had not just one woman ruler, but two: first Edward's half-sister Mary, who soon died, too, then his half-sister Elizabeth. She was an extremely successful and powerful queen, ruling for almost half a century.

Bringing up baby

There were no such things as Tudor baby-gro outfits. In fact, babies were wrapped up so tight, it was as if their parents wanted to *stop* them from growing! For the first months after birth, they were bound in cloth bandages that made it impossible for them to move the head or arms. After four months or so, their arms were freed, but not yet their legs.

Swaddling

Infants were wrapped up, or 'swaddled' like this for medical reasons. Tudor people believed that 'the tender limbs of a child may easily and soon bow and bend and take various shapes.' The tight cloths were meant to help them to grow straight. Many people also feared that unless babies were swaddled, they might do terrible damage to themselves – like ripping off their own ears! Wrapping up babies suited Tudor parents, too. Modern experiments have shown that swaddling slows down a baby's heartbeat, makes it sleep longer and cry less. Tudor parents also kept their babies out of harm's way by hanging the swaddled bundles up on wall pegs!

These wealthy sisters from the Cholmondeley family hold their first-born babies in a picture from around 1600. It is unlikely that either the women or their children wore such fine clothes when not posing for a painting!

This early Tudor rocking cradle had solid sides, which protected the baby from draughts.

Mother or nurse?

Modern mothers can choose whether to breast-feed their new babies or give them formula milk (a substitute for milk made from powder) in bottles. Some Tudor mothers had a different choice – whether to feed their infants themselves, or hire a **wet nurse** to feed them. Upper-class mothers might send their babies away for up to eighteen months to be fed and looked after in this way.

The children of richer Tudor families had to get used to seeing little of their parents. After being wet-nursed, many were brought up mainly by nurses, governesses and tutors, and some might then be sent to boarding school at age ten.

Sad results of wet-nursing

Wet-nursing was not always a happy experience for children. In a book called *Civil Conversation* (1581), the writer Stephen Guazzo tells the story of a child that says to its mother: 'You carried me for only nine months in your belly, but my wet nurse kept me with her for two years … As soon as I was born, we were separated, so I never got to know you.' The historian Lawrence Stone also points out that wet-nursed babies seemed twice as likely to die as babies fed by their own mothers.

Children without parents

Not all Tudor children were lucky enough to have two parents alive. Maybe 20 per cent of children under ten suffered the death of a mother or father and many became orphans.

If a child's parent married again, the child would get a stepmother or stepfather. But it seems that few children actually lived with their step-parents. Instead they went off to live with grandparents or uncles and aunts. If they had no relatives to support them, local officials had to make sure they were cared for, at places like Christ's Hospital in London. Some Tudor children had only mothers, even though their fathers were still alive. Divorces were not allowed by the Church, but parents did split up. In the city of Norwich in 1570, 8.5 per cent of the poor women in a survey had been deserted by their husbands.

Elizabeth I as a young princess. Her father Henry VIII grew tired of her mother, Anne Boleyn, and had her executed in 1536. Their marriage was declared 'null and void', which meant that Elizabeth became officially illegitimate. But she still became queen in 1558.

Henry Fitzroy, the illegitimate son of King Henry VIII by his lover Elizabeth Blount. He died aged seventeen. Some said he was poisoned by Henry's queen at the time, Anne Boleyn.

Punishing unmarried parents

Then there were **illegitimate** children. Their parents never got married at all. In Tudor times, if a child was born without married parents, it was seen as a bad thing. Such a child was called 'baseborn', meaning that its parents were sinners, so it was sinful, too. In Terling, Essex, between 1570 and 1640, 71 illegitimate births were recorded. In 61 of these cases, the parents were made to appear in court. If convicted, they were whipped and put in the **stocks**. Even if the mother had expected to marry the father and was abandoned, she was still punished.

Why were local officials so harsh about this? Partly they were concerned about expense. If an illegitimate child was poor, then the other families of the **parish** had to look after it. Partly too they feared that God would be displeased, and 'pour down His **wrath**' on the whole community.

Help from godparents

It was usual for Tudor boys to have two godfathers and a godmother. Tudor girls had a godfather and two godmothers. Such people might help out if their godchildren became orphans. We know from wills that people often left them money or goods. A Devonshire **yeoman** William Honeywell left £6 to his godson in his will, while in 1602, during a dinner visit to his god-daughter, he gave her a shilling. And in a letter of 1611, Lady Elizabeth Grey sent 'my most dearest love to my sweetest god-daughter' – showing that such relationships could be affectionate, too.

Staying alive

Alice George was an ordinary Oxford woman, born in 1572. She told a clergyman, John Locke, that 'she was married at thirty, and had fifteen children; that is, ten sons and five daughters **baptized**, besides three **miscarriages.**' Many of these children died before growing up. In the Devon village of Colyton, nearly a third of all children born between 1550 and 1750 died before they were fifteen years old. And in crowded, germ-ridden towns and cities, it was even harder to stay alive. During the reign of Elizabeth I, a person could expect to live on average for just 37 years.

Poor hygiene, widespread disease

Disease was a constant fact of life for Tudor children. Poor children, especially town-dwellers, were the most at risk. Living in cramped, unhygienic conditions, and suffering from bad diets, they often fell ill. Doctors were few and expensive. Even they did not really know how to diagnose or treat most diseases. Disastrous **epidemics** swept whole regions. Attacks of influenza (flu) in 1557 and 1558 killed about five per cent of the population. Those who died had already been weakened by hunger after serious harvest failures in 1555 and 1556.

These Tudor tombs can be found in Westminster Abbey, London. Only wealthy parents could afford to mark their children's deaths in this way.

Sanitation in most homes was poor or non-existent. Men and women seldom washed, and children seem not to have been toilet trained by adults. (But evidence survives of bed-wetters being made to drink a pint of their own urine – as a 'lesson'!)

Many parents, however, behaved fondly towards growing children. The modern historian Lawrence Stone writes that they tended 'to treat children from about two to seven as amusing pets' for the entertainment of grown-ups. 'It was,' he goes on, 'the one period in a child's life when his parents and other adults treated him other than harshly or with **indifference**.'

Skulls and earthworms

Only children from wealthy families could afford to be treated by doctors. Yet some Tudor doctors' cures had little to do with medical science. For **gout**, live earthworms were put on the affected skin until they began to smell. Other medicines might include powdered human skull. Many people worked out their own theories about illnesses and cures. If a root, leaf, nut or plant *looked* like a part of the human body, then it might bring health to that part. So walnuts, for example, were supposed to be good for the brain and for mental disease.

Home from home

Sir Simonds D'Ewes was born to upper-class parents in late Tudor times. As a man he wrote an **autobiography**, describing his childhood. Other boys from wealthy families may have had similar experiences. After several months with a **wet nurse**, he went to live with his grandparents for seven years. His parents visited him only twice, and he was brought up mainly by servants. He was sent to five different boarding schools. Then finally, aged sixteen, he went to St John's College, Cambridge, to be a student. He had spent almost all his young life away from home.

'Fostering out'

Tudor children of all classes had to get used to living in other people's houses. In early Tudor times, noble and other well-to-do parents often sent their children to live in households similar to their own. There they would learn how to behave at court. But in later Tudor times, boys like Simonds D'Ewes more usually went to private boarding schools, which only the rich could afford.

Rich farmers and merchants might also send their sons away – and even some daughters – to be **apprentices**. This would happen between the ages of seven and seventeen. Apprentices would live in their masters' houses, even if these houses were not very far away.

Absent fathers

In some wealthy Tudor families, the fathers – not the children – were 'exported' to homes elsewhere. **Courtiers** spent more time with their **monarchs** than with their children. Another man who chose to live apart from his family for long periods was the playwright William Shakespeare. Born in 1564 and brought up in Stratford-upon-Avon, Shakespeare lived and worked mainly in London through the 1590s. So his three children – who stayed in Stratford with their mother – saw little of their famous father. Sadly the only boy, Hamnet, died in 1596, at the age of just eleven.

Craftspeople and **artisans** usually apprenticed their sons to others, rather than give them work at home. And the children of labourers might be sent away to be farm servants or **domestic** servants in their early teens.

Only English parents seem to have 'fostered out' or 'exported' their growing children in this way. They began to do it in **medieval** times, but historians are still not quite sure why. It must have had a big effect on relationships between the generations.

Lady Tasburgh of Norfolk, pictured with her children. Married Tudor noblewomen, unlike their husbands, were not expected to spend time at court. Their children grew up in the country, seeing little of their father.

Skills for life

Hugh Latimer was the son of a **yeoman**. He went on to become the Bishop of Worcester. He remembered that his father taught him how to use a bow and arrow as a boy. 'As I got older and stronger,' he wrote, 'he brought me bigger and bigger bows.' People believed you could become a good archer only if you learned what to do while you were growing up.

In earlier Tudor times, it was vital that boys *did* learn this skill. Since 1285, all men from sixteen to 60 had a duty to fight for their **monarch** in times of emergency. The kind of weapons they used varied depending on how rich or poor the fighter was. For most, it was bows and arrows. Under Queen Elizabeth I, weapons like **pikes** and **harquebuses** became more common – and special training was given to young men who showed skill in using them.

Preparing for court

On pages 28 to 33, you can find out what schooling Tudor boys and girls were given. But either in or out of school, they were also meant to pick up other useful skills for life. For wealthy Tudors this included training for court.

Dancing was learned in the early years, not just for enjoyment but also – in the words of Lord Herbert of Cherbury – 'since it encourages suppleness and agility in the limbs.'

Swimming

There were no swimming pools in Tudor England. But children who lived near rivers or the sea still had the chance to swim. 'It is fit for a gentleman to learn how to swim, unless he gets cramps easily. However, I must confess that I myself cannot swim. For since I once nearly drowned while learning to swim, my mother forbade me to continue …' From the **autobiography** of Lord Herbert of Cherbury (1583–1648).

According to Roger Ascham, who tutored Queen Elizabeth as a girl, 'to ride, **joust**, use all weapons, run, leap, dance, sing and play all instruments tunefully, **hawk**, hunt and play tennis are all necessary for a **courtier**. He should also learn several languages.'

This preparation was only for boys though. Wealthy young ladies were expected to learn music, singing, dancing and needlework. With these, they could expect to attract a suitable husband. Poorer girls had to learn as soon as possible how to cook, clean and run a household. This prepared them for when they married and set up homes of their own.

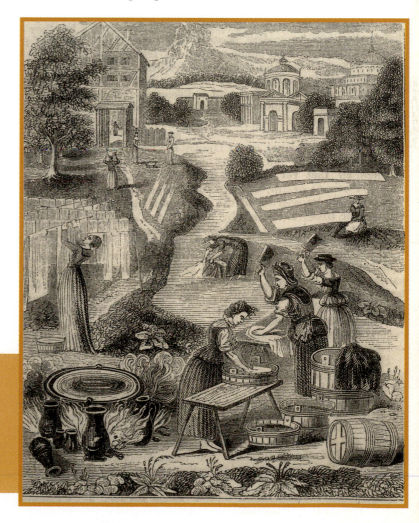

Peasant girls were trained in domestic duties from an early age. These women are washing cloth, beating it out, then hanging it up to dry or laying it out to bleach in the sun.

Children or adults?

When do children start being adults? When they get a full-time job? When they leave home? When they start to vote? When they get their driving licences? Different people would give different answers. But most people now would agree that there *is* a period of time called 'childhood'. And during that period, children have their own kinds of clothing, interests and activities. In Tudor times, it was not quite like that.

Growing up fast

Even small Tudor children were trained to behave like miniature adults. They looked like miniature adults, too. Little rich girls were stuffed into **bodices** and **corsets** reinforced with iron and whalebone. These were meant to shape their bodies in a way that the Tudors found attractive. Yet they could also cripple growing girls, breaking ribs and preventing the lungs from developing.

Boys might wear smocks (overalls, like shirts) until they were 'breeched'. This was when they got their first pair of knee-length trousers or 'breeches'. After this important moment, around the age of six, they were expected to be men in all but name.

Showing respect

Tudor children were rarely allowed to be 'childish', yet they had to show great respect to their parents. When at home, they had to kneel and ask for their parents' blessing every morning. They still had to do this when they visited as adults. Even grown-up sons had to keep their hats off in their parents' presence. Later in the 1600s an Oxford University student began his letters home with 'Most honoured father.' His father's replies began with the single word, 'Child'!

Wealthy Tudor children in clothing that made them look like 'miniature adults'. The girl was only 23 months old. The boy in knee-length trousers had been 'breeched' around the age of six.

Confirmation

The next key stage in growing-up came when children were **confirmed** in church. This happened between the ages of fourteen and sixteen. By sixteen, boys could also be 'called up' to fight for their **monarch**. Many of these boys – and their sisters – had already been doing adult work for five years or more.

It is hard to say exactly what a 'Tudor childhood' was. Most Tudor children had little time to themselves – and little space, too, since only the rich had separate rooms for each family member. Unlike today, very few products were made for just children to enjoy – even toys were far more rare. In Tudor times you were expected to grow up fast – then stay grown-up.

Children in need

'In the **parish** of St Stephen's there lives John Burr, 54 years old, who is too sick to work any more. His wife Alice, 40, spins. They have seven children, aged 20, 12, 10, 8, 6, 4 and 2. They can all spin wool, and have always lived in his house.'

That comes from a **census** of the poor in the city of Norwich in 1570. Many town and city families were terribly poor. In earlier Tudor times local officials often made door-to-door collections to help them out. Wealthier people were also generous in giving to the poor. But the problem was so great that from 1563, Tudor governments *made* the more fortunate support the poor of the parish. By law, people now had to pay a regular 'rate' or amount. This rate varied, according to how well-off they were themselves.

Children on the roads

Some poor families moved around the country – begging, looking for work, sometimes stealing. Tudor officials treated such people more harshly – returning them to their home parishes by force, among other punishments. By a law of 1547, **vagran**t children could be seized by anyone prepared to teach them a trade.

A Tudor family takes to the roads. As the population rapidly grew, there were not always enough jobs to go round. Some fathers took their wives and children with them on a search for work. But they could be confused with wandering criminals and beggars, and punished severely.

Beware vagrants!

In 1566 the writer Thomas Harman published a **pamphlet** warning people about the tricks that Tudor rogues and pickpockets got up to. Some vagrant children, he wrote, looked ill or wounded. But he said their beggar-parents might well have injured them on purpose – so that people would give them money out of pity. Vagrant babies were tied in sheets and carried on their mothers' backs. 'They bring the children up savagely,' wrote Harman.

Boys might then be **apprenticed** until they were 24, girls until they were 20. The children's parents had no say in this at all. If a child ran away and was recaptured, he or she could be treated as a slave.

Orphaned children had difficulties, too, if they could not prove where their home parish was. Local officials were unsure where a poor girl named Catherine Boland had been born. She spent some time in Northamptonshire and some in the city of Leicester. But both **parishes** refused to take responsibility for her, and shuffled her back and forth. In the end, government officials called **Justices of the Peace** ordered both parishes to share the cost of her upkeep.

Wealthy townspeople, like Humphrey and Elizabeth Bridges in Cirencester, gave very generously to the poor. The words on their tomb in the parish church mention how generous they were.

Working children

Many people today go to university after school. They do not usually start regular jobs until they are over twenty. In Tudor times almost all children began to work at a much younger age.

In 1563 a law called the Statute of **Artificers** was passed. The law said that any poor, unemployed male from 12 to 60 years of age could be *made* to work in farming. Boys and men could, for example, be forced to work in the fields during the hay or corn harvests.

Training for the future

The law of 1563 also set new rules on **apprenticeship**. Unless a young man had been trained by a master for seven years, he was not allowed to be employed in any specialist trade or craft. If a boy wanted to become a **draper**, a goldsmith or a merchant – all of them 'superior' jobs – he could do so only if his father did the job already, or if his family was quite wealthy.

All over Europe, girls and boys helped to gather in the autumn hay before rain could spoil it. Hay was used as food for animals over the long winter months. Farm-workers' young children also did jobs like chasing away birds, watching sheep, milking cows and making butter and cheese.

This is an 'indenture' – a written agreement between a master and an apprentice, setting out what will happen during the apprenticeship.

Boys could be as young as seven when they agreed to train with a master. Sometimes their apprenticeships lasted for up to ten years. For most of this time, they were not paid for their work. So, by the end, they could be doing a man's work for no wages.

Why was the government so keen on this lengthy training? Partly it wanted to ensure that adult butchers, bakers, clockmakers or shipbuilders worked only to the highest standards. Partly, too, it did not want too many boys training for a limited number of jobs.

Apprentices were not just taught by their masters. They were housed, fed and clothed by them, too. Some masters treated their apprentices well, and gave them a good education. In the 1580s, 82 per cent of boy apprentices in London and Middlesex could read and write. Other masters were so harsh that the boys ran away.

Small children, big earners

'In English cities every child of six or seven years old is forced to some art in which he earns his own living and something else to enrich his parents or master. In the city of Norwich, children aged six to ten make fine knitted stockings. Every child over 7 is able to earn 4 shillings a week at that trade.' The Tudor writer Thomas Wilson made these remarks in *The State of England in 1600*. It is highly unlikely that these child workers were allowed to keep much of the money they earned for themselves.

Schools for all?

According to the Tudor schoolmaster and writer Richard Mulcaster, education was meant to train every person 'to perform those functions in life which his position shall require.' Most men needed no book-learning to work at their jobs in the fields, so, as boys they got little or no schooling. And since most adult women were expected to concentrate on 'good **housewifery**', girls were not usually educated either. But as you will see over the next six pages, there were several changes in Tudor education – and more children than before benefited from them.

Religious-based education

In the Middle Ages almost all England's schools were run by the Church. 'Song' and 'grammar' schools were attached to cathedrals or abbeys. Boys went to them to train to sing in church services or train to be priests. During the 1500s, local rich men paid to start up schools that were less religious. But teachers still had to get a licence to teach from their local bishop. And any teacher who tried to 'keep a school' without a licence could be **excommunicated** – a very serious punishment.

A child learning the alphabet. Schools did not always have highly-qualified staff. In Falmouth, in Cornwall, poor Tudor children got a basic education from the local bellringer.

Younger children used a 'hornbook', like this. Inside the wooden frame was a single page, protected by a thin clear sheet of horn.

By the end of Tudor times, young boys (aged five or six in towns, seven or eight in the country) might go to 'petty' schools for a short time. There they learned first reading, then writing. Some girls might go to these schools, too. But by 1600, 72 per cent of men and 92 per cent of women could still not sign their own names.

At 'grammar schools', older boys learned Latin and maybe some Greek until they were fifteen. Poor children were allowed to go to these schools for free, but often parents needed them to work to bring in extra money. Meanwhile, wealthy parents paid fees for their sons to be boarders at new private secondary schools.

University education

There were just two universities in Tudor England, at Oxford and at Cambridge. In early Tudor times, boys went to the colleges there when aged fourteen or fifteen. By 1600, new students tended to be older and there were about 2000 students in all at each university. William Harrison wrote in 1577 that the colleges were built 'at first only for poor men's sons, whose parents were not able to bring them up to learning. But now … the rich take many of the places.' Some gentleman students then completed their education by studying law at the 'Inns of Court' in London.

At grammar school

In his play *As You Like It*, William Shakespeare described:
'… the whining schoolboy, with his satchel
And shining morning face, creeping like snail
Unwillingly to school.'
Was he writing from personal experience? If so, from the age of about six he probably went to the King's New School in his home town of Stratford-upon-Avon. In southern England, many new grammar schools like it began to appear after 1550. Between 1558 and 1603, 136 were founded. More of the masters were well-trained at university, too. Boys like the young Shakespeare (from families of **yeomen**, craftspeople, merchants or tradespeople) were now able to get a good education.

The gateway to all knowledge

Teaching varied from school to school, but most schoolwork was based on the study of Latin – the gateway to 'all knowledge whatsoever'. Across western Europe Latin was still written and spoken by clergymen, scholars, politicians, officials, lawyers and doctors. Schoolboys read and translated comedies by Ancient Roman playwrights, as well as the work of great poets like Ovid. There were few books, so long passages were learned by heart.

This photo shows the schoolroom at the Grammar School, Stratford-upon-Avon, set up much as it would have looked in Tudor times. The pupils had to attend lessons up to ten hours a day, six days a week. No wonder school holidays were sometimes called 'remedies'!

Tudor pupils used small, cheap books like this to learn simple Latin phrases. During Tudor times, English began to take the place of Latin as the language used for education.

Some of the classwork was acted out in short plays. There might also be a little Greek, if the masters were qualified to teach it. But history, geography, arithmetic and English barely figured as separate subjects.

As in the home, discipline was usually strict. Some masters struck a naughty pupil's hand or mouth with a 'ferrula' – a flat piece of wood, pear-shaped at the end, with a hole in the middle. Others beat the pupil's naked bottom with a bundle of birch twigs. According to a popular Dutch author called Batty, God had *designed* the human buttocks to be severely beaten without causing serious injury to the victim!

Westminster School rules, 1560

Tudor schools were quite small compared to today's. At Westminster School there were only two masters. Their duties were: 'to teach and examine in Latin, Greek and Hebrew grammar, and the **humanities**, poets and **orators**. Also to see that the boys behave properly in church, school, hall and chamber, as well as in all walks and games, that their faces and hands are washed, their heads combed, their hair and nails cut, their clothes both linen and woollen, gowns, stockings and shoes kept clean, neat, and like a gentleman's … They shall choose **monitors** from among the most serious scholars to stop anything dirty being done.'

Learning at home

No law said Tudor parents *had* to send their children to school. Some wealthy families paid teachers to give lessons in the home. Henry VIII's chief minister Thomas Cromwell employed a full-time tutor to educate his son, Gregory. Around 1530, the tutor described a typical day they spent together. The pupil must have missed the company of other boys his own age:

After prayers, Gregory looked at a passage called 'Youthful **Piety**' by the great Dutch scholar Erasmus. He had to read it in Latin and in English, then compare the two. Then he practised writing for one or two hours, and spent the same amount of time reading a history of England by Robert Fabian. The rest of the day he spent playing the **lute** and **virginals**. 'When he goes riding,' his tutor added, 'I talk to him on the way about Roman or Greek history. Then I ask him to tell it back to me. To relax he goes hunting and **hawking** and shoots his long bow, very skilfully.'

A rare picture of an unusual sight in Tudor times: a female teacher with a female pupil. Some girls from wealthy families became great scholars.

This painting is thought to be of Lady Jane Grey (1537–1554). She was famous for her learning, writing to leading scholars in Europe by the time she was fourteen, and reading Greek for fun!

New learning for girls

'I do not see why girls should not learn as well as boys,' wrote the scholar and politician Sir Thomas More. Several other experts in education agreed with him. So, from about 1520 to 1560 tutors taught a number of upper-class English girls Latin, Greek, French and Italian to a very high level.

Later in the century, however, educational fashions changed again. Girls were now expected to return to learning 'social graces' like music, painting, drawing, dancing and needlework. They were also not meant to 'challenge' their menfolk in the home. Maybe educated women seemed threatening to men! Whatever the reason, the experiment in girls' education did not continue.

Top scholar

In his book *The Schoolmaster*, the tutor Roger Ascham (1515–1568) described one of his pupils – a girl – as 'one example for all the gentlemen of this [royal] court to follow.' 'One maid goes beyond you in excellence of learning and knowledge of many languages … Besides her perfect fluency in Latin, Italian, French and Spanish, she now reads more Greek every day than some priests read Latin in a whole week. And best of all, she has worked hard … to understand, speak and write more cleverly than almost anyone at the two universities.' Who was this amazing scholar? Henry VIII's daughter, later Queen Elizabeth I!

Special days

Tudor children did not have holidays like ours. But they had plenty of time off work or school to celebrate special days in the Church calendar. Most fell in the six months between 24 December and 24 June. Writer John Aubrey looked back and described the Tudor village festivals of his grandfather's time:

'In every **parish** there is, or was, a church house. Inside it were spits, crockery, all kinds of **utensils** for making a feast. Here the housekeepers met, and were merry and gave charity to the poor. The young people came there too, and had dancing, bowling, shooting at targets, etc, while the older folk sat watching … Such joy and merriment took place every holiday.'

Festival fun and games

The longest festival period was the twelve days of Christmas, from 25 December to 6 January. Then there would be decorations, singing, house visits, plays put on by mummers (silent actors) and games of football. More Church festivals and saints' days followed – like Plough Monday, Shrove Tuesday, St Valentine's Day and Easter – until the high excitement of May Day. At that time young and old people alike would spend the night celebrating out of doors, then bring home a maypole to dance around.

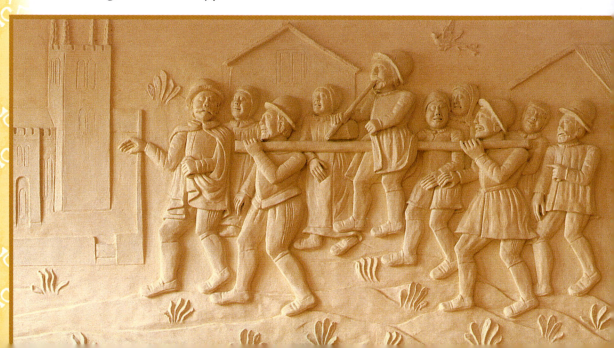

Boy Bishops

In some cathedrals, abbeys and university colleges at Christmas, a boy was chosen to dress up as a bishop and take some church services for fun. At Salisbury Cathedral the choirboys chose one of their own number to be the 'Boy Bishop'. At King's College, Cambridge, he wore a small costume including a white wool coat, a scarlet gown with a white fur hood, fine knitted gloves, gold rings, with a **crozier** and a **mitre**. Even some local parishes had Boy Bishops. They led processions through the streets, collecting money that was then handed over to the church.

Not everyone was so keen on the fun. 'There is a great Lord among them all,' wrote John Stubbes, a pamphlet (small booklet) writer from the 1580s, 'namely Satan, prince of hell.'

Stubbes obviously disapproved of such 'pastimes and sports'. So did other strict Christians like him, known as Puritans. But old customs were not easy to get rid of. And some were not just an excuse for merry-making. On Midsummer Eve, for example, people lit bonfires made of bones (this is where we get the word bonfires or 'bone-fires'). The stench was supposed to drive away various kinds of evil. This included both diseases that infected humans and wet weather or **blight** that ruined crops.

Even when no special festival was being celebrated, Tudor villagers could still let off steam. Husbands who let their wives 'henpeck' them – like the one being carried here – were paraded around the area. As they were taken on this 'skimmington ride', people played rough music and mocked them.

Having fun

Older relatives have probably said to you, 'When we were young, we had to make our own entertainment.' For poorer Tudor children with time to spare, that was certainly true.

Only wealthy parents could afford to buy carved and painted wooden toys – the most expensive dolls and toy ships often came from abroad. Nor did poor children get the chance to go riding, **hawking**, hunting or shooting like the better-off. But in the countryside they had more opportunity than most modern children to roam around and to swim or fish in local rivers and lakes.

Great shows

There were, of course, no televisions, cinemas, pop festivals or massive sporting events. But the Tudor **monarchs** laid on lavish **pageants** and processions to impress their subjects, sometimes by torchlight. In 1539 Henry VIII staged a mock-battle on large flat boats called barges on the River Thames in London. Actors playing 'the King's men' defeated those playing 'the **Catholic Pope's** men' and threw them all overboard. (This was just after Henry VIII had stopped England being a Catholic country.)

This wooden rocking horse has survived since Tudor times. It must have belonged to a wealthy family.

This 1560 painting from the Netherlands, called *Children's Games*, could almost be showing a playground scene in a modern school. But Tudor children somehow had to survive without mobile phones, personal stereos and replica football kits!

For more gruesome entertainment, children could join the crowds that watched public executions. And at festivals like Shrovetide (from the seventh Sunday before Easter until the end of the following Tuesday) some brutal street sports were played in the towns. One was football, which rarely had either teams or rules. According to Sir Thomas Elyot in 1531 it was 'nothing but beastly fury and extreme violence'. Another was 'cock-threshing' – in which a cockerel was tied up by one leg, while people threw missiles to knock it over or kill it. King Henry VII even had cockerels delivered to his palace at Shrovetide in 1493, so that he could watch them fight each other to the death!

Tudor drama

In earlier Tudor times, children could watch special Christian plays on Corpus Christi Day in June. These were called 'mystery plays'. They were put on by groups of tradespeople, and showed the history of the world from Adam and Eve to the present time. Children would have enjoyed the rude jokes and everyday language. The plays were last performed in England at Coventry in 1580. But children could still enjoy shows put on by bands of travelling actors. And some could afford to pay a penny and watch plays at the first purpose-built theatres – like The Globe on the South Bank of the River Thames in London.

Children on the throne

King Henry VIII tried hard to make sure his crown passed to a male heir. Only a king, he believed, could successfully rule England. Henry achieved his aim. When he died in 1547 he was succeeded by his son, who now became King Edward VI. Unfortunately Edward was just nine years old. 'Woe to thee, O land, where the king is a child,' said Bishop Hugh Latimer in a sermon in 1549. Why did he say this?

This painting from around 1568 shows Henry VIII on his deathbed in 1547. He points to the son who would become king after him – Edward VI. The man next to Edward is his uncle, the Duke of Somerset, who briefly ruled in his name.

The need for personal rule

Today a queen or king has little real power. But in Tudor times a ruler really had to rule. A mighty king like Henry VIII was able to strike fear and respect into his subjects (a bit like a headteacher!). They would then think twice before disobeying him. They also believed *God* would punish any disobedience, since all true kings had the blessing of Heaven. With a boy-king, things were different.

Edward VI was still a schoolboy. He was a good pupil in Latin, French and Greek, loved music and astronomy, and was deeply interested in religion. But his studies left him little time to rule. Besides, he was too young to inspire fear and respect. So his uncle the Duke of Somerset ran the kingdom for him. But some of Somerset's **policies** proved unpopular. People showed how unhappy they were by rebelling in several parts of England in 1549. They might not have rebelled against a real king. But they did rebel against the rule of Edward's 'evil **councillor**', Somerset.

Somerset was removed and the Duke of Northumberland took his place. But some now saw *him* as an 'evil councillor'. There could have been more rebellions, but in 1553 Edward died of **consumption**, aged only fifteen. No child would ever rule England again.

A child Queen of Scots

Mary Stuart was even younger than Edward VI when she became Queen of Scotland. When her father King James V died in 1542, she was just one week old. Talks began at once to arrange a marriage with the future King Edward of England. Royal children were often **betrothed** very early, to form a friendly link between their kingdoms. But in 1548 Mary sailed abroad instead to marry the future king of France. They married when she was sixteen. He died when she was only eighteen. Her sad story did not get any happier. She was executed for plotting against Edward VI's half-sister, Queen Elizabeth I of England, after spending nearly 20 years in prison.

Growing up into adults

Most Tudor parents strictly controlled their children. Many Tudor fathers decided what jobs their sons should do. Some also had a big say in whom their children would marry. In this way, children still felt their parents' influence long after they became adults.

Choosing whom to marry

Children from wealthy families tended to get married quite young. For this, they needed their parents' **consent**. Often the parents arranged 'good' marriages for them. Queen Elizabeth I's **Chancellor of the Exchequer**, Sir Walter Mildmay, chose a fourteen-year-old girl for his son Anthony to marry – against his son's own wishes!

Lord Burghley, Elizabeth I's chief minister, had this advice for his younger son: 'Take great care in the choice of your wife, for she may be the cause of all the good or ill that happens to you; and, as in warfare, you can make only one mistake … Find out about her character, and what her parents were like when they were young. Let her not be poor … yet do not choose someone ugly just because she is rich …'

Arranged marriages

In 1514 a Lancashire girl was forced by her **yeoman** relations to marry a man she deeply disliked. If she refused, they told her, she would lose her **inheritance** in land. But her new husband beat her badly, and she ran away from him, demanding a separation. 'I would not have stayed with him for an hour,' she explained, 'but I did not want to lose my land.' Another girl, Margery Shaftoe, found her future mapped out like this in her father's will of 1599: 'To my daughter Margery: 60 sheep, and I give her in marriage to Edward, son of Reynold Shaftoe of Thockerington.'

Staying single longer

Tudor people usually lived shorter lives than us, but most of them did not get married earlier. The average age for a bride was 26, for a groom it was around 28. By marrying quite late, people could limit the number of children they had.

Not all upper-class arranged marriages turned out to be loveless or unhappy. In 1584 Robert Sidney married Barbara Gamage. They had almost certainly never met before. But they enjoyed a happy life together until Robert died in 1626. This painting shows Lady Sidney with her children.

Many poorer children lived away from home. Without their parents watching over them, they were freer to choose their partners for life. But they still had to wait until they had finished their **apprenticeships**, and had enough money to set up a home. Then, when they could look after themselves and earn a living at last, they could start up families of their own.

How do we know? – Parish registers

In 1538 Thomas Cromwell, the chief minister of King Henry VIII, sent out royal 'injunctions' or orders to every **parish** priest. These injunctions ordered the priests to set up a parish register. In it they were to record information about the parish such as **christenings**, marriages and deaths. It provides a vital source of information about Tudor children for modern historians. This is what the injunctions said:

'You shall keep a register, in which you shall write the day and year of every wedding, christening and burying made within your parish. And every priest who comes after you must do likewise … For the safe keeping of this register, the parish shall supply one good **coffer** with two locks and keys ... Every Sunday you shall take this register out and … record all the weddings, christenings and burials made during the week before. Then the register must be locked up again. Failure to do this will result in a fine of 3s 4d, to go towards keeping the church in good repair.'

Valuable records

From about 1550 onwards, more and more parish registers survive. They were not always kept accurately, and historians have to be careful that the information they take from them is correct. But they can help us to see how life changed for children during the later Tudor period.

Single mothers in Morebath

The parish register of Morebath, a village in Devon, survives from 1558. In it, we can trace the arrival of every new child in the village. Not all these children, however, may have been very welcome. In March 1566 a son John was born to Margaret Morsse. And in November 1568 a son James was born to Mary Timewell. Neither Margaret nor Mary were married, for there is no record of their weddings in the register. Therefore their children were **illegitimate**. This was disapproved of by many Tudor people (see page 15).

We can tell, for example, that by 1600 the **birth rate** was rising. Partly this was because the average age of people getting married was falling. Partly it was because fewer children were being killed by the plague or a type of flu called 'the sweating sickness'.

A plague *did* strike Stratford-upon-Avon in the summer of 1564. The burial register shows that it probably killed more than 200 people. (From 1 January to 20 July, 22 burials were recorded. For the rest of the year there were 237.) One person who escaped the plague was a newly **baptized** baby – the future playwright, William Shakespeare. Like the parish registers, young William survived. Today we can also use *his* plays as a source of information on life in Tudor times.

This entry in the Stratford parish register tells us that William Shakespeare was christened on 26 April 1564. It says in Latin, 'William, son of John Shakespeare'. Babies were usually christened three days after they were born. But we cannot be sure of Shakespeare's exact birth date.

Timeline

1485	Tudor family begins to rule over England and Wales
1492	Christopher Columbus reaches America
1509–47	Reign of Henry VIII
1529–39	England stops being a Roman **Catholic** country
1536	King Henry VIII begins to close down the monasteries and nunneries, including some schools in these places
1538	**Parish** registers kept from now on
1542	Mary Queen of Scots is born
1547	Very harsh law passed against **vagrant** children
1547–53	Reign of boy-king Edward VI
1553–58	Reign of Mary I
1558–1603	Reign of Elizabeth I 136 new grammar schools set up
1563	First Tudor Poor Law passed, helping poorest families; Statute of **Artificers** passed, setting new rules on **apprenticeship** and work
1564–1616	Life of William Shakespeare
1577–80	Francis Drake becomes first English sea-captain to sail around the world
1580	Last 'mystery plays' in England performed at Coventry
1587	Mary Queen of Scots is executed by order of Elizabeth I
1588	English navy beats invading Spanish Armada (fleet of ships)
1603	End of Tudor period

Sources and further reading

Sources

The author and Publishers gratefully acknowledge the publications from which sources in the book are drawn. In some cases the wording or sentence structure has been simplified to make the material appropriate for a school readership.

Birth, Marriage and Death, David Cressy (Oxford, 1997)

Elizabeth I and Her Reign, Ed. Richard Salter (Macmillan Documents and Debates, 1988)

Elizabethan People, Ed. Joel Hurstfield and Alan G.R. Smith (Edward Arnold Documents of Modern History, 1972)

The Elizabethan Underworld, Gamini Salgado (Alan Sutton, 1984)

The Family, Sex and Marriage in England 1500–1800, Lawrence Stone (Pelican, 1979)

The Later Tudors, Penry Williams (Oxford, 1995)

Poverty and Vagrancy in Tudor England, John Pound (Longman, 1971)

The Sixteenth Century, Patrick Collinson (Oxford, 2002)

Tudor England, 1485–1603, Ed. Roger Lockyer and Dan O'Sullivan (Longman Sources and Opinions, 1993)

The Tudor Image, Maurice Howard (Tate Gallery, 1995)

The Voices of Morebath, Eamonn Duffy (Yale University Press, 2001)

Further reading

A Tudor School, Peter Chrisp (Heinemann Library, 1997)

Tudor World, Haydn Middleton (Heinemann Library, 2001)

Tudor Children, Jane Shuter (Heinemann Library, 1996)

Tudor Family Life, Jane Shuter (Heinemann Library, 1997)

Websites

www.heinemannexplore.co.uk – contains KS2 History modules including the Tudors.

www.brims.co.uk/tudors/ – information on Tudors for 7–10 year olds.

Glossary

apprentices young people learning a craft from a master

apprenticeship practice of learning a craft from a master

artificers craftsmen

artisans skilled men who work with their hands

astrologer someone who studies the heavens to make predictions

autobiography someone's life-story, written by him- or herself

baptism ceremony in which a child is made a member of the church

baptize make a child a member of the church

betrothed engaged to be married

birth-rate number of births per every 1000 people each year

blight plant disease caused by parasites

bodice part of a dress or undergarment above the waist

Catholic only Christian faith in western Europe until the 1520s, when people began to follow the new Protestant faith

census counting up of all the people in a country

Chancellor of the Exchequer person who deals with all money matters for a monarch or government

christen make a child a member of the church

confirmed going through the service of 'confirmation' in church, as long as you have been baptized before

consent agreement

consumption common Tudor disease affecting the lungs

coffer box for keeping valuable things in

corset tight-fitting undergarment

councillor adviser to the king or queen

courtier person who spent time at a king or queen's court as a companion or adviser

crozier long hooked staff carried by a bishop

domestic at home, in the home

draper seller of cloth

epidemics widespread diseases

excommunicated not allowed to worship in church any more; cut off from the Christian religion

gout disease affecting the joints and feet

harquebus early kind of gun that could be carried

hawking hunt birds or animals with a hawk

housewifery all the jobs done by a woman around the house

humanities study of non-scientific subjects

indifference lack of interest in someone or something

inheritance belongings and land received from another person

illegitimate child born to parents who are not married

joust competition to fight an opponent on horseback

Justices of the Peace local Tudor officials

legitimate born to married parents

lute guitar-like musical instrument

medieval during the Middle Ages (just before Tudor times)

midwife nurse who helps women give birth to their babies

miscarriage death of a baby before it is due to be born

mitre pointed hat of a bishop

monarch king or queen

monitor person who helps to keep order and organizes things

orator great public speaker

Ottoman Turks Turkish people who conquered large parts of eastern Europe and Asia

pageant procession for entertainment

parish local area with its own church and own church official

piety deep religiousness

pike Tudor weapon, like a spear

policies actions planned and carried out by a government

Pope head of the Catholic church. He lives in Rome.

population number of people in a country

Protestant religious faith of people who turned away from the teachings of the Catholic church

sanitation flushing toilets and drains

smite hit

stocks timber frame that criminals were locked up in, to be viewed in public by passers-by

utensils tools, objects used for a certain purpose

vagrant poor, wandering person

virginals Tudor musical instrument like a harpsichord

wet nurse woman who breast-feeds someone else's baby

wrath anger

yeoman rich farmer with his own land

Index